Using Forensics

Using Forensics

Wildlife Crime Scene!

By Laura M. Sanders Arndt

NATIONAL SCIENCE TEACHERS ASSOCIATION

Arlington, Virginia

NATIONAL SCIENCE TEACHERS ASSOCIATION

Claire Reinburg, Director
Judy Cusick, Senior Editor
Andrew Cocke, Associate Editor
Betty Smith, Associate Editor
Robin Allan, Book Acquisitions Manager

ART AND DESIGN
Will Thomas, Jr., Director
Tim French, Senior Graphic Designer—Inside Design
D.W. Miller, Illustrations

PRINTING AND PRODUCTION
Catherine Lorrain, Director

NATIONAL SCIENCE TEACHERS ASSOCIATION
Gerald F. Wheeler, Executive Director
David Beacom, Publisher

LIBRARY OF CONGRESS CATALOGING-IN-PUBLICATION DATA
Arndt, Laura M. Sanders, 1960-
  Using forensics : wildlife crime scene! / by Laura M. Sanders Arndt.
    p. cm.
  Includes bibliographical references and index.
  ISBN 978-0-87355-270-7 (alk. paper)
  1. Wildlife crime investigation. 2. Forensic sciences. I. Title.
HV8079.W58A76 2007
363.25'98--dc22
                    2007030774

Only if we understand

can we care.

Only if we care

will we help.

Only if we help

shall they be saved.

—*Jane Goodall*, noted English primatologist, ethologist, and anthropologist and founder of the Jane Goodall Institute

---

We, as educators and parents, have the vital task of helping our students, children, and all people understand the essential role wildlife plays in the health and balance of our natural ecosystems. Our own survival and quality of life is dependent on this balance. When we care, we are willing to step up and speak out to give animals a voice. When we humans and animals have one voice, then wildlife will be saved and we will all thrive from the Earth's diverse, enriching, balanced ecosystems.

Contents

Section 1:
Wildlife Crimes Overview

Section 2:
Training in Forensic Techniques

National Science Teachers Association

Section 3:
Investigating and Solving a Wildlife Crime 185

Section 4:
Evaluations and Assessments 293

Appendixes 317

Additional Resources 333

Index 335

Acknowledgments

The number of individuals who have contributed to this curriculum is humbling. My sincere thank-you goes out to each of those teachers, scientists, wildlife officers, students, friends, and family.

The authenticity of this updated version of the curriculum rested with the Colorado Divison of Wildlife's (DOW) Jeff Rucks. He patiently answered question upon question about wildlife crime and animal identification diagnostics. If he did not know the answers, he knew who would.

Mark Cousins (DOW), Steve Lucero (DOW), Warren Gartner (DOW), Jeff Stephenson (Denver Museum of Nature and Science), David Armstrong (University of Colorado at Boulder), and Julia Rainer (DNA lab scientist) all generously offered their expertise.

A former police officer and detective, my sister-in-law, Linda, helped me understand and incorporate the intricacies and language of investigating a crime from the moment an officer is sent to the crime scene to the presentation of the case in court. She facilitated consultations with various judges, prosecutors, and law enforcement officials across the country.

My career-long gratitude goes out to Anne Tweed, my teaching partner for many years. She has given me endless encouragement to follow my dream of publishing this book. Her knowledge and enthusiasm for sound, issue-based science education made her invaluable in this project.

I wrote the original version of this curriculum in the early 1990s. The Division of Wildlife's Liza Hunholz and Mark Lamb guided my creation of the first wildlife crime. Bernadette Antencio (U.S. Fish and Wildlife Service) gave insight into the national and international wildlife trade issues that became integral to the curriculum.

Niki Kigerl worked with me to teach, revise, and teach again the original version to hundreds of students in our outdoor naturalist classes at Eaglecrest High School (Cherry Creek School District) in Colorado. Many other teachers have been trained in the original curriculum and now teach it in their own classes. Their comments and support have been my inspiration to publish it for others.

A team of teachers, students, and adults interested in CSI (crime scene investigation) came together for a weekend workshop to pilot this updated curriculum. Their teaching expertise and creativity helped strengthen the final version. I sincerely thank Julia Rainer, Sung Baek, Lisa Johnson, Jessica Boline, Barbara Jones, Maria King, Nadyne Orloff, Henry Barrett, and Aron Villanyi. I also thank the people who reviewed this curriculum for NSTA Press: Paul Kuerbis, Bill Leonard, Steve Metz, Dennis Mucenski, Jeff Rucks, Howard Schindler, and Anne Tweed. I respectfully thank the NSTA Press team who worked on this book—Robin Allan, Judy Cusick, Tim French, Catherine Lorrain, and Claire Reinburg—for transforming the curriculum into a book for the science classroom.

I so appreciate my family (Roger, Erik, and Cory), my editor/mom Pat Sanders, and personal and professional friends who have been patient with my endless hours of writing and researching. I could not have done this without you.

Scientific and Law Enforcement Advisers

Antencio, Bernadette, Eagle Repository, U.S. Fish and Wildlife Service, Denver, CO.

Armstrong, David, ecology and evolutionary biology, University of Colorado at Boulder.

Arndt, Linda, former police officer and detective.

Cousins, Mark, hunter education coordinator, Colorado Division of Wildlife, Denver, CO.

Gartner, Warren, conservation education supervisor, Natural Resources Education Center, Fort Harrison State Park, Indianapolis, IN.

Hunholz, Liza, area wildlife manager, Colorado Division of Wildlife, Denver, CO.

Lamb, Mark, district wildlife manager, Colorado Division of Wildlife, Fairplay, CO.

Lucero, Steve, education coordinator, Colorado Division of Wildlife, Colorado Springs, CO.

Rainer, Julia, molecular and cellular biologist, secondary science educator, Golden, CO.

Rucks, Jeff, manager of education and outreach, Colorado Division of Wildlife, Denver, CO.

Stephenson, Jeff, zoology department collections manager, Denver Museum of Nature and Science, Denver, CO.

Tweed, Anne, principal consultant, McREL (Mid-continent Research for Education and Learning), Denver, Colorado. NSTA President 2004–2005.

About the Author

Laura M. Sanders Arndt taught high school outdoor naturalist, environmental science, and biology classes for nine years in Colorado's Cherry Creek School District (Eaglecrest High School).

She originally wrote and taught this wildlife forensics curriculum in the early 1990s for her outdoor naturalist classes. Since 1993 she has given workshops to many teachers to show them how to use the curriculum in their sixth–twelfth-grade classes.

Laura's inspiration for writing the curriculum came from a life-long love and concern for wildlife. She has volunteered in international mountain gorilla conservation education since the mid-1980s, has written three curricula on gorillas for the United States and Africa, and has helped establish conservation education programs in Rwanda and Uganda. Project Wild and Project Learning Tree, as well as Colorado Geographic Alliance, set her path for writing issue-based, inquiry science units. Before beginning her teaching career, she worked as an educational ranger at Roxborough State Park, chose a master's internship at Chicago's Brookfield Zoo, and volunteered at the Denver Zoo and at an organization caring for permanently injured raptors (Raptor Education Foundation).

Today Laura develops and facilitates hands-on inquiry science workshops, teaches science and nature enrichment classes and programs, writes science curricula, works with The Wildlife Experience museum on developing education programs, and continues efforts to support mountain gorilla conservation projects in Uganda and Rwanda.

She lives with her family, husband Roger and children Erik and Cory, in the ponderosa pine forest and wildflower-rich land of Franktown, Colorado.

About the Illustrator

D. W. Miller likes to aid scientists and student-scientists in their exploration and explanation of the natural world. In addition to appearing in numerous textbooks and magazines, his work has been used in displays for the American Museum of Natural History in

New York, the Smithsonian Institution in Washington, DC, and the National Museum of Science and Industry in London. Miller, who lives in Bellingham, Washington, studied at Montserrat School of Visual Art in Massachusetts, Olympic Park Institute in Washington, and the Art Students League in New York.

Foreword

How do we get student's attention … and keep it? In science classrooms, posing a really interesting question or beginning with a mystery is a good way to begin. Students can't help but ask, Why did that happen? How can that be true?

By creating a wildlife crime mystery that students have to solve, this curriculum gives students the opportunity to ask questions as they conduct their investigation. Teams of student scientists pursue their promising leads, they follow clues—and they sometimes hit dead ends. Robert Cialdini, a social psychologist at Arizona State University, believes that there are significant benefits to teaching using mysteries since "the process of resolving mysteries is remarkably similar to the process of science" (2005. What's the best secret device for engaging student interest. *Journal of Social and Clinical Psychology* 24 (1): 22–29).

Scientific mysteries exist wherever there are questions without obvious answers. What is causing global climate change? Why is it so hard to get some species of animals to breed in captivity? With a scientific question, students know where they are headed but don't know for sure how they'll get there. This uncertainty has been the power of using CSI (crime scene investigation) strategies in science classrooms. CSIs get students to make careful observations, collect specimens for analysis, and conduct experiments to provide additional data. The result is classrooms where students question their own assumptions and ask questions about each other's ideas.

As professionals, we must ask ourselves some important questions: How can our teaching practices help students to think and act like scientists? What are the best ways to motivate students to learn? And finally, what do my students need to have me do to promote curiosity and excitement while they learn? As the research on student learning shows, one clear goal is to engage students with the content. This book will provide teachers with an opportunity to do just that. And it is no mystery why students like to learn this way. It is fun and exciting to experience some of the wonder and awe that go with uncovering the mysteries and puzzles of science.

Anne Tweed
Principal Consultant, McREL
(Mid-continent Research for Education and Learning)
NSTA President, 2004–2005

Introduction

The mystery and intrigue of crime scene investigations (CSIs) have captured the attention of the general public. Each week, millions of TV viewers marvel as a team of scientists uses forensic science to recreate the scene, track down suspects, and piece together the clues that solve a crime. The heroes of these shows aren't the traditional muscle-bound men finding answers with their fists. Rather, they are men and women with strong backgrounds in science, solving crimes with their minds. While the focus of CSI is on human crime, many of the same techniques can be applied to crimes against wildlife.

Poaching (illegally hunting animals) is one of these crimes. Poaching means more than hunting out of season for meat. Poachers kill wildlife for a variety of reasons. Some kill for the thrill and power of it and do not even take the bodies. Others kill to have the trophy parts of animals. Still others kill animals to show their anger at wildlife laws, a person, or a situation. Last, but far from least, a large number of poachers kill for the money. Annual international wildlife trade is a multi-billion-dollar business involving millions of plants and animals. People involved in illegal wildlife trade may kill or capture the animals themselves or hire others to do that job. In some poor countries, wildlife trade criminals become invisible middlemen by hiring local people to kill the animals. After paying them a small fee, the middlemen turn around and sell the animals or animal parts for large profits. Many are willing to do anything to get and sell their animal merchandise.

Forensic lab techniques can be used to solve these crimes. The National Fish and Wildlife Forensics Laboratory in Ashland, Oregon, consists of a team of scientists working with national and international officials to investigate wildlife crimes. "The job of the lab is to determine the species source and analyze forensic evidence that could link it to a violation of wildlife law—and a human suspect"(Pahl 2003).

This book, *Using Forensics: Wildlife Crime Scene!*, combines two popular topics—using forensic science for crime scene investigations and studying wildlife issues—to create a complex scientific investigation that can only be solved using inquiry-based strategies.

Investigating a wildlife crime in the classroom allows students to solve cases in the same way as the new breed of TV heroes. Students will learn about such wildlife topics as ecosystems, species identification, biodiversity, and endangered species. They'll then put that knowledge to use in the lab, using forensic investigation to collect the clues and catch the criminal.

Authenticity in the Crime and in the Lab

The news reports of wildlife crimes that appear at the beginning of each lesson in Section 2 are actual offenses committed in the United States and internationally. The procedures used in the lessons to investigate these crimes are many of the same performed in forensic labs to solve crimes against both wildlife and humans. The lessons in Section 2 and the wildlife crime investigation in Section 3 were written with assistance from Colorado Division of Wildlife officers and education staff, U.S. Fish and Wildlife staff, city and county law enforcement officers and detectives, and scientists from the Denver Museum of Nature and Science.

Field-Tested Curriculum

The original version of this curriculum was written in the early 1990s and taught to hundreds of high school students by the author. Over 100 middle and high school teachers have also tested it in their classrooms. The updated curriculum presented here was piloted and reviewed by a dozen teachers and several wildlife officers and scientists.

A Brief Outline of the Book

Section 1, "Wildlife Crimes Overview": Students are introduced to issues and facts about crimes against wildlife. Students identify human actions that threaten specific kinds of animals, compare wildlife laws, and read about international wildlife trade.

Section 2, "Training in Forensic Techniques": Students learn the specific skills required to investigate crimes. The lessons are independent of each other and may be taught in any order. They may be used as a series of lessons or as single units introduced during the school year as the material applies to the curriculum. The connections between each lesson and specific National Science Education Standards are given.

- Lesson 1: Antlers and Horns—Practice observation skills by describing, measuring, drawing, and identifying antlers and horns.

- Lesson 2: Blood Typing—Use card drawings of blood antigens and antibodies to construct blood types and determine safe transfusions for donors and recipients. Then conduct a lab using simulated blood to test for blood types and Rh factors of four fictitious people.

- Lesson 3: DNA Fingerprinting—Use a paper model of DNA to simulate laboratory steps to create a DNA fingerprint by cutting the DNA with an enzyme (scissors). Graph the DNA pieces to show how they were separated on a paper gel box model.

- Lesson 4: Fingerprints—After each student makes and identifies a set of his or her own ink fingerprints, lab groups make a set of unidentified fingerprints on a variety of surfaces. These unknowns are exchanged for another group to identify.

- Lesson 5: Hair Identification—Use a microscope to examine, compare, and classify hair from classmates and other mammals.

- Lesson 6: pH and pH Indicators—Learn about pH and pH indicators through a series of inquiry activities. Then conduct a lab using pH indicators to determine the pH ranges of known household solutions.

- Lesson 7: Mammal Skulls—Distinguish among teeth patterns of a variety of mammal skulls and categorize them by predicting what they eat. Then use a dichotomous key to identify mammal skulls.

- Lesson 8: Tracks and Trace Fossils—Unravel the stories shown on mystery track pattern cards. Identify mammal tracks found in a fictitious new protected wilderness area. Create a brochure to teach visitors about the wildlife. Food web and biodiversity extensions are described.

Section 3, "Investigating and Solving a Wildlife Crime": Students investigate a wildlife crime involving bears. They interview a cast of crime suspects and witnesses, played by volunteer school staff and parents, and work in teams to explore all facets of the investigation. This case can be adjusted to fit the curriculum. Any forensic procedures not studied in Section 2 may be omitted from the investigation without affecting the investigation's impact.

- Investigation Day 1: Has a Wildlife Crime Been Committed? Students are introduced to the wildlife crime. Their investigative teams review the initial crime reports and other support papers, record information in their Investigator Notebooks, and begin filling out the timeline on the crime.

- Investigation Day 2: Interviewing the Cast of Characters (Suspects and Witnesses). Investigative teams gather information from the suspects and witnesses.
- Investigation Day 3: Sharing Interview Notes. Investigative teams talk about information gathered by interviewers, record interview summaries, and begin to piece together the crime.
- Investigation Day 4: Forensic Lab Tests of Evidence. Investigative teams analyze crime evidence at ten lab stations.
- Investigation Day 5: Forensic Lab Tests Continue. Investigative teams share forensic lab test findings on evidence and discuss new ideas about the crime before completing their assigned labs.
- Investigation Day 6 and 7: Summarizing Findings and Charging Suspects. Teams work together to determine criminal offenses, suspects, and victims.
- Investigation Day 8: Presentation of Case to the Prosecuting Attorney. Teams present their case to the prosecuting attorney (teacher) to explain the evidence that supports the charges being made. The team with the most accurate case will make the arrest.

Section 4, "Evaluation and Assessment": Upon completion of the wildlife crime investigation, the teacher can use the tools in Section 4 to evaluate both the student teams and individual students.

- Investigator's Summary Packet—Students individually summarize their forensic labs from Investigation Day 4, interviews, and case results and bind their papers in a case report packet. They also evaluate themselves.
- Group Evaluation—Investigative teams evaluate team members on their contributions to solving the crime.
- Lab Practical Assessment—Students individually demonstrate their knowledge and skills in forensic lab techniques and solving the wildlife crime on a 30-question lab practical assessment. An answer key is provided.
- New Wildlife Crime: You're in Charge—Students choose an online article about a current wildlife crime (from state operation game thief programs or from international animal trade news reports) and outline a plan for investigating the crime.

Connections to the National Science Education Standards and to Inquiry Science

The connections between each lesson in Section 2 and the National Science Education Standards are given at the beginning of the lesson. In addition, the following standards are addressed in this book.

Standard Connection	Category	Lesson
Content Standard F— Population, resources, and environment (grades 5–8) Natural resources (grades 9–12)	Science in Personal and Social Perspectives	Students will explain international legal and illegal wildlife trade and the impact of wildlife trade on bears. They will describe a variety of national and international wildlife laws and their role in protecting species and ecosystems.
Content Standard F— Risks and benefits (grades 5–8)	Science in Personal and Social Perspectives	Students will compare the costs and benefits of capturing or killing wildlife to society, the natural environment, and the individual.
Content Standard G— Nature of science (grades 5–8) Nature of scientific knowledge (grades 9–12)	History and Nature of Science	Students will work in investigative teams to simulate actual law enforcement and forensic science procedures. They will repeatedly modify and refine explanations of the crime as they continue to gather and analyze more layers of physical, written, and verbal evidence. Their final step is to make an arrest based on scientifically analyzed physical evidence connecting the suspect, victim, and laws broken.

The entire process of investigating the wildlife crime—from reading the initial crime reports to arresting the suspect—requires students to demonstrate the full spectrum of steps and levels in scientific inquiry. Investigative teams can only solve the crime if they can connect dozens of discrete pieces of physical, verbal, and written evidence to the suspect, victim, and laws broken. In *Inquiry and the National Science Education Standards: A Guide for Teaching and Learning* (NRC 2000), the authors identify five essential features of classroom inquiry (see column 1 in the table below); all of these features are found in this book.

Essential Feature of Classroom Inquiry	Inquiry Feature as Found in This Book
1. Learner engages in scientifically oriented question.	1. Students compose, revise, and respond to questions to guide the steps of their investigation.
2. Learner gives priority to evidence.	2. Students collect and analyze physical, verbal, and written evidence.
3. Learner formulates explanations from evidence.	3. Students must decide and explain how the evidence relates, or does not relate, to the crime. They must determine which evidence is weaker and which is stronger and then use the strongest to build their case connecting the suspect, victim, and laws broken.
4. Learner connects explanations to scientific knowledge.	4. Students discover that they can only make an arrest if they have strong connections between scientifically tested physical evidence and the suspect and laws broken. They cannot arrest based only on interviews and circumstantial evidence.
5. Learner communicates and justifies explanations.	5. Students must share information daily with their investigative teams. They must help each other understand results from lab tests and interviews in order to solve the crime. Every piece of the crime investigation is important. Students must summarize their findings for both class presentations and written assessment.

Frequently Asked Questions and Concerns

About the Curriculum in General

How is this forensic curriculum different from others?

The focus of this curriculum is on wildlife crimes rather than the human murders of other forensic curricula. The curriculum trains students as wildlife investigators and forensic scientists. They study wildlife laws and analyze case studies of crimes against wildlife. Many of the forensic labs in Section 2 relate to ecology and wildlife identification (mammal hair, tracks, antlers, and skulls), in addition to the traditional forensic labs on blood, DNA, and fingerprints. Students use their knowledge of forensic and wildlife laws to investigate and analyze evidence in a common crime against wildlife (bear deaths and dismemberment).

By focusing on crimes against wildlife instead of humans, the curriculum can complement course topics such as endangered species, ecology, ecosystems, and environment science.

Everything I teach must be standards-based. How do I rationalize spending over a week of class time letting students solve a crime?

National Science Content Standard A of the National Science Education Standards (NRC 1996) reads, "Science as Inquiry: All students should develop abilities necessary to do scientific inquiry [and] understandings about scientific inquiry" (p. 121). Solving the crime requires a large-scale, inquiry-based scientific investigation. Students apply their knowledge of scientific content and lab procedures to real-life issues. By the time they have solved the crime, they know how to do scientific inquiry at all levels and understand the important steps of scientific investigation. Students realize they can "do science," meaning they can figure out scientific mysteries and conduct investigations on their own. They recognize a reason to learn the scientific concepts of the course or unit and they are inspired to choose careers that use science.

More specifically, in the Teacher Guidelines for each training lesson in Section 2, you will find the connections between that lesson and specific content standards.

Why doesn't the curriculum start with the initial crime report and suspect and witness interviews? That would generate student interest prior to the training lessons.

Great idea. As a matter of fact, when I first wrote this curriculum, I did just that. Unfortunately, it was not effective in the long run. (Maybe you would have better luck!) The students were so excited when they read the first crime report that they wanted to "solve the crime NOW!" That enthusiasm got stalled, and frustration set in, when they realized they had to go through many days of learning forensic content background and training labs. They lost the momentum and focus. Even if written down, facts and ideas for solving the crime were forgotten or confused. The crime lost its realism because they kept switching between being investigators and students.

By keeping the crime uninterrupted from beginning to end in Section 3, students feel as if they are investigating and solving the crime in real time. They discover new facts with every new report, interview, and lab test. Their enthusiasm, motivation, and focus stay high, and the competition among investigative teams is palpable as they huddle up to discuss their latest findings and try to piece the crime puzzle together. They even track down the cast members they have interviewed to question them further on their own time.

I already have a full curriculum. How do I fit this in?

Here are some ways that teachers have used the material in this book:

- In both middle school classes and high school (biology, environmental science, and criminology) classes, teachers have incorporated the training lessons into their required curriculum throughout the year by blocking out time in advance to teach those concepts. Any training lessons not covered by their required curriculum are taught right before the wildlife crime investigation is used as a culminating activity.
- Some teachers use only training lessons that fit into their curriculum. This personalizes the crime to their class. The crime investigation may be conducted as an end-of-the-year assessment or taught sequentially from training lessons during the crime investigation.

About Section 2: Training in Forensic Techniques

Why do some of the training lessons in Section 2 look like labs I already teach?

That is on purpose! I intentionally mimicked labs commonly taught in science classes to reduce the amount of new content that teachers would have to add to their classes. If you already teach labs like these, you will have an easier time incorporating the crime investigation, which is the unique piece that adds relevance to all the labs. The large-scale scientific investigation allows students to apply their knowledge of your course content and lab procedures.

My students need more rigorous content and labs. Can I use the lab investigations and content I already teach in my class?

Certainly! The labs in lessons 1–8 are basic labs. They are not meant to be a comprehensive study of the science content. That information can be found in many other science texts and resources. If you already teach the content found in one of the training lessons, you can use your own materials or incorporate the forensic lab or background as needed.

If you do not normally teach the concepts of a training lesson, but still want students to analyze the crime evidence, then spend a day or two going through the background and labs. This will give them enough information to analyze the evidence.

Note: Many of the labs in Section 2 model the actual lab procedures required to analyze the evidence presented in Section 3. If you do not model this, students might need more guidance during the crime investigation.

I don't have time to teach all the training lessons in Section 2. How can I shorten the curriculum?

You can cut out labs from the training lessons according to your time constraints, student ability levels, and course focus. If you cut out a training lesson, you will just give the students the lab results for the evidence during the crime investigation. I would wait until the teams have completed all or most of the other labs. Then give them the evidence results to the entire class, saying the analysis report was done by a different forensic lab.

About Section 3: Investigating and Solving a Wildlife Crime

The set-up for the crime investigation requires a lot of prep time. How can I get everything ready without sacrificing other teaching responsibilities that compete for my time?

The prep work for the crime investigation does take extra time. But once this is done, the students do all the work. You become a facilitator for the full crime investigation. You explain their next steps, hand out papers, answer their questions with guiding inquiry questions, remind them of their team responsibilities, walk around, and watch them DO science.

The prep work is greatly reduced the second or third time you teach the curriculum. Keep crime materials organized together. I have labeled containers holding materials for each training lesson and steps of the crime investigation. Each container also has a list of materials needed. When I am ready to teach the curriculum again, I pull out the containers, check the lists, and add whatever materials are stored in other locations. Prep time is minimal!

Another way to reduce prep time is to have students read the suspect and witness reports instead of conducting interviews. Although the interviewing is a favorite part of the investigation for most students (as I discuss in the answer to the next question), it does add on organization time because of the need to find and prepare the cast of characters (i.e, the suspects and witnesses) and organize the interview day.

How can I make the crime as realistic as possible?

As I said above, although the crime investigation can be shortened by eliminating the suspect and witness interviews and having the students simply read the suspect and witness reports, the interviews make the crime feel very realistic. I have always had students do the actual interviews. One middle school teacher who teaches the curriculum to seventh graders selects eighth graders to play the cast members. Students absolutely love this part because they are "real investigators" and get the characters' statements firsthand. Student interview teams write interview questions, find and interview the characters in predetermined locations around the school, call characters back in for follow-up

REFERENCES

National Research Council (NRC). 1996. *National science education standards*. Washington, DC: National Academy Press.

National Research Council (NRC). 2000. *Inquiry and the national science education standards: A guide for teaching and learning*. Washington, DC: National Academy Press.

Pahl, M. April 2, 2003. U.S. "animal detectives" fight crime in forensics lab. *National Geographic Today*. *http://news.nationalgeographic.com/ news/2003/04/0402_030402_tvwildlife crimes. html*

SCIENCE NOTEBOOK RESOURCES

Campbell, B., and L. Fulton. 2003. *Science notebooks: Writing about inquiry*. Portsmouth, NH: Heinemann.

Fulwiler, B. R. 2007. *Writing in science: How to scaffold instruction to support learning*. Portsmouth, NH: Heinemann.

Gilbert, J., and M. Kotelman. 2005. Five good reasons to use science notebooks. *Science and Children* (Nov./Dec.): 28–32.

Klentschy, M. 2005. Science notebook essentials. *Science and Children* (Nov./Dec.): 24–27.

Section 1

Wildlife
Crimes
Overview

Crimes Against Wildlife

Teacher Guidelines

Overview

This section sets the stage for upcoming forensic training lessons (Section 2) and the crime investigation (Section 3). Activities and readings introduce students to issues and facts about crimes against wildlife by identifying human actions that threaten specific types of animals, comparing wildlife protection laws, and exploring issues of legal and illegal international wildlife trade.

Time Required

3–5 class periods

Materials

Each student will need a copy of each of the following handouts:

- "Essential Questions About Crimes Against Wildlife: Keeping an Investigator Notebook" (Handout A, p. 4)
- "Surrounded by Threats: Wildlife's Challenge to Survive" (Handout B, pp. 5–6)
- "Agencies and Organizations With a Focus on Wildlife Crimes and Endangered Species" (Handout C, pp. 7–8)
- "The Billion-Dollar Market of International Wildlife Trade" (Handout D, pp. 9–14)
- "National and International Wildlife Laws and Agreements" (Handout E, pp. 15–19)

Teaching Plan

1. Students begin their Investigator Notebooks by responding to "Essential Questions About Crimes Against Wildlife: Keeping an Investigator Notebook" (Handout A).

2. Assign each student, or let each student pick, an animal from "Surrounded by Threats: Wildlife's Challenge to Survive" (Handout B) to research online or in print material. Also give

each student "Agencies and Organizations With a Focus on Wildlife Crime and Endangered Species" (Handout C), which includes websites they can use in their research.

3. After doing the research, students share information about their animal(s) and, as a class, they group the animals according to categories of threats (some categories of threats would be the following: use as pets, leather products, fur, jewelry, decorations, food/bushmeat, or medicines; the loss of their habitats; being seen as undesirable pests).

4. Students read and discuss "The Billion-Dollar Market of International Wildlife Trade" (Handout D).

5. Give students copies of "National and International Wildlife Laws and Agreements" (Handout E) to learn about and compare regulations protecting wildlife. As outlined on the first page of the handout, students first do a K-W-L in their Investigator Notebooks.

    The teacher then decides if students will simply read and discuss the brief descriptions of wildlife laws and agreements on pages 16–19 or if students will go online, using the forensic links on pages 7–8, to find out more. Another possibility is to make this a jigsaw activity by putting students into groups and assigning each group one of the 11 laws and regulations to read and/or research further. Then divide the groups so that one member of each group forms a new group to share findings. Have students make a data table (name of law, description, other important information) in their Investigator Notebooks to summarize the laws.

Handout A

Essential Questions About Crimes Against Wildlife: Keeping an Investigator Notebook

Name _____ Date _____

Students write responses to all or selected questions in their Investigator Notebooks* and discuss in small groups.

- CRIME SCENE - DO NOT CROSS - CRIME SCENE - DO NOT CROSS - CRIME SCENE - DO NOT CROSS - CRIME SCENE - DO NOT CROSS - CRIME SCENE - DO NOT CROSS -

1. Use the **K-W-L** format to answer the following questions (**K-W-L** stands for: What I **K**now–What I **W**ant to know–What I **L**earned):

   - *What do I <u>know</u> about crimes against wildlife? (Put a star by information you are not sure is accurate.)*
   - *What do I <u>want to know</u> about crimes against wildlife?*
   - *What did I <u>learn</u> about crimes against wildlife? (Your teacher will tell you when it is time to answer this last question.)*

2. Why do people poach (kill animals illegally)? See Handout D, "The Billion-Dollar Market of International Wildlife Trade," for information on this topic.

3. Why should a person care about crimes against wildlife?

4. Do crimes against wildlife affect the balance of an ecosystem? Justify your answer.

5. Does legal hunting or collecting of animals affect the balance of an ecosystem? Justify your answer.

6. List a variety of crimes against wildlife in a table (column 1: Animal; column 2: Crime against this animal). Is one type of crime more serious than another? Explain.

Note to the Teacher: For more information on the notebooks, read "Keeping an Investigator Notebook" on pages xxv–xxvi.

National Science Teachers Association

Handout B
Surrounded by Threats: Wildlife's Challenge to Survive

Name _____ Date _____

- CRIME SCENE - DO NOT CROSS - CRIME SCENE - DO NOT CROSS - CRIME SCENE - DO NOT CROSS - CRIME SCENE - DO NOT CROSS - CRIME SCENE - DO NOT CROSS -

Animals are fighting for survival in most ecosystems, countries, and bodies of water across the world. Who is their common competitor? Humans.

Pick one or more animals from the list below, as approved by your teacher. Search online or in printed resources for answers to the questions that follow the list. (For online resources, see Handout C, "Agencies and Organizations With a Focus on Wildlife Crime and Endangered Species.") When done, report your findings to your class.

Partial List of Animals Threatened by Human Actions

(Related animals faced by similar threats are grouped together.)

- Alligator, caiman, or crocodile
- Antelope, bushbuck, or other antelope species
- Apes: gorilla, chimpanzee, orangutan, or gibbon
- Bears: black, grizzly, polar, spectacled, sun
- Birds: cockatiel, cockatoos, parrots, macaws
- Butterflies: rainforest species, monarchs
- Cats: jaguar, leopards, lions, ocelot, tigers
- Coral
- Elk, deer
- Elephant: African, Asian
- Fish: bluefin tuna, orange roughy, cod, caviar
- Fish: salmon
- Fish: tropical (coral reef) fish, sea horses

- Frogs
- Hermit crabs
- Insects
- Lizards
- Manatees and dugongs
- Monkeys
- Raptors: eagles, hawks, owls, falcons
- Rattlesnakes
- Rhinoceros
- Seals, sea lions, walruses
- Sea otters
- Sea turtle
- Sharks
- Shellfish
- Songbirds: hummingbirds, tanangers
- Spiders: tarantulas
- Whales

Handout B
Surrounded by Threats: Wildlife's Challenge to Survive

For each animal:

1. What is the species?

2. Where does the animal live?

3. What is its ecosystem home?

4. How is this animal threatened, harmed, or killed by human actions?

National Science Teachers Association

Handout C

Agencies and Organizations With a Focus on Wildlife Crime and Endangered Species

Name _____ Date _____

- CRIME SCENE - DO NOT CROSS - CRIME SCENE - DO NOT CROSS - CRIME SCENE - DO NOT CROSS - CRIME SCENE - DO NOT CROSS - CRIME SCENE - DO NOT CROSS -

Government Agencies

National Fish and Wildlife Forensics Laboratory, U.S. Fish and Wildlife Service. *www.lab.fws.gov*

U.S. Fish and Wildlife Service, Department of the Interior. *www.fws.gov*

International Monitoring Organizations

CITES (Convention on International Trade in Endangered Species of Wild Fauna and Flora). *www.cites.org*

TRAFFIC (Wildlife trade monitoring network). *www.traffic.org*

World Conservation Union. *www.iucn.org*

World Wildlife Fund TRAFFIC, United Kingdom. *www.wwf.org.uk/wildlifetrade/trade.asp*

Organizations

African Wildlife Foundation. *www.awf.org*

Bushmeat Task Force. *www.bushmeat.org*

Caviar Emptor. *www.caviaremptor.org*

Conservation International. *www.conservation.org*

Defenders of Wildlife. *www.defenders.org*

Humane Society of the United States. *www.hwus.org*

International Fund for Animal Welfare. *www.ifaw.org*

Handout C
Agencies and Organizations With a Focus on Wildlife Crime and Endangered Species

International Gorilla Conservation Program. *www.igcp.org*

International Primate Protection League. *www.ippl.org*

Jane Goodall Institute. *www.janegoodall.org*

Mountain Gorilla Veterinary Project. *www.mgvp.org*

National Wildlife Federation. *www.nwf.org*

Naturewatch. *www.naturewatch.org*

Sea Turtle Restoration Project. *www.seaturtles.org*

Wildlife Conservation Society. *www.wcs.org*

Wildlife International. *www.wildlife-international.org*

World Wildlife Fund (Global Environmental Conservation Organization). *www.panda.org*

Wildlife Lists, Field Guides, and Interactive Games

Animal Diversity Web. *http://animaldiversity.ummz.umich.edu/site/index.html*

Colorado Division of Wildlife. *http://wildlife.state.co.us/WildlifeSpecies*

eNature, National Wildlife Federation. *http://enature.org*

Kids page, Federal Bureau of Investigation. *www.fbi.gov/fbikids.htm*

Monterey Bay Aquarium's Seafood Watch Program. *www.mbayaq.org/cr/seafoodwatch.asp*

Wildlife Conservation Society's Go Fish Program. *www.wcs.org/gofish*

World Wildlife Fund (Biodiversity Basics). *www.biodiversity911.org* (includes games and interactives for learning about wildlife trade and sustainable seafood)

National Science Teachers Association

Handout D
The Billion-Dollar Market of International Wildlife Trade

Name _____ Date _____

- CRIME SCENE - DO NOT CROSS - CRIME SCENE - DO NOT CROSS - CRIME SCENE - DO NOT CROSS - CRIME SCENE - DO NOT CROSS - CRIME SCENE - DO NOT CROSS -

Why Do People Poach Wildlife?

Poachers are people who illegally kill wildlife. Some kill wildlife for the thrill and power of killing and leave the animal bodies in the field. Others kill in order to collect and display trophy parts of animals. Still others kill wildlife to show their anger at wildlife laws, a person, or a situation.

Last, but far from least, a large number of poachers kill for the money. Annual international wildlife trade is a billion-dollar business involving millions of plants and animals. People involved in illegal wildlife trade may kill or capture the animals themselves or hire others to do that job. In some poor countries, wildlife-trade criminals become invisible middlemen by hiring local people to kill the animals. After paying them a small fee, the middlemen turn around and sell the animals or animal parts for large profits. Many are willing to do anything to get and sell their animal merchandise (TRAFFIC/Wildlife trade-monitoring network. *www.traffic.org/wildlife/wild2. htm*).

Hundreds of millions of animals and plants (tens of thousands of species) are taken from their natural habitats each year to meet the demand. Some animals are captured for pets or live animal exhibits; others are killed for products such as clothing (fur, leather), jewelry, souvenirs, decorations, trophy parts, and medicines. Some wildlife are considered pests and killed to keep them out of areas inhabited by humans. Recently, the illegal or commercial trade in bushmeat (wildlife killed for food) in parts of Africa has passed habitat loss as the biggest threat to such animals as elephants, gorillas, forest antelope, and crocodiles (Bushmeat Crisis Task Force. *www.bushmeat.org/whatis.html*.)

What Is Legal Wildlife Trade?

Most animals can be legally hunted, captured, and traded by following local, national, or international laws. Special permits are required to trade endangered or threatened wildlife and wildlife in fragile ecosystems. (An "endangered" species is one that is threatened with extinction. A "threatened" species is one that has an uncertain chance of survival—that is, it is likely to become an endangered species.) The common goal of the laws is to keep the number of animals in a species or population high enough to protect the ecosystem's health and to keep the species from going extinct.

Handout D
The Billion-Dollar Market of International Wildlife Trade

Why Do People Engage in Illegal Wildlife Trade?

People begin hunting, capturing, and trading wildlife illegally when

- Buyers can not find the product legally.
- There are more buyers than there are wildlife products available to buy.
- The wildlife is rare and hard to hunt or capture.

Wildlife Trade Fact

Wildlife trade is by no means always a problem and most wildlife trade is legal. However, it has the potential to be very damaging; populations of species on Earth declined by about 40%, on average, between 1970 and 2000—and the second-biggest threat to species survival, after habitat destruction, is wildlife trade. (TRAFFIC/Wildlife trade-monitoring network: *www.traffic.org/wildlife/wild2.htm*)

What Role Do YOU Play in International Crimes Against Wildlife?

Most of us believe we never directly or intentionally harm animals. Unfortunately, though, simply by living in today's world we may be contributing to wildlife crimes by unknowingly supporting the people who commit them. The key to breaking support for these illegal activities is increasing public awareness of the types of crimes committed against wildlife, the laws protecting wildlife, and the ways we may be contributing to these crimes.

Are You Breaking Wildlife Protection Laws When You Shop?

Without looking very hard, it's possible to find and purchase either illegal products or illegally obtained live animals in most communities in the United States. When we travel abroad, we may find beautiful unique souvenirs for sale. Ivory carvings, coral jewelry, leather belts and wallets, fur rugs or coats, wall decorations of feathers and shells, or collections of butterflies are tempting gifts.

We also might eat at a restaurant that offers exotic foods like sea turtle soup, shark steaks, songbird eggs or caviar. Markets in some parts of the worlds sell living and dead primates, antelope, and many other native animals for meat. Bushmeat, meat from wildlife used as food, is often taken illegally and sold for profit. The general term *bushmeat* covers a diverse range of species, including monkeys, porcupines, rats, lions and even elephants. Purchases of any of these items can support crimes against wildlife. In some parts of the world,

Handout D
The Billion-Dollar Market of International Wildlife Trade

bushmeat trade has become a more serious threat to wildlife populations than habitat loss!

Though it may not be illegal to buy these items or food in other countries, it is illegal to bring them into the United States. If customs agents find illegal animals, animal parts or products, they will confiscate them. The person possessing them could be fined or arrested.

How Do Your Purchases Support the Illegal Sales of Wildlife, Wildlife Parts, and Products?

Look around your house, school, and favorite stores and restaurants. You might find an item made from an animal protected by law. Most people never realize they have bought something illegal. Others may say, "It does not matter. It was already dead." or "Someone else would have bought it if I didn't."

The truth is that every purchase of an illegal animal, animal part, or product increases the incentive for sellers to get more. Sellers will always find a way to meet the demand.

Local people are often hired to kill or capture animals for the seller. Your purchase adds to the demand for poachers to take more animals, dead or alive, from their natural habitat.

What Animals, Animal Parts, or Products Are Illegal to Have?

All threatened and endangered animals and plants are protected by international and national laws. In rare instances some of these animals and animal parts are allowed to come into the United States with a special government permit. Is your favorite animal endangered? The U.S. Fish and Wildlife Service maintains the Threatened and Endangered Species database System (TESS), listing all animals and plants classified as protected under American and international law. The database is updated daily and may be viewed online at *www.fws.gov/Endangered/wildlife.html#Species*. The table on the next page is only a sampling of protected animals and some reasons they are killed or captured. Many species of plants are also threatened.

Handout D
The Billion-Dollar Market of International Wildlife Trade

Animal	Examples	Products made from these animals
Bears	Polar, black, grizzly	Paws for soup, gall bladders for traditional medicine, claws for jewelry, fur for rugs, wallets, clothes, and decorative items. Mounted trophies.
Birds	All migratory songbirds, raptors (hawks, eagles, owls, falcons), parrots, macaws, cockatoos	Many sold as pets. Feathers used in decorations. Mounted trophies.
Cats	Jaguars, tigers, African lions, leopards, ocelots, margays	Fur rugs, coats, purses, wallets, decorations. Mounted trophies.
Elephants	African and Asian elephants	Tusk ivory carved into trinkets, jewelry, and other decorative products. Feet made into stools and trashcans. Skin made into leather products.
Marine fish and invertebrates	Many species of fish and clams	Live animals for saltwater aquariums, decorations, and meat.
Marine Mammals	Walruses, whales, seals, sea lions, manatees, porpoises, sea otters	Purses, wallets, and clothing made from sealskin and sea otter fur. Scrimshaw (etching) or carvings from walrus ivory, narwhal bone, or whalebone. Mounted trophies.
Reptiles	Sea turtles, crocodiles, alligators, caiman, many lizards and snakes	Many skin products such as hatbands, shoes, belts, and wallets. Eggs and meat of some are eaten as delicacies. Mounted trophies.
Sharks	Great White shark, nurse shark, whale shark	Meat, skin for shoes, teeth for decorations and jewelry.

National Science Teachers Association

Handout D
The Billion-Dollar Market of International Wildlife Trade

What Laws Are Protecting Wildlife?

Animals are protected by international laws and individual country laws. The Convention on International Trade in Endangered Species of Wild Fauna and Flora (CITES) set laws to protect international trade of threatened and endangered species. More than 160 countries participate. In the United States, the Lacey Act makes it illegal to have any wildlife that was taken in violation of state, federal, foreign, or Indian tribal law. Many other laws protect specific groups of animals (see "National and International Wildlife Laws and Agreements" [Handout E] for more information).

Who Is Poaching?

Poaching rings and black market sales can be very profitable. In the United States poachers can be people you regularly see working at businesses, restaurants, hospitals, and schools. Their reasons for hunting illegally vary from making extra money, to showing their anger at wildlife laws, to feeling the thrill of hunting and killing. Worldwide, poaching is a serious ongoing problem that governments are working to control. The demand for ivory enticed poachers to hunt the African elephant despite protective laws. As a result, the elephant population in Africa was reduced by over 50% between 1977 and 1997, from 1.3 million to 600,000 (*Source*: de Seve, K. 2001. *The elephants of Africa*. From the television series *Nature*, by Thirteen/WNET: New York. Text available online at *www.pbs.org/wnet/nature/elephants/poaching.html*.)

Who Is Protecting Our Wildlife?

Wildlife protection spans from national agencies and organizations to the actions of one person. Internationally, the organization TRAFFIC monitors wildlife trade. Nationally, the U.S. Fish and Wildlife Service employs wildlife inspectors and agents to uncover illegal wildlife activity. Every state has a department of natural resources with state wildlife officers and managers.

Many nonprofit organizations, such as the International Primate Protection League, work to protect animals and educate the public about wildlife concerns. Many of these organizations rely on individual citizens like you to report illegal activity.

What Can I Do?

You can also help protect wildlife from crimes. If you see any suspicious activity when you are in a natural area, report it to local

Handout D
The Billion-Dollar Market of International Wildlife Trade

wildlife officers or police. If you see products being sold that you suspect are made from protected animals, report it. When you shop, find out what the product is made of before buying. Do not buy pets taken from the wild. Follow the suggested buying rule, "If in doubt, do without."

For more information, visit the websites listed in Handout C, "Agencies and Organizations With a Focus on Wildlife Crime and Endangered Species," especially the websites under "International Monitoring Organizations."

How Can You Monitor Your Own Environment?

Ask yourself the following questions:

1. What types of items have I seen or heard about in my community that might have been made illegally from animal parts?

2. What kinds of animals have I seen or heard about in my community that are sold at pet stores or that people have as pets?

3. How can I help reduce crimes against these animals?

Handout E
National and International Wildlife Laws and Agreements

Name _____ Date _____

- CRIME SCENE - DO NOT CROSS - CRIME SCENE - DO NOT CROSS - CRIME SCENE - DO NOT CROSS - CRIME SCENE - DO NOT CROSS - CRIME SCENE - DO NOT CROSS -

Student Overview

For over 100 years, people have protected our wildlife by establishing state, national, and international laws. These protective measures can be credited with bringing many species back from the brink of extinction. Wildlife officers and investigators must understand the laws and be able to recognize when they have been broken. In this activity, students will choose one or more national or international wildlife laws to read about (or research in more depth) and describe to classmates.

Instructions

1. Use the **K-W-L** format to answer the following questions in your Investigator Notebooks about laws that protect wildlife. (**K-W-L** stands for: What I **K**now–What I **W**ant to know–What I **L**earned):

   - *What do I <u>know</u> about laws that protect wildlife? (Put a star by information you are not sure is accurate.)*
   - *What do I <u>want to know</u> about laws that protect wildlife?*
   - *What did I <u>learn</u> about laws that protect wildlife? (Your teacher will tell you when it is time to answer this last question.)*

2. Use the following forensic links to conduct research on the 11 laws and agreements listed on pages 16–19.

   - Bushmeat Crisis Task Force. *www.bushmeat.org*
   - CITES (Convention on International Trade in Endangered Species in Wild Flora and Fauna). *www.cites.org*
   - *Digest of Federal Resource Laws of Interest to the U.S. Fish and Wildlife Service.* U.S. Fish and Wildlife Service. *www.fws.gov/laws/lawsdigest/indx.html*
   - Endangered Species Handbook. *www.endangeredspecieshandbook.org/legislation*
   - *Federal Laws and Related Laws Handbook.* New Mexico Center for Wildlife Law. *http://ipl.unm.edu/cwl/fedbook/airhunt.html*
   - TRAFFIC (The Wildlife Trade Monitoring Network). *www.traffic.org*

Using Forensics: Wildlife Crime Scene!

15

Handout E

National and International Wildlife Laws and Agreements

1. CITES: Convention on International Trade in Endangered Species of Wild Fauna and Flora

The Convention on International Trade in Endangered Species of Wild Fauna and Flora (CITES) is a voluntary international agreement between 169+ international governments. It provides varying amounts of protection to more than 33,000 plant and animal species whose survival is threatened by international trade of the species.

Appendixes I, II, and III to the convention are lists of species given different levels or types of protection from over-exploitation. Appendix I lists about 800 species that are threatened with extinction, and CITES generally prohibits commercial international trade in specimens of these species. However, trade may be allowed under exceptional circumstances, for example, for scientific research. Appendix II lists about 32,500 species that are not necessarily now threatened with extinction but may become so unless trade is closely controlled. The species can only be traded with import and export permits. On Appendix III, the approximately 300 species are not threatened by extinction globally, but one country has asked other countries for help in controlling the trade.

2. African Elephant Conservation Act

This act, passed in 1988, helps protect the African elephant by assisting African countries to enforce laws in places where the elephant is native. It also established the African Elephant Conservation Fund. The act prohibits countries from importing raw African elephant ivory or products made from this ivory. The act was successful in stopping the large international elephant ivory market. In 1989, African elephants were listed as endangered (CITES Appendix I; see #1 above), which ended the international legal trade of their ivory.

3. Airborne Hunting Act

This act, a section of the Fish and Wildlife Act of 1956, prohibits harassing, capturing, or killing birds, fish, and other animals from aircraft. Specifically, while flying in an aircraft, you can not shoot or attempt to shoot any bird, fish or other animal; you can not use an aircraft to harass any bird, fish or other animal; and you can not knowingly participate in using an aircraft for any of these purposes.

Handout E
National and International Wildlife Laws and Agreements

4. Antarctica Conservation Act

The federal law, enacted in 1978, protects the plants and animals of Antarctica as well as Antarctica's ecosystems that the animals depend on for survival. Certain products cannot be taken onto land or ice shelves or into water in Antarctica. Waste can not be left on ice-free land areas or put in water, and cannot be burned in a way that puts pollutants into the air. All vessels coming to Antarctica must follow the regulations in the Act to Prevent Pollution from Ships. All expeditions must be government-approved, and all members of an expedition must know about the environmental protection regulations of this act.

The following activities are only permitted by special permit: disposing of waste that is not approved by the Act to Prevent Pollution from Ships; introducing any nonnative species; entering any Antarctic Specially Protected Area; and capturing, transporting, buying, selling, or possessing any native animal or plant.

5. Eagle Protection Act

This act, passed in 1940, protects the bald and golden eagles in the United States. It is illegal to import, export, harm, capture, or bother the eagles. It is prohibited to sell, purchase, or exchange body parts, nests, eggs, or products made from these animals. Permits may be given for scientific research, exhibits, or Native American spiritual purposes. Violators may be fined from $100,000 to $500,000 and be sentenced to up to two years in prison.

6. The Endangered Species Act

The Endangered Species Act of 1978 prohibits bothering, harming, chasing, hunting, capturing, and collecting those species that are listed as endangered or threatened with CITES (see #1 above). It also prohibits selling, transporting, and possessing a listed species illegally taken within the United States (land, fresh water, and ocean). The regulations are applied to living or dead animals, their body parts, and products made from their body parts. Special permits may be given.

When species are listed by CITES as endangered, it has been shown that they are in danger of extinction in their natural habitats. Species classified as threatened could become endangered if current threats to their survival are not controlled. The Endangered Species Act gives additional protection to species that look similar to those listed as endangered or threatened.

Violators of the Endangered Species Act may be fined up to $50,000 and/or sentenced to one year in prison for crimes involving endangered species and $25,000 and/or six months in prison for crimes involving threatened species.

Handout E

National and International Wildlife Laws and Agreements

7. Humane and Healthful Transport Regulations

The Humane and Healthful Transport of Wild Mammals and Birds into the United States regulations took effect in 1992 under the Lacey Act (#8 in this list). The purpose is to stop the high death rate and inhumane treatment of live animals being imported into the United States. Almost 350,000 caged birds arrived dead in the United States between 1980 and 1991. These regulations require that birds and other animals transported to this country are in cages with plenty of space and are given adequate food and water. They also require that, during the travel period to the United States, the animals are inspected frequently to ensure their healthy arrival.

8. Lacey Act

Before 1900, European and U.S. fashion featured hats decorated with beautiful bird feathers (plumes). Tens of thousands of birds across the world were killed to supply this demand. The Lacey Act of 1900 was passed to stop this enormously damaging trade of bird parts, as well as the killing and trading of deer and other animals for the meat trade. The act strengthened existing laws by prohibiting transporting, buying, and selling wildlife and wildlife body parts across state lines. Before the act's regulations went into effect, people in one state would kill the animals illegally and then cross into another state where the animal was not native to legally sell it. The Lacey Act prohibits transporting, buying, selling, importing, and exporting of any wildlife or plants that are obtained illegally.

Amendments to the act in 1981 raised maximum penalties under the act to sentences of up to one year in jail and/or fines of up to $100,000 for misdemeanors, and five years imprisonment and/or fines up to $250,00 for felonies. Maximum fines for organizations in violation of the Lacey Act are $200,000 for misdemeanor violations and $500,000 for felonies. In addition, vehicles, aircraft, and equipment used in a violation, as well as illegally obtained fish, wildlife, and plants, may be subject to forfeiture. Persons who provide information on violations of the Lacey Act may be eligible for cash rewards.

9. Marine Mammal Protection Act

Before the Marine Mammal Protection Act was passed in 1972, millions of dolphins were drowned in nets set for tuna. The act prohibits harassing, hunting, capturing, killing, importing, or exporting marine mammals (sea otter, walrus, polar bear, dugong, whales, sea lions, and seals). Marine mammals are protected in any ocean or sea or on land controlled by the United States. A permit can be granted

Handout E

National and International Wildlife Laws and Agreements

to zoos or scientific research programs for the capture of marine mammals.

Importing and exporting marine mammals is strictly controlled by permit. U.S. ports and harbors cannot import or export any illegally-taken marine mammal; they cannot possess any illegally taken marine mammal, body parts, or products; and they cannot transport, buy, or sell any marine mammal, body parts, or products.

10. Migratory Bird Treaty Act

The Migratory Bird Treaty Act prohibits the killing of non-game, native migratory birds to be sold for meat or feather trade. First signed in 1918, it now is an agreement among the United States, Canada, Mexico, Japan, and Russia.

The regulations prohibit killing, harming, capturing, possessing, buying, or selling any migratory bird, its feathers or other body parts,

nests, eggs, or products made from body parts. Migratory bird hunting regulations allow the taking of ducks, geese, doves, woodcock, and some other species during established hunting seasons. Special permits may be granted for birds bred in captivity.

Violators can be fined up to $500,000 and sentenced to up to two years in prison.

11. Wild Bird Conservation Act

The Wild Bird Conservation Act of 1992 restricts the huge business of importing wild birds into the United States for the cage bird trade. This law bans the importation of most wild-caught birds, including wild parrots, hummingbirds, and birds of prey. Special permits may be granted to zoos and captive breeding programs. Bird imports have been dramatically reduced because of enforcement of this act.

Section 2

Training
in Forensic
Techniques

Overview

The eight forensic training lessons can be taught in any order. Each also stands alone.

National Science Teachers Association

Handout F
U.S. National Fish and Wildlife Forensics Laboratory: The Real Thing

Name _____ Date _____

- CRIME SCENE - DO NOT CROSS - CRIME SCENE - DO NOT CROSS - CRIME SCENE - DO NOT CROSS - CRIME SCENE - DO NOT CROSS - CRIME SCENE - DO NOT CROSS -

An Overview by Ken Goddard

Veterinary pathologists in the National Fish and Wildlife Forensics Laboratory conduct necropsies (autopsies of animals) on [upper right] a cougar and [upper left] an eagle. The two dead wolves on the floor are waiting to be necropsied to determine how they died. Both were later determined to have been shot, as were the cougar and the eagle.

"The National Fish and Wildlife Forensics Laboratory is the only lab in the world dedicated entirely to examining and identifying evidence from wildlife victims of national and international crime. Opened in 1989, it is run as a typical police crime laboratory. Its unique challenge is to research and develop new animal characteristics that allow scientists to identify a species from body pieces, parts, and products. Staff must be able to prove that the evidence came from one of thousands of possible animal species in the world.

What exactly goes on here? Well, pretty much the same thing that goes on in a regular crime laboratory. But in case you're still curious, all crime laboratories—whether they are police or wildlife oriented—do two things:

- They examine, identify, and compare evidence items using a wide range of scientific procedures and instruments.

- In a triangular manner, they attempt to link suspect, victim, and crime scene with physical evidence.

The only real difference between our wildlife crime lab and a 'typical' police crime laboratory is that our victim is an animal. And we must keep in mind that, every now and then, our suspect will turn out to be an animal also. For obvious reasons, it's important that we not confuse the natural events of 'Mother Nature'—one animal killing another for food or territory—with human violations of wildlife laws."

Ken Goddard is director of the National Forensics Laboratory, U.S. Fish and Wildlife Service, 1490 E. Main St., Ashland, OR 97520-1310. www.lab.fws.gov.

Handout G
Essential Questions
About Crime Scene Investigations

Name_____ Date_____

- CRIME SCENE - DO NOT CROSS - CRIME SCENE - DO NOT CROSS - CRIME SCENE - DO NOT CROSS - CRIME SCENE - DO NOT CROSS - CRIME SCENE - DO NOT CROSS -

Have students write responses to these questions in their Investigator Note-books* and discuss in small groups.

1. Use the **K-W-L** format to answer the following questions (**K-W-L** stands for: What I **K**now—What I **W**ant to Know—What I **L**earned):

   • *What do I <u>know</u> about crime scene investigations? (Put a star by information you are not sure is accurate.)*

   • *What do I <u>want to know</u> about crime scene investigations?*

   • *At the end of the crime investigation (Section 3): What did I <u>learn</u> about crime scene investigations?*

2. How is forensic science different from other kinds of science?

3. Is one type of evidence better than another? Explain.

*For more information on the use of Investigator Notebooks see pages xxv–xxvi.

Topic: forensics
Go to: *www.scilinks.org*
Code: UF01

National Science Teachers Association

Handout H

Your First Wildlife Crime: Moose Slaughter in Maine

Name _____ Date _____

- CRIME SCENE - DO NOT CROSS - CRIME SCENE - DO NOT CROSS - CRIME SCENE - DO NOT CROSS - CRIME SCENE - DO NOT CROSS - CRIME SCENE - DO NOT CROSS

"A $10,000.00 reward is being offered to anyone who can provide information that leads to the arrest of whoever is responsible for the killing of nine moose northwest of Greeneville on or around the 23rd of October. People with any information regarding this case should call the Game Thief Hotline at 1-800-ALERT-US (1-800-253-7887).

"'This is one of the most despicable wildlife killings in the history of this state,' said Lieutenant Pat Dorian of the Maine Warden Service. 'This slaughter defies description.'

"The slaughtered moose carcasses were discovered in a three-mile radius on a logging road in Soldiertown township northwest of Greeneville. The moose were believed to be killed on or around Saturday, October 23, a week before deer season and two weeks after the close of the moose season. If someone saw anyone the weekend of 10/23/99 around Center Pond, we would be very interested in knowing what they saw.

"After the discovery of the nine carcasses, wardens searched the area for physical evidence by foot and with K-9 units. Hunter Checkpoints were established and game wardens patrolled the area. Wardens have also been to area sporting camps, lodges, and area motels seeking information about the nine dead moose.

"We had nearly the entire division working on this when discovered for about ten days. We have brainstormed every night. We know that it is someone who is very familiar with the country up here, because the location where the moose were shot is very remote and off the beaten path.

"Inland Fisheries and Wildlife biologist Doug Kane inspected the dead animals and determined that there was one bull moose, four mature females and four moose calves under a year old.

"Over 100 people were interviewed in conjunction with the killing and more will be as we find more leads. There is a list of suspects and a considerable amount of physical evidence but more information is needed to wrap up this case. There is no question that more than one person was involved in this slaughter.

"'We take each and every wildlife crime seriously,' said Joe Maslach, game warden in Eureka. 'These crimes deprive sportsmen of the opportunity to legally hunt these animals, and these crimes also hurt our wildlife management efforts.'"

—*Operation Game Thief, Maine Department of Inland Fisheries and Wildlife.* www.maine.gov/ifw/aboutus/wardenservice/operationgamethief/index.htm

Handout H
Your First Wildlife Crime: Moose Slaughter in Maine

Student Questions

1. What do the authorities know about the crime?

   a. Whom do they suspect? (general characteristics)
   b. What was the crime?
   c. When was the crime?
   d. Where was the crime?

2. How could the following types of evidence help solve this crime?

   • Antlers
   • Human blood
   • DNA
   • Fingerprints
   • Animal and human hair
   • Unidentified liquid and powders
   • Animals skull
   • Animal tracks

3. What are the next steps the investigators should take?

Lesson 1:
Antlers and Horns

The Crime: "Trophy Hunter Caught"

"Thanks to an Operation Game Thief tip, a wildlife officer was tipped off to the person that poached a trophy deer buck out of season. The officer investigated the case that [occurred] over 1 year ago. Thanks to the sketch by a deer enthusiast and a concerned tipster, the officer was able to unravel this case and retrieve this illegally taken magnificent trophy. On December 29, [the suspect] pled guilty to illegal killing, possession and unlawful transport of game."

New Mexico Game and Fish (state agency). www.wildlife.state.nm.us/enforcement/operation_game_thief/index.htm

Investigator Questions

1. What was the crime?

2. The deer was killed for trophy parts. What does that mean?

3. How did the sketch help in solving this crime?

Lesson 1: Antlers and Horns

Teacher Guidelines

Overview

Animals across the world are killed legally and illegally for their antlers and horns. These trophy parts—an entire antler or head mount, or a piece made into a knife handle or ground into medicines—can become crucial pieces of evidence to prove a crime has been committed. In this lesson, students will practice different parts of scientific inquiry by differentiating among different species' antlers and horns. They will describe, measure, and draw the specimens; communicate their observations; and analyze other students' work.

Connections to the National Science Education Standards

Standard	Category	Lesson Connection
Content Standard A—Abilities necessary to do scientific inquiry (grades 5–12)	Science as Inquiry	Students examine antlers and horns, and distinguish among them by writing qualitative and quantitative data. Students critique other students' data and use references to identify the species of the antlers and horns.
Content Standard C—Structure and function in living systems (grades 5–8)	Life Science	Students compare (1) structure and function of antler and horn tissue layers and (2) changing structure and function of antlers and horns at different times of the year or of the animal's lifetime.
Content Standard C—Behavior of organisms (grades 9–12)	Life Science	Students explain male behavior as it relates to testosterone levels, time of year, antler growth.

Time Required

1 50-minute class

Materials

- Handouts (one for each student):
  - "Antlers and Horns: Student Lab Investigation" (Handout 1-A, p. 32)
  - "Specialized Headgear: Antlers and Horns" (Handout 1-B, p. 35)
  - "Antlers Through the Seasons" (Handout 1-C, p. 39)
- Antlers and horns from eight North American mammals (preferably, antlers of a mule deer, whitetail deer, elk, moose, and caribou; horns of a mountain goat, bighorn sheep, and American pronghorn)
- 4 or 5 sets of "Animal Headgear Information" cards (one set for each group) (see pp. 42–43)
- Approximately 20 half-sheets of unlined paper (to be used as "observation sheets" by students)
- Tape measures, or string and rulers

Teaching Plan

Getting Ready

1. Get a variety of antlers and horns from eight different North American mammals (see "Materials" list). These can be borrowed from

   - Local nature centers
   - Your state department of natural resources, division of wildlife
   - Hunters or taxidermists
   - Natural history museums
   - Hunting and fishing stores

   Note: If you can not get actual antlers and horns, use photos of the animals (copy from books, wildlife magazines, or an internet image search).

2. Set up "headgear" lab stations. Each should have

   - One numbered antler or horn
   - Tape measure, or string and ruler

Section 2: Training in Forensic Techniques

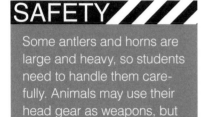

SAFETY

Some antlers and horns are large and heavy, so students need to handle them carefully. Animals may use their head gear as weapons, but students should not.

3. Prepare the eight "Animal Headgear Information" cards (one set for each group) by cutting along dotted lines on pages 42–43. Laminate the cards if you plan to use them repeatedly.

Guiding Students

1. Read aloud and discuss "The Crime: 'Trophy Hunter Caught'" (p. 27).

2. Use the K-W-L format. Have students respond to the following questions in their Investigator Notebooks:

   • *What do I know about antlers and horns? (Put a star by information you are not sure is accurate.)*
   • *What do I want to know about antlers and horns?*

3. Explain that a forensic scientist (the students) must examine the antler or horn evidence, identify the animal species, and defend his or her analysis. To do this, the forensic scientist compares the evidence with drawings, descriptions, and measurements of known antlers and horns.

4. Put students in groups of 2–4 so all have an assigned "headgear" lab station. As you go over lab instructions (see "Antlers and Horns: Student Lab Investigation," p. 32), talk about the meaning of qualitative data (e.g., drawings, descriptions) and quantitative data (e.g., measurements, counts) as they relate to what the students will do.

5. Have students do the lab.

6. After students complete the lab, read and discuss "Specialized Headgear: Antlers and Horns" (Handout 1-B).

7. Read and discuss "Antlers Through the Seasons" (Handout 1-C) to learn about the role of testosterone in antler growth and male behavior.

8. Revisit "The Crime: 'Trophy Hunter Caught'" as a class to see if students have new insights.

National Science Teachers Association

Extensions

- Look at field guides or websites to compare antlers and horns of other animals not included in the lab investigation.
- Invite a wildlife officer, nature center speaker, or hunter to talk with the class about local animals with antlers and horns.
- Do the lab activity "Measuring Antlers" in *Wild About Elk: An Educator's Guide* by Project Wild, Western Regional Environmental Education Council, Inc., and Rocky Mountain Elk Foundation. (Available from Project Wild, 5430 Grosvenor Lane, Bethesda, MD 20814, 301-493-5447, e-mail *natpwil@igc.apc.org*.) OR Rocky Mountain Elk Foundation, 2991 W. Broadway, P.O. Box 8249, Missoula, MT 59807-8249.)

WEB LINKS

Play a matching game at the "Official Kidsite of Yellowstone National Park." Practice your skills at matching an animal with the correct antler or horn. *www.nps.gov/yell/kidstuff/AHgame/ahdiffer.htm*

Animal Diversity Web. Extensive animal field guide. *http://animaldiversity. ummz.umich.edu/site/index.html.*

Lewa Wildlife Conservancy (LWC). 2006. Uses of rhino horn. *www. lewa.org/rhino-horn-uses.php*

REFERENCES

Burt, W. H., and R. P. Grossenheider. 1998. *A field guide to mammals: North America north of Mexico.* Peterson Field Guides series. Boston: Houghton Mifflin.

Harrell, A. 2006. *Point Reyes (California) Light.* Park rangers are after elk antler poachers who sell the aphrodisiac to black-market shops in Chinatown. March 2.

Wild about elk: An educator's guide. 1994. Missoula, MT: Rocky Mountain Elk Foundation. Project Wild, Western Regional Environmental Education Council.

Handout 1-A
Antlers and Horns:
Student Lab Investigation

Name _____ Date _____

· CRIME SCENE · DO NOT CROSS · CRIME SCENE · DO NOT CROSS · CRIME SCENE · DO NOT CROSS · CRIME SCENE · DO NOT CROSS · CRIME SCENE · DO NOT CROSS ·

Your Job

In groups, examine antlers and horns at lab stations set up by your teacher. Show how each horn or antler at the station is unique through your descriptions, measurements, and drawings. Exchange your written analysis with another group's and check the accuracy of their analysis by comparing it with the antler or horn they observed. Finally, determine the species of the headgear using the Animal Headgear Information Cards that your teacher will give you after you have analyzed the antlers/horns at at least three stations.

Your Steps

1. Go to your assigned lab station. Choose a member of the group to be a recorder. The recorder, with the group's help, writes down the following on a half-sheet of paper—your "observation sheet." *Note:* Do not record the antler or horn number that your teacher has assigned to the lab station on your observation sheet. Make a key with this information on a separate piece of paper.

    • Names of people in the group.
    • Qualitative data (You want other students to be able to read your observations and identify which specimen you are describing.)
      ▪ Write a description of the antler/horn.
      ▪ Draw the design and shape of the antler/horn.
    • Quantitative data
      ▪ Make a measurement of the antler/horn.
      ▪ Count something on the antler/ horn (be sure to write down what it is that you have counted).
      ▪ Give size comparisons or ratios between parts on the antler/horn (example: _____ is two times as long as _____).

2. Visit at least three lab stations. Use a new sheet of paper at each new station. When finished, give your written observations to the teacher.

National Science Teachers Association

Handout 1-A
Antlers and Horns:
Student Lab Investigation

3. Your teacher will pass out the observations, making sure that groups do not get their own. Read the written observations of another group and find the specimen described. Check for accuracy of all parts of the observations. Write the specimen number on the top of the matching observations.

4. Return the papers to the group recorders for them to check.

5. Get a set of "Animal Headgear" information cards. Working in your groups, determine the species for each antler and horn. Record your decisions in a two-column table (column one: lab station number; column two: species).

6. Discuss or write answers to the following questions:

What Did You Discover About Antlers and Horns?

1. Which was easier—writing a descriptive observation of the specimens or checking the accuracy of another group's observations? Why?

2. When you wrote your descriptions, which antler/horn was the easiest to describe? Why? Which was the hardest? Why?

3. When you checked the accuracy of other observations, which description was easiest to match with the specimen? Why? Which was hardest to match? Why?

4. Which type of information was most helpful in matching the description to the correct antler or horn: written word description, drawing, measurement, or counts? Why?

5. How would these observation skills be important for solving a wildlife crime?

6. Read your comments on antlers and horns in your Investigator Notebook (*What do I know…*, *What do I want to know…*). Now answer this question: *What have I learned about antlers and horns?*

Handout 1-A
Antlers and Horns: Student Lab Investigation

STUDENTS: TAKE A CLOSER LOOK

- One person claims a new species has horns and someone else says it has antlers. How could they find the correct answer by observing the animal for a year?
- When would a female deer choose to mate with a male who is not the strongest and does not have the largest antlers or horns? Defend your answer.
- How does testosterone affect changes in both antler growth and male behavior?

National Science Teachers Association

Handout 1-B
Specialized Headgear: Antlers and Horns

Name _____ Date _____

Public Demand For Antlers and Horns

The antlers and horns of many different animals across the globe are popular both for their ornamental beauty and their perceived medicinal value. The demand for these antlers and horns has fueled illegal hunting and the trafficking (buying and selling) of these items. In some countries in the Middle East, rhinoceros horns are still used to make dagger handles. Ground into a powder, rhino horn is prescribed to treat fevers in traditional Chinese medicine in parts of the world today (LWC 2006). Pieces of elk antler are sold illegally as an aphrodisiac (a food or drug that people believe arouses sexual desire), priced as high as several hundred dollars an ounce. The market for this item has become a problem in America's national parks, where rangers have reported finding dead (obviously killed) elk with sawed-off antlers (Harrell 2006).

What Does the Forensic Scientist Need To Know?

Forensic scientists are often sent items made from animal parts that were collected in police seizures. In order to determine if a crime has been committed, scientists must first identify from which animal the antler or horn came. Even a small portion of this material can be enough to determine the species of origin. Thus, such material is valuable evidence in wildlife crime investigation.

Deer and elk can only be killed during certain seasons. Therefore, scientists must be able to tell the season the antler was taken. Federal law states that antlers in velvet (skin that allows the antler to grow) must be treated with formaldehyde to make the velvet useless for traditional Asian medicines. Since it is illegal to have untreated velvet antlers, scientists must run chemical tests to determine if formaldehyde treatment has been done.

Anatomy of Antlers And Horns

What animals have horns?

Bighorn sheep, white sheep, mountain goats, bison, musk ox, American pronghorn.

What are horns?

Horns are a permanent part of the animal's skull and have three layers (Figure 1.1). The inner layer extends up from the skull as a bony core (Figure 1.2). It is covered by a thin layer of blood-vessel-rich tissue that supplies blood to the outer layer of the horn, called the sheath. This

Handout 1-B
Specialized Headgear: Antlers and Horns

third layer is made of keratin, a protein that is also in fingernails and hair. The sheath continues to grow throughout the animal's life and is what people are referring to when they use the term *horn* (Figure 1.3).

1.1

A: Core
B: Sheath
C: Keratin

1.2

Skull showing the bony core.

1.3

Outer keratin layer—the "horn" as we know it.

Both males and females have horns, though the females' are usually smaller. Horns are not shed except in American pronghorns, who shed the keratin sheath once each year.

What animals have antlers?

White-tail deer, mule deer, elk, caribou, moose

What are antlers?

Antlers grow from the skull (Figure 1.4), and are shed once each year. They are made of bone that grows from two disc-shaped bumps on the skull, called pedicles. During the months when the antler is growing, the soft cartilage is covered by blood-vessel-rich skin called velvet. When the antler is finished growing, this tissue dies, the cartilage hardens to bone and the velvet falls off. In all but one species, the caribou, only males grow antlers. Both sexes of caribou have antlers, though the females' are smaller.

How big do antlers and horns grow?

The size of a male's antlers or horns tells a story. To grow large antlers or horns, a male must be healthy and well fed—and strong enough to carry the weight of this specialized headgear. Elk antlers can weigh up to 25–40 pounds (11–18 kg). Male bighorn sheep horns can weigh as much as 30 pounds (14 kg). That is

Handout 1-B
Specialized Headgear: Antlers and Horns

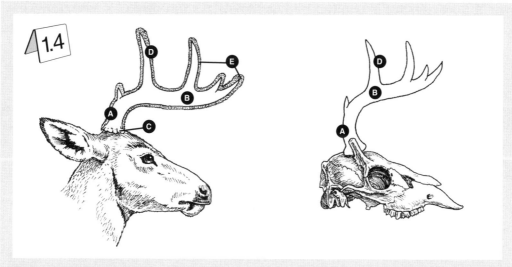

Antler

A: Base—the raised rounded end of the main beam that is attached to the skull.
B: Main beam—the part of the antler that grows from the base and supports the branching tines (points).
C: Pedicle—disc-shaped bumps of bone on the skull from which antlers grow.

D: Prong or Tine—a point on an antler that is at least 1 inch long and longer than it is wide.
E: Velvet—layer of blood-vessel-rich skin that covers the outside of a growing antler and supplies it with blood.

more that the weight of all other bones in his body!

What's the Purpose of Antlers and Horns?

Rutting (mating) season is the one time during the year that males gather with the female herds. Drama unfolds as the males battle each other with their horns and antlers for territory closest to the females. Holding onto this choice spot means a male has more chances of mating with a female when she is ready. Even though the stronger, larger males

STUDENTS: TAKE A CLOSER LOOK

- What are anatomical differences between antlers and horns?
- If an animal has antlers or horns, it must be a male. Agree or disagree. Defend your answer.
- An animal has to be killed to get its antlers or horns. Agree or disagree. Defend your answer.

Handout 1-B
Specialized Headgear: Antlers and Horns

stay busy chasing the other males away from the females, they do not have exclusive access. Females will mate with other males if the larger male's attention is distracted or if a less dominant male is closer and more convenient to the female.

REFERENCES

Harrell, A. 2006. *Point Reyes (California) Light.* Park rangers are after elk antler poachers who sell the aphrodisiac to black-market shops in Chinatown. March 2.

Lewa Widlife Conservancy (LWC). 2006. Uses of rhino horn. *www.lewa.org/rhino-horn-uses.php*

Handout 1-C
Antlers Through the Seasons

Name _____ Date _____

SS - CRIME SCENE - DO NOT CROSS - CRIME SCENE - DO NOT CROSS - CRIME SCENE - DO NOT CROSS - CRIME SCENE - DO NOT CROSS - CRIME SCENE - DO NOT CROS!

How can males grow huge antlers in just a few months? Why do antlers always begin growing in the spring, lose their velvet in the fall, and fall off the male's head in the winter? Why do new antlers begin growing as soon as the full-grown antlers fall off? The answer to all these questions is … hormones, hormones, and more hormones!

Antlers in the Spring to Mid-Summer

Spring signals the start of new antlers. Soft layers of cartilage, growing from the pedicle on the head, are covered by velvet (Figure 1.5). This thin layer of living tissue is filled with blood vessels. Antlers grow rapidly—moose antlers, for example can grow up to one inch a day. Although antlers can be damaged during this growing stage, the velvet provides some protection while supplying blood to the growing tissue.

Why do the antlers grow?

An increase in daylight triggers the body to make high levels of the male hormone testosterone. This hormone stimulates the growth of antlers.

Antlers in Late Summer

Antlers begin to harden into bone and the velvet begins to fall off. This is when males can be seen rubbing their antlers against trees to shed their velvet (Figure 1.6).

Deer with velvet antlers.

Elk rubbing velvet strips on tree.

Handout 1-C
Antlers Through the Seasons

Why do the antlers stop growing?

Blood stops flowing through the velvet to the antlers, causing the living tissue to die. The antlers stop growing, and change from soft cartilage to hard bone.

Antlers in Early Fall

The antlers, cleaned of all velvet, are marked with grooves and ridges where blood vessels once lay. The antlers are firmly attached to the pedicle on the animal's skull. This is the season of rut, when males use their antlers to battle for the territory closest to the females. Claiming and defending this prime location gives them more chances to mate.

Why do the antlers remain in place?

Testosterone remains high in early fall. This keeps the antlers firmly attached to the skull. It also affects the male's behavior during the rutting season. Males become more aggressive and willing to fight for territory next to the females (Figure 1.7).

Antlers in Late Fall Through Early Winter

Rut and mating season ends. The males stop battling for territory, leave the females, and go off on their own.

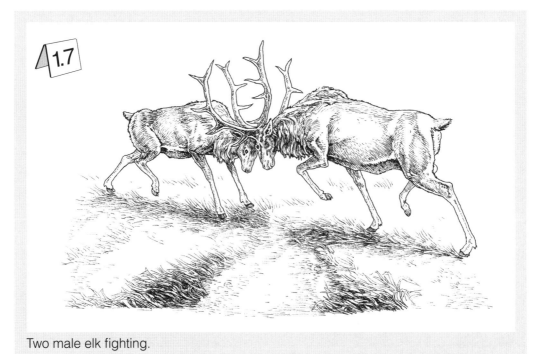

1.7

Two male elk fighting.

Handout 1-C

Antlers Through the Seasons

Why do males stop battling?

Testosterone levels begin to drop, and so does the male's aggressive mating behavior.

Antlers in Late Winter

Antlers fall off (are shed). Like kids wiggling loose teeth, males can be seen rubbing partially attached antlers on trees. It is not unusual to see a male with one antler hanging or missing (Figure 1.8). In a few months the cycle will begin again as a new set of antlers begins to grow.

Why do antlers fall off?

Testosterone levels drop to their lowest points, causing the antler to detach from the pedicle.

1.8

Deer with one antler.

Mule deer

The male's antlers have prongs that branch out in pairs. There is not a main beam from head to tip.

Whitetail deer

The male's antlers have prongs that extend up from a main beam. The main beam curves forward over the head.

Elk

The male has wide branching antlers as long as 1.1–1.5 m from tip to tip. The main beam curves toward the elk's back with prongs extending up from the beam.

Moose

Males have massive flat antlers with fingerlike prongs around the edges. The antler spread can measure up to 2 meters from tip to tip. These are the largest antlers of any animal in the world.

National Science Teachers Association

Bighorn sheep

The male's massive horns curve back, down, and out, and then forward again to make a complete circle. They can weigh as much as 14 kg. A female's horns are much smaller and only slightly curved. Interesting fact: Bighorn sheep have double-layered skulls to protect themselves from powerful head poundings during male rut battles.

American pronghorn

Its horns are unique. The outer, pronged horn is actually a keratin sheath of hair that is shed every year. Under the sheath is a pointed bone extending from the skull. Male horns (average 25 cm) are larger, black, and pronged. Female horns (average 12 cm) are shorter and rarely pronged.

Caribou

All males, and more than half the females, have antlers that are partially flattened (palmated) with fingerlike prongs around the edges. One flattened section comes down over the nose. Female caribou, whose antlers are smaller than the males, are the only females to grow antlers.

Mountain goat

Both males and female have thin, pure black horns (20–30 cm long) that curve backwards.

Using Forensics: Wildlife Crime Scene!

Lesson 2:
Blood and Blood Typing

SCiLINKS
THE WORLD'S A CLICK AWAY

Topic: blood types
Go to: *www.scilinks.org*
Code: UF02

The Crime: "Deer Poachers Found"

"ELKO, Nev.—Investigations by Nevada Department of Wildlife [NDOW] game wardens have led to the conviction and sentencing of three men for wildlife crimes in Northern Nevada. The two separate cases covered illegal taking of wildlife and needless waste of a game animal.

"'The success of these cases hinged on information provided by concerned sportsmen,' said Rob Buonamici, chief game warden at NDOW. 'We cannot be everywhere at every moment, so we rely heavily on tips from those sportsmen and women who really care about ethical hunting and Nevada's wildlife resources.'

"In [one] case, two men shot and killed a two-point mule deer buck in a remote portion of Elko County with no valid tag and well outside of hunting season. They shot the animal near a jobsite where they were both working. The men took the hindquarters for meat, but left the rest of the animal to waste...."

Source: "Game Warden Investigations Lead to Numerous Convictions." May 3, 2006. Nevada Department of Wildlife. www.ndow.org/about/news/pr/050306poaching_convictions.shtm

Investigator Questions

1. What is the crime?

2. How could blood from the deer be used as evidence?

3. If a forensic scientist found a small amount of human blood on the deer parts that were left in the field, how could this become useful evidence?

Lesson 2: Blood and Blood Typing

Teacher Guidelines

Overview

Blood collected at the scene of a wildlife crime can be identified through a lab test as human or nonhuman. If human, a quick blood-typing test will let investigators begin building a description of a suspect.

In this lesson, the students will use blood antigen (agglutinogen) and antibody (agglutinin) diagram cards to construct blood types and determine safe transfusions for donors and recipients. Then they will apply their knowledge by (1) conducting a lab using simulated blood to test for blood types and Rh factors of four fictitious people and (2) explaining the role of blood type identification in solving crimes.

Connections to the National Science Education Standards

Standard	Category	Lesson Connection
Content Standard A—Abilities necessary to do scientific inquiry (grades 5–12)	Science as Inquiry	Students • discover and demonstrate understanding of blood antigens and antibodies through independent or guided activities with manipulative items. • conduct a pre-designed lab to test for unknown blood types and explain how they identified blood types.
Content Standard C—Structure and function in living systems (grades 5–8) The cell (grades 9–12)	Life Science	Students demonstrate understanding of the structure and function of blood antigens and antibodies as they are found naturally in the body and as they interact during a blood transfusion.

Content Standard E— Understandings about science and technology (grades 5–12)	Science and Technology	Students explain how people have benefited from technological advances that led to the discovery of blood antigens and antibodies, accurately identifying donors and recipients.

Time Required

2 50-minute class periods

Materials

- Handouts (one for each student):
  - "Unlocking the Mysteries of Blood Types" (Handout 2-A, p. 52)
  - "Matching Blood Types" (Handout 2-B, p. 55)
  - "Blood Types: What Did I Discover?" (Handout 2-C, p. 61)
  - "Are You My (Blood) Type? Student Lab Investigation" (Handout 2-D, p. 64)
- Simulated blood kit
- "Blood Antigen and Antibodies" cutouts (see Teaching Plan [Getting Ready, #2]) and 4 or 5 ziplock plastic bags to hold the cutouts
- "Rh Antigens and Antibodies" cutouts (see Teaching Plan [Getting Ready, #2]) and 4 or 5 ziplock plastic bags to hold the cutouts

Teaching Plan

Getting Ready

1. Order simulated blood kit from science supply company (e.g., Carolina Biological Supply Company).

2. For each group of four students, make three copies of "Blood Antigens and Antibodies" (p. 47). Laminate. Cut out (or have students cut out) each piece (RBCs and antibodies) and put in a ziplock plastic bag. One bag will go to each student group. (For additional distinctions, you can color code the antigens and antibodies [e.g., antigen and antibody A = red; antigen and antibody B = blue].)

Blood Antigens and Antibodies

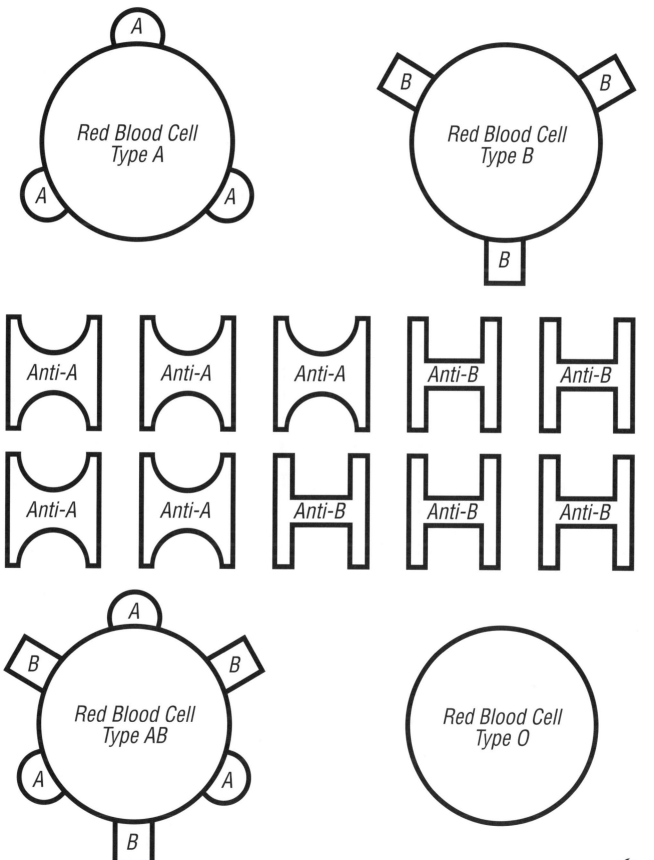

Rh Antigens and Antibodies

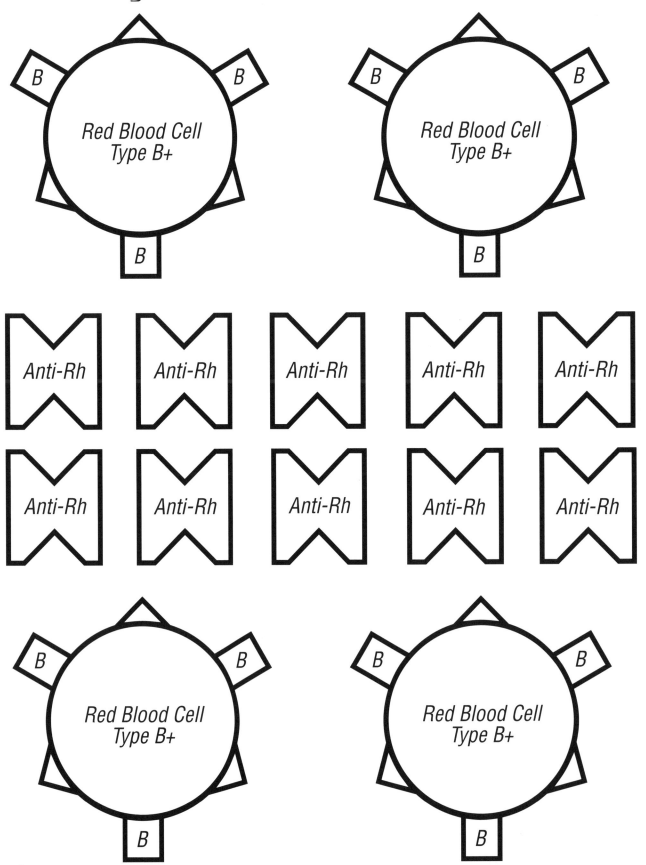

3. Follow the same steps for "Rh Antigens and Antibodies" cut-outs (p. 48).

Guiding Students

1. Read aloud and discuss "The Crime: 'Deer Poachers Found'" on page 44.

2. Use the K-W-L format. Have students respond to the following questions in their Investigator Notebooks:

   • *What do I <u>know</u> about blood typing? (Put a star by information you are not sure is accurate.)*
   • *What do I <u>want to know</u> about blood typing?*

Introductory Inquiry Lab

3. Give a spot plate to each small group of students, along with one bottle of simulated blood and antibody sera for type A, type B, and Rh (anti-A, anti-B, and anti-Rh).

4. Have them fill three spot plate wells with two drops of blood each.

5. Have them add two drops of anti-A serum (antibody A) to one well, two drops of anti-B serum to the second, and two drops of anti-Rh serum to the third.

6. Ask students to draw and describe in their Investigator Notebooks what happens over the next few minutes and to give possible reasons for the results.

Note: Depending on the knowledge level of your students, you can use the word *agglutinogen* for *antigen* and *agglutinin* for *antibody*.

Blood Types

7. Give each group one bag of the "Blood Antigens and Antibodies" cutouts. Also give *each student* a copy of Handouts 2-A, 2-B, and 2-C.

8. Have groups work together to complete the activity in "Unlocking the Mysteries of Blood Types" (Handout 2-A) with

teacher guidance or independently. They should assign group roles:

- Person who will read aloud the procedures for "Unlocking the Mysteries of Blood Types."
- Person who passes out and collects the cutouts.
- Person who will read aloud selected portions of "Matching Blood Types."
- Person who will check for accuracy, encourage participation, and ask for teacher clarification if needed.

Simulated Blood Typing Lab

9. Set up lab materials. Give each student a copy of Handout 2-D. Have students complete the lab by testing for antigen A, antigen B, and antigen Rh in simulated blood samples. *Note:* Information about Rh disease could be included after the lab, if it fits the curriculum.

Conclusion

10. Revisit "The Crime: 'Deer Poachers Found'" as a class to see if students have new insights.

STUDENTS: TAKE A CLOSER LOOK

Family members are the first people asked to donate blood if a relative needs a transfusion. Ask members of your immediate and extended family if they know their blood types. Figure out who could donate blood to whom. Who could you donate to? From whom could you receive blood?

Extensions

Contact guest speakers or field trip guides who could make presentations about:
- Blood typing and Rh disease (Contact blood donation center, hospital, doctor's office, March of Dimes)
- Use of blood typing in crime investigation (Contact sheriff or police department, state division of wildlife, U.S. Fish and Wildlife Service, attorneys)

WEB LINKS ⊂⊃⊂⊃⊂⊃⊂⊃⊂⊃⊂⊃⊂⊃⊂⊃⊂⊃⊂⊃⊂⊃⊂⊃

Australian Red Cross. n.d. All about blood, blood types: What are they. *www.arcbs.redcross.org.au/Donor/aboutblood/bloodtypes.asp*

Blood Typing Interactive Game. *www.nobelprize.org/medicine/educational/landsteiner/index.html*

"I would like to donate blood—Do they need all blood types or just certain ones?" How Stuff Works. *www.howstuffworks.com/question593.htm*

Handout 2-A
Unlocking the Mysteries of Blood Types

Name _____ Date _____

Your Job

Use cutouts of red blood cell (RBC) surface antigens and plasma antibodies to find the make-up of each blood type. Determine the donors and recipients for each blood type.

Your Steps

Part 1: Blood Antigens and Antibodies

1. Get a "Blood Antigens and Antibodies" cutout set for your group of four. Take the red blood cells (RBCs) with attached antigens out of the bag. Put one type (A, B, AB, or O) in front of each person.

2. In "Matching Blood Types" (Handout 2-B), read aloud through the end of the section "What Determines Blood Type?"

3. In "Blood Types: What Did I Discover?" (Handout 2-C), answer #1 and #2.

4. Put the the antibodies in the center of the table. From the handout "Matching Blood Types," read aloud the section "What Are Blood Antibodies?" and answer #3 in the handout "Blood Types: What Did I Discover?"

5. Look for an antibody that fits the shape of your RBC's antigen. Fit the two together and show your group. Then show how your same three RBC antigens can be locked together by several antibodies and cause the blood to clot.

Part 2: Donating and Receiving Blood

1. From the handout "Matching Blood Types," read aloud the section "Is This Blood Friend or Foe?" and answer #4 and #5 in the handout "Blood Types: What Did I Discover?"

2. Put all the antibodies back into the center of the table. Look at the shapes and figure out which antibodies will be found naturally in your blood type's plasma. *Remember:* These antibodies should not cause clotting, so they can not match the shape of the antigens.

National Science Teachers Association

3. In the handout "Blood Types: What Did I Discover?" answer #6 and #7.

4. When can a person with one blood type safely donate to a person with a different blood type? *Answer:* A donor should not give RBC antigens to a recipient if the antigens will clot with the recipient's plasma antibodies. If the blood clots, the recipient could die.

    To demonstrate this:

    a. Lay the RBC antigen and antibody cutouts for one blood type in front of each person.
    b. If you are the student with type A, you are the first donor. Hold your antigen card next to each of the blood types, including your own. Ask your group, "Can type A donate to (this blood type) and not cause clotting?" Look at the antibodies.
    c. Record your answers in #8 (table) in "Blood Types: What Did I Discover?"
    d. Repeat this process using the other three blood types as donor blood types.

5. From the handout "Matching Blood Types," read aloud the section "Who Can a Person Donate Blood To?"

6. When can a person with one blood type safely receive blood from a person with a different blood type? *Answer:* A recipient is the person who receives a donor's antigens. The recipient's antibodies should not clot with the donor's antigens.

    To demonstrate this:

    a. Lay out the cutouts as you did in Step 4 above.
    b. If you are type B, you are the first blood recipient. Have each student hold the RBC antigen card for his or her blood type next to the RBC antigen and antibody combination for your blood type. Ask your group, "Can type B receive antigens from this blood type and not clot?"
    c. Record your answers in #9 (table) in "Blood Types: What Did I Discover?".
    d. Repeat this process using the other three blood types as recipients.

7. From the handout "Matching Blood Types," read aloud the section "Who Can a Person Receive Blood From?"

Handout 2-A
Unlocking the Mysteries of Blood Types

8. From the handout "Matching Blood Types," read aloud the section "What Is the Rh Factor in Blood?"

   To demonstrate this:

   a. Put the other cutouts away and get the "Rh Antigens and Antibodies" cutouts from your teacher.
   b. Set an RBC antigen in front of each student. Use the antibodies for Rh to show how clotting can occur.

9. Answer #10, #11, #12, and #13 in "Blood Types: What Did I Discover?"

10. From the handout "Matching Blood Types," read aloud the section "How Is Blood Type Used to Solve Crimes?" and answer #14 in "Blood Types: What Did I Discover?"

Handout 2-B
Matching Blood Types

Name _____ Date _____

- CRIME SCENE - DO NOT CROSS - CRIME SCENE - DO NOT CROSS - CRIME SCENE - DO NOT CROSS - CRIME SCENE - DO NOT CROSS - CRIME SCENE - DO NOT CROSS -

The history of blood research and the role of blood in medicine are marked by trial and error. In 1799, an elderly George Washington was treated by a team of physicians who recommended bloodletting to remove the impurities making him ill. Over a nine-hour period, they removed approximately 3.75 liters—over half the blood in his body! He died the next day (Vadakan 2004).

From its earliest attempts in the 1600s and over hundreds of years following, blood transfusions between people did not have a high rate of success due to the lack of knowledge about the concept of different blood types. It was not until the early 20th century, when Austrian physician Karl Landsteiner announced he had discovered three main types of human blood groups (he was awarded the Nobel Prize for Medicine for this discovery), that people began to understand the vital importance of blood types (EBC 2002).

Today, blood-type identification has uses outside the hospital walls. It can help forensic scientists narrow suspect pools and point to probable suspects involved in crimes, and it can help match parents with children when parentage is in question.

What Does the Forensic Scientist Need to Know?

Forensic scientists distinguish between blood types and know what will happen if different blood types are mixed. In the lab, they can recognize and explain the chemical reactions observed in testing for blood types. Finally, they understand how blood typing can be used as evidence in a crime investigation.

What Determines Blood Type?

A person has the same blood type throughout his or her lifetime. The four different types of human blood (A, B, AB, and O) each have a different combination of proteins attached to the red blood cell (RBC) (Figure 2.1). The two proteins (called antigens or agglutinogens) are called antigen A and antigen B. The type of antigens present give the name of the blood type. Antigen A is found in type A blood; antigen B is found in type B blood; type AB RBCs have both antigens; and type O RBCs have no antigens.

What Are Blood Antibodies?

Blood antibodies are like bodyguards flowing through the plasma in our

Handout 2-B
Matching Blood Types

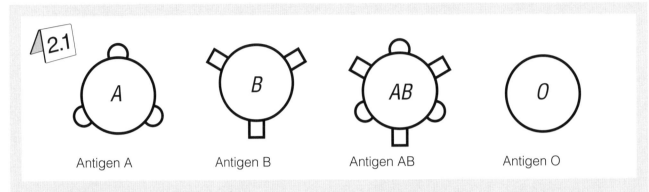

2.1

Antigen A   Antigen B   Antigen AB   Antigen O

RBCs with antigens attached (except for Type O, which has no antigens).

blood vessels. Part of the immune system, they attack foreign RBC antigens by locking onto them like a lock and key (Figure 2.2). This causes the blood to clot and can lead to death. These antibodies begin to form in a baby's blood plasma shortly after birth.

The body makes antibodies for any antigen that is not found naturally on the body's RBCs (Figure 2.3). For example, if the blood has antigen A (type A), the person would make antibody B to attack any foreign antigen Bs that might enter the blood stream. If the blood has antigen B (type B), the person would make antibody A to attack foreign antigen As. If the blood has both antigens A and B (type AB), the person would make *no* blood antibodies. Type O RBCs have no antigens, so the person would make both antibodies A and B.

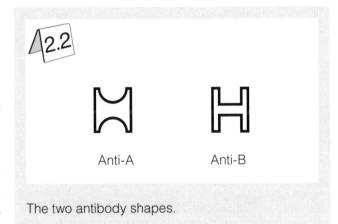

2.2

Anti-A   Anti-B

The two antibody shapes.

Is This Blood Friend or Foe?

A blood transfusion means blood is taken from one person and put directly into another person's blood vessels. Before 1900 many patients mysteriously died from blood transfusions, while others lived. Doctors had no way of determining the blood types of the donor and the recipient of a transfusion, but they knew that transfusions were more successful when the donor

Handout 2-B
Matching Blood Types

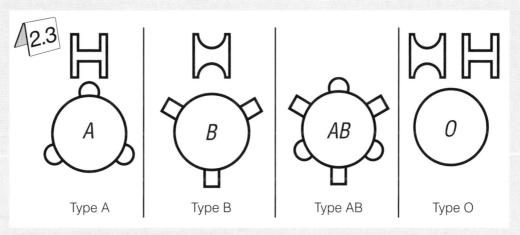

Antigens and antibodies for the four blood types.

was a close relative. In fact, blood type is inherited from parents.

Eventually, technology and lab tests gave doctors and scientists a way to identify the antigens and antibodies in blood. They found that if the donor's red blood cells had antigens that matched the antibodies in the recipient's blood, the antibodies would lock onto the foreign antigens, causing the blood to clot (Figure 2.4). The

result was often the death of the person receiving the blood.

Who Can a Person Donate Blood to?

The discovery of the structure and function of blood antigens and antibodies helped doctors to safely match donors and recipients. The type of antigens on the donor's red blood cells is the important factor in

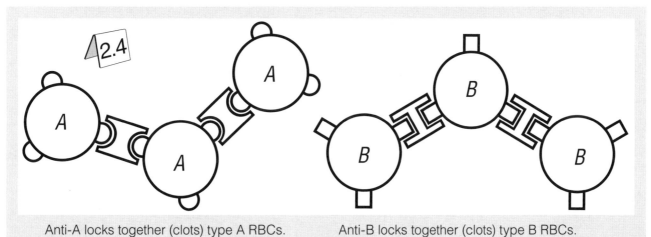

Anti-A locks together (clots) type A RBCs.   Anti-B locks together (clots) type B RBCs.

Handout 2-B
Matching Blood Types

deciding who can donate blood. For instance, a person with antigen A (type A) can donate blood to another person with antigen A (type A and type AB) (Figure 2.5). The donor's antibodies are minimal in a transfusion and do not cause life-threatening harm to the recipient. Type O has no antigens, so no antibodies can lock onto antigen A or antigen B to cause clotting. Type O is called the "universal donor" because it is safe for all recipients.

Who Can a Person Receive Blood From?

A person who needs a blood transfusion can safely receive blood with antigens that match his or her own blood or blood with no antigens (type O). If the patient receives blood with antigens that match his or her plasma antibodies, the blood will clot

and the patient could die (Figure 2.6). For example, if a person has type A (antigen A and antibody B), she can receive type A because the donor's antigen A will not clot with her antibody B. She can also receive type O because it has no antigens to react with her antibodies (Figure 2.7).

If a person has type AB blood (antigens A and B), he can receive any type of blood because his plasma has no antibodies. If a person has type O, he has both antibody A and B in the plasma. The only safe donor is another type O with no antigens.

What Is the Rh Factor of Blood?

The Rh factor is another protein antigen found on the surface of red blood cells. It is either present (+) or absent (-). It was first discovered in, and then

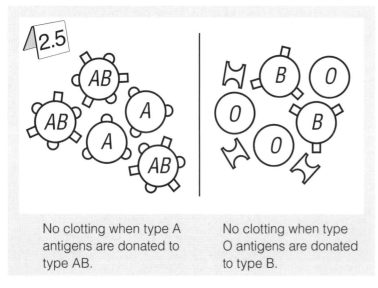

No clotting when type A antigens are donated to type AB.

No clotting when type O antigens are donated to type B.

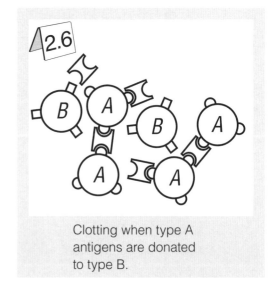

Clotting when type A antigens are donated to type B.

Handout 2-B
Matching Blood Types

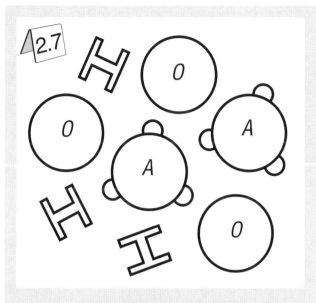

Type A can receive blood from type O.

How Is Blood Type Used to Solve Crimes?

All people fit into one of four blood-type categories. In the United States, 45% of people have type O, 39% have type A, 12% have type B, and 4% have type AB. In terms of forensics, this means blood type can only be used as indirect or circumstantial evidence to classify a suspect with a larger group of people who have the same blood type. It cannot be matched to one individual. For example, if the blood at the crime scene is type O and the suspect's blood is type O, all that can be concluded is that the suspect is in the group of individuals having the blood type of the evidence. If the blood type from

named after, the rhesus (RH) monkey. There is no relationship between a person's blood type and the presence of the Rh-antigen. Each blood type is either Rh+ or Rh-, with 85% of the U.S. population being Rh+.

If a person has the Rh antigen (Rh+), he will not have the Rh antibody in his plasma (Figure 2.8a). An Rh- (no antigen) woman who is pregnant with an Rh+ baby will begin making Rh antibodies if her blood mixes with the baby's. These antibodies will lock onto the baby's Rh antigens and cause the blood to clot. This serious medical condition, called Rh disease, can threaten the lives of her future children (Figure 2.8b). This is also a problem if an Rh- person receives a transfusion of Rh+ blood.

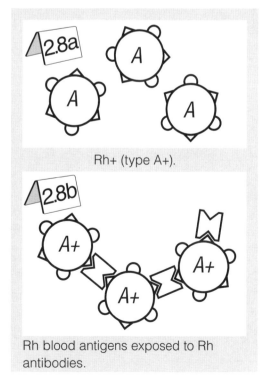

Rh+ (type A+).

Rh blood antigens exposed to Rh antibodies.

Handout 2-B
Matching Blood Types

the scene of a crime is different from that of the suspect, however, it could support a plea of innocence.

A stronger identification test using blood would be to isolate the DNA from the blood and create a DNA fingerprint. These results could be reliably matched to a single individual.

REFERENCES

Educational Broadcasting Corporation (EBC). 2002. Blood history: Discovery and exploration timeline. From the PBS program "Red Gold: The Epic Story of Blood." Timeline available online at *www.pbs.org/wnet/redgold/history/timeline3.html*

Vadakan, V. V. 2004. The asphyxiating and exsanguinating death of President George Washington. *The Permanente Journal* 8 (2): 76–79.

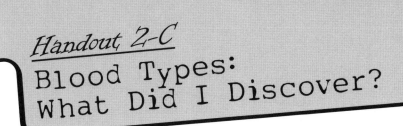

Handout 2-C
Blood Types:
What Did I Discover?

Name _____ Date _____

- CRIME SCENE - DO NOT CROSS - CRIME SCENE - DO NOT CROSS - CRIME SCENE - DO NOT CROSS - CRIME SCENE - DO NOT CROSS - CRIME SCENE - DO NOT CROSS -

1. How is blood typing helpful?

2. What are antigens and where are they found?

3. What are antibodies and where are they found?

4. Draw RBCs with antigen(s) for each blood type. Draw and name the antibodies that will lock onto each blood antigen.

Type A	Type B	Type AB	Type O

5. What would happen if your blood had matching RBC antigens and antibodies, as shown in #4?

6. Draw the combination of antigens and antibodies found naturally in each blood type. (They cannot lock together to cause clotting.)

	Type A	Type B	Type AB	Type O
RBC antigen(s)				
Antibodies naturally found in blood plasma				

61

Handout 2-C
Blood Types:
What Did I Discover?

7. If you have antigens A and B, what is your blood type?

    If you have antibodies A and B, what is your blood type?

8. Each blood type can donate to _____. Mark donor matches with a "yes." *Reminder:* The donor's antigens should not clot with the recipient's antibodies.

	Type A	Type B	Type AB	Type O
Type A can donate to___.				
Type B can donate to___.				
Type AB can donate to___.				
Type O can donate to___.				

9. Each blood type can receive blood from _____. Mark recipient matches with a "yes." *Reminder:* The recipient's antibodies should not clot with the donor's antigens.

	Type A	Type B	Type AB	Type O
Type A can receive blood from ___.				
Type B can receive blood from ___.				
Type AB can receive blood from ___.				
Type O can receive blood from ___.				

National Science Teachers Association

Handout 2-C
Blood Types:
What Did I Discover?

10. What is the Rh factor?

11. Complete this table on Rh factor reactions in blood by putting an X in the correct boxes.

Blood type	Has antigen Rh	Can make antibody Rh	Will clot if antigen Rh is donated
Rh+			
Rh-			

12. Draw the RBC antigens for

   - B+
   - AB+
   - O+

13. Write the blood types, including Rh, for the first set of blood cards you worked with.

14. Blood typing has its limits in identifying an individual in a crime.

   a. Why can't a blood sample be matched to a specific person after comparing blood types?

   b. What additional blood test could give a match to a specific individual?

Handout 2-D
Are You My (Blood) Type?
Student Lab Investigation

Name _____ Date _____

- CRIME SCENE - DO NOT CROSS - CRIME SCENE - DO NOT CROSS - CRIME SCENE - DO NOT CROSS - CRIME SCENE - DO NOT CROSS - CRIME SCENE - DO NOT CROSS -

Your Job

Use simulated blood of four fictitious people to test for blood type and Rh factor.

What You Need to Know

A person's blood type is tested by mixing samples of blood with laboratory solutions that contains anti-A serum (antibody A), anti-B serum (antibody B), and anti-Rh serum (antibody Rh). Clotting proves that a particular antigen was in the blood. For example, if blood clotted with anti-A serum and anti-Rh serum, but did not clot with anti-B serum, then antigens A and Rh were in the blood. The blood type would be A+.

Blood typing is based on a chemical reaction that causes precipitates (solids) to form in specific ionic solutions. In blood typing tests, a precipitate (clot) forms when a particular antigen is present in the blood.

Your Steps

1. Work in pairs to complete the following reference table. Use it to determine blood types from your results.

Reference Table

Complete the table by putting an X in boxes to show when clotting will occur for each blood type. These are the results you should expect to see during the blood typing activity.

Blood type	Add anti-A serum	Add anti-B serum
Type A		
Type B		
Type AB		
Type O		

2. Set the spot plate on a larger-sized paper towel. Trace around the spot plate and label the rows and columns as shown in the "Blood Type Results" diagram.

National Science Teachers Association

Handout 2-D
Are You My (Blood) Type?
Student Lab Investigation

Blood Type Results

Record test results by writing "clot" in the cups that clotted. Based on the three anti-sera tests, determine the blood type for each individual.

Antibody Serum

Blood Sample	Anti-A	Anti-B	Anti-Rh	Blood Type

3. Draw this lab set-up in your Investigator Notebook or lab notes as a diagram or a data table.

4. Put 2–3 drops of the first person's simulated blood in each of the three anti-sera wells for that individual.

5. Test the blood's reaction to each anti-serum by putting 2 drops of anti-A serum into the first well, 2 drops of anti-B serum into the second, and 2 drops of anti-Rh serum into the third.

6. Complete steps 4 and 5 for the other three blood samples.

7. Stir with a toothpick and let the blood mixture sit for 3–5 minutes. Use a magnifying lens to determine if a precipitate has formed. A positive result will show a darkened clumping at the bottom or a crystallized web on the top. (The precipiate appearance will vary depending on the type of blood test kit used.)

8. Record the results and determine the blood type of each individual.

Handout 2-D
Are You My (Blood) Type?
Student Lab Investigation

What Did You Discover About Blood and Blood Typing?

1. Why do some blood types form precipitates when mixed with anti-sera, while others do not?

2. What type antigen is present if a precipitate forms with

   • anti-A serum?

   • anti-B serum?

   • anti-Rh serum?

3. Pick one blood sample and summarize in several sentences your procedure and interpretation of the results. Use the words *antigen, antibodies, anti-serum,* and *precipitate.*

4. Read your comments on blood typing in your Investigator Notebook (*What do I know about blood typing? What do I want to know about blood typing?*). Respond to the following question: *What have I learned about blood typing?*

National Science Teachers Association

Lesson 3: DNA Fingerprinting

The Crime: "Record Ivory Cache Traced to Zambia Elephants, DNA Shows"

Topic: DNA
fingerprinting
Go to: *www.scilinks.org*
Code: UF03

Topic: structure of DNA
Go to: *www.scilinks.org*
Code: UF04

Topic: DNA: structure
and function
Go to: *www.scilinks.org*
Code: UF05

"A trail of DNA has helped investigators trace the largest shipment of contraband ivory ever seized to African savanna elephants from Zambia. The size of the shipment—more than 500 whole tusks and thousands of individual pieces—means that elephants from a single region have been hit hard.

"In June 2002 customs agents in Singapore intercepted a 20-foot (6-meter) container holding 13,000 pounds (5.9 metric tons) of elephant ivory. Investigators wanted to identify which populations of African elephants the ivory had come from, and for that they needed a 'fingerprint' that would lead them to the animals that were killed.

"Two years ago [Sam] Wasser [a wildlife biologist at the University of Washington in Seattle] and his colleagues at the University of Washington published a continent-wide map of genetic fingerprints for African elephants ....To make this map, Wasser's team had sequenced DNA recovered from nearly 500 samples of dung collected from elephants in 23 African countries. Ample roughage [plants] in the elephants' diets helps slough off plenty of cells from the intestines, making DNA easy to extract from dung. Wasser's team found that they were able to identify which country—even which game preserve—new dung samples came from.

"Bill Clark, secretary for the Interpol Working Group on Wildlife Crime, asked Wasser to match DNA from the seized ivory to his genetic map. But getting DNA out of the tusks proved to be a challenge. When Wasser's team compared 75 samples from the illegal shipment to their genetic map, they found that all of the ivory came from Zambia.

"Meanwhile the illegal trade continues. On May 10 customs officials in Hong Kong announced they had confiscated a shipment of 600 African elephant tusks."

Source: Brown, S. "Record Ivory Cache Traced to Zambia Elephants, DNA Shows." August 18, 2006. National Geographic News: Animals and Nature." http://news.nationalgeographic.com/news/2006/08/060817-ivory-DNA .htm/

Investigator Questions

1. What was the crime?

2. How was DNA fingerprinting used to solve the crime?

National Science Teachers Association

Lesson 3: DNA Fingerprinting

Teacher Guidelines

Overview

Courtroom evidence has been forever changed by the development of DNA fingerprinting procedures and the introduction of DNA evidence in a case. A DNA match between a piece of evidence and an individual is as strong a connection as two matching fingerprints. Suspects are regularly convicted or found not guilty of crimes based on DNA evidence.

In this lesson, students will make a visual model for each step of the gel electrophoresis technique for creating a DNA fingerprint. First, they will use scissors to show the actions of a restriction enzyme on a paper DNA strand. Next, they will sort the different-sized DNA pieces on a gel box diagram and graph the DNA pieces' size distribution for the final DNA fingerprint. After comparing and matching classmates' DNA fingerprints, they will explain how DNA fingerprinting can be used to solve crimes.

Note: If appropriate to your class content, a DNA extraction lab or actual DNA electrophoresis lab would be a good follow-up to this unit.

Connections to the National Science Education Standards

Standard	Category	Lesson Connection
Content Standard A—Abilities necessary to do scientific inquiry (grades 5–12)	Science as Inquiry	Students discover and demonstrate, through an independent or teacher-guided paper model simulation, the steps to create a DNA fingerprint through gel electrophoresis. They compare their techniques with actual lab procedures.
Content Standard E—Abilities of technological design (grades 5–12)	Science and Technology	

Standard	Category	Lesson Connection
Content Standard A—Understandings about scientific inquiry (grades 5–12)	Science as Inquiry	Students explain how DNA fingerprint lab techniques allow scientists to match the evidence to one individual and why this is beneficial.
Content Standard C—Reproduction and heredity (grades 5–8) Molecular basis of heredity (grades 9–12)	Life Science	Using a paper model of DNA, students show the organization of nucleotides and the reason why DNA (and the DNA fingerprint) is unique in each individual organism.
Content Standard C—The cell (grades 9–12)	Life Science	Students demonstrate and explain the role of restrictive enzymes in the lab procedure to create a DNA fingerprint.

Time Required

2 50-minute class periods

Materials

- Handouts (one for each student):
  - "Creating a DNA Fingerprint: Student Lab Investigation" (Handout 3-A, p. 73)
  - "Your DNA Strand" (Handout 3-B, p. 79)
  - "DNA: The Golden Key of Forensic Evidence" (Handout 3-C, p. 80)
- Gel box diagram (p. 74)
- Clear tape
- Scissors
- Graph paper (10 divisions/inch or smaller)

Teaching Plan

1. Read aloud and discuss "The Crime: 'Record Ivory Cache Traced to Zambia Elephants, DNA Shows.'"

2. Use the K-W-L format. Have students respond to the following questions in their Investigator Notebooks:

   - *What do I <u>know</u> about DNA fingerprints? (Put a star by information you are not sure is accurate.)*

National Science Teachers Association

• *What do I <u>want to know</u> about DNA fingerprints?*

3. Give each student the student lab investigation "Creating a DNA Fingerprint: Student Lab Investigation" (Handout 3-A) and each pair of students "Your DNA Strand" (Handout 3-B). Read aloud the subsection "Getting the DNA From the Cells" from the Student Lab Investigation (Handout 3-A) and let students create their DNA strand for testing.

   Note: To save time or to guarantee DNA fingerprint matches within the class, you can tape the strands together before the lab.

4. Read and discuss "DNA: The Golden Key of Forensic Evidence" (Handout 3-C).

5. Instruct students to independently complete the lab in pairs, or guide them through the procedure as a class, discussing each step along the way.

6. When their DNA fingerprint "photographs" are completed, students should post them next to each other in the room, compare the images, and identify any matches.

7. Revisit "The Crime: 'Record Ivory Cache Traced to Zambia Elephants, DNA Shows'" as a class to see if students have new insights.

Extensions

• Conduct a lab that isolates actual cellular DNA into a visible substance.
• Conduct a DNA gel electrophoresis lab to create an actual DNA fingerprint.
• Visit a lab that creates DNA fingerprints or have a scientist visit the classroom.
• Invite an attorney, scientist, and/or law enforcement officer to talk to the class about DNA evidence.

WEB LINKS

Bergen County Technical Schools. June 2004. Background and theory. The Forensics Project. *www.bergen.org/EST/Year5/theory.htm*

DNA fingerprints. *http://en.wikipedia.org/wiki/DNA _fingerprints*

REFERENCES

Friend, T. 1995. DNA fingerprinting: Power tool. *National Wildlife* (Oct./ Nov.): 17–23.

Nunley, K. F. 1996. Making DNA fingerprints. *The Science Teacher* (March): 32–25.

Handout 3-A
Creating a DNA Fingerprint: Student Lab Investigation

Name _____ Date _____

- CRIME SCENE - DO NOT CROSS - CRIME SCENE - DO NOT CROSS - CRIME SCENE - DO NOT CROSS - CRIME SCENE - DO NOT CROSS - CRIME SCENE - DO NOT CROSS -

Your Job

To re-create the procedures used in a real forensic lab for making a DNA fingerprint, you will use paper, scissors, and graph paper.

Your Steps

1. Getting the DNA From the Cells

   In a Real Forensic Lab

   DNA can be isolated from small pieces of hair, skin, blood, saliva, or other body tissue or fluid. In plants, animals, fungi, and protists, DNA is found in the cell nucleus (Figure 3.1). The first step in the procedure is to destroy the cellular and nuclear membranes so that the heavy DNA molecules can be separated from the rest of the cellular material (Figure 3.2).

   Your Re-Creation

   Cut apart the columns of DNA nucleotide base pairs on "Your DNA Strand." Then randomly tape them together end-to-end to form one long continuous strand. There should be no gap between nucleotides when taped together. Read "DNA: The Golden Key of Forensic Evidence," compare the information to your DNA strand, and discuss these questions.

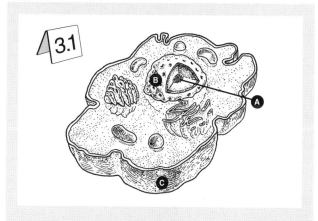

3.1

A: DNA
B: Nuclear membrane
C: Cell membrane

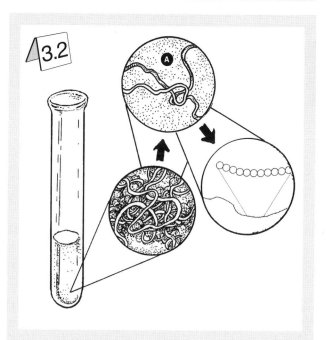

3.2

Test Tube With DNA in Liquid.
A: Extracted DNA

Handout 3-A
Creating a DNA Fingerprint:
Student Lab Investigation

- What does each letter represent?
- What are the four combinations of letters?
- Where can DNA evidence be found?
- Do you need to look at all the DNA to tell individuals apart? Explain your response.

2. Making the DNA Fingerprint

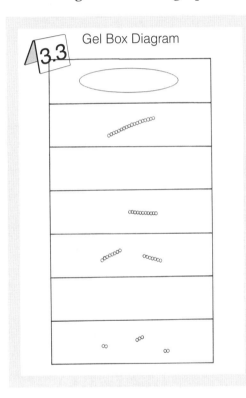

Gel Box Diagram

In a Real Forensic Lab: Cutting DNA with Enzymes

In the lab, scientists use restriction enzymes to cut the DNA strands in very specific ways. When a restriction enzyme is mixed with the DNA, it targets and cuts the double strand at specific nucleotide base pairs. The resulting "breakdown" will have DNA fragments of differing lengths (Figure 3.3).

Your Re-Creation

Scissors take on the role of the restriction enzyme. Starting at the top of "Your DNA Strand," cut the paper after every **GC** pair. Do this for the entire strand. When done, you will have a pile of different-sized DNA pieces.

In a Real Forensic Lab: Sorting DNA Segments in the Gel Box

The DNA breakdown is put into the starting well of a gel box. When an electrical current is applied, the pieces move across the gel toward the far end of the box. The smaller pieces will move quickly through the gel, traveling a greater distance than the longer, heavier pieces. Some pieces might be so large that they do not move out of the starting well.

Your Re-Creation

Set all DNA pieces at the starting well of the gel box diagram (Figure 3.4). Count the nucleotide base pairs for each DNA piece and move it into the corresponding gel box section. For instance, pieces with 1 to 3 pairs are light

74

Handout 3-A
Creating a DNA Fingerprint: Student Lab Investigation

and move to the end of the gel box. Pieces 19 or more pairs long are too heavy to move out of the starting well.

In a Real Forensics Lab: Creating the DNA Fingerprint "Photograph"

Once all of the pieces are separated, the gel is stained and "photographed," showing a pattern (Figure 3.5). The DNA pieces are seen as dark bands of different sizes in each section of the gel. Parts of the banding pattern are the same for all individuals of one species, while other parts are different for every individual.

Your Re-Creation

After all DNA pieces have been moved to their correct location in the gel box, count the number of pieces in each section. Record your data in the gel box summary, showing the number of nucleotide base pairs in a gel box section and the number of DNA pieces in each section.

Gel Box Summary

# nucleotide pairs	# DNA pieces
19+	_____
16-18	_____
13-15	_____
10-12	_____
7-9	_____
4-6	_____
1-3	_____

Gel Plate for DNA Electrophoresis* /3.4\

12+ cm (19+ pairs)	Starting Well
10–12 cm (16–18 pairs)	
8–10 cm (13–15 pairs)	
6–8 cm (10–12 pairs)	
4–6 cm (7–9 pairs)	
2–4 cm (4–6 pairs)	
0–2 cm (0–3 pairs)	

* This is a sample diagram. Teachers will have to re-create it at approximately 8 1/2" × 11" for student use.

(Arrow = Electric current moves DNA pieces across gel lane.)

/3.5\ DNA Fingerprints

Individual 1   Individual 2

Handout 3-A
Creating a DNA Fingerprint: Student Lab Investigation

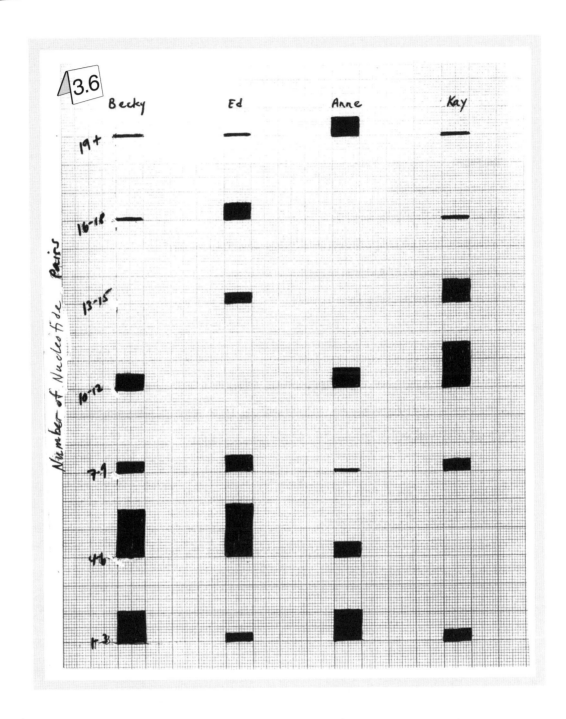

Handout 3-A
Creating a DNA Fingerprint: Student Lab Investigation

Make a "photograph" of the DNA fingerprint shown on your gel box by using graph paper to draw a graph that looks like the bands (see Figure 3.6). For each section, draw a band that matches the number of DNA pieces.

3. Identifying an Individual by a DNA Fingerprint

In a Real Forensic Lab

The result of this procedure is called a DNA fingerprint because, like actual fingerprints, the image can be matched to only a single individual (Figure 3.7). If similar or identical images are obtained from different samples, the DNA came from the same individual or from genetically similar individuals. Scientists can also compare DNA fingerprints of different species and identify the banding pattern that members of a species have in common.

Scientists can try to match a DNA fingerprint from blood, hair, skin, or other tissue found at the scene of a crime to a DNA fingerprint from suspects or victims. They can also match parts of a child's DNA to that of "unidentified" parent (i.e., in situations where parentage is uncertain) or other potential relatives. Still another use for this procedure is classifying organisms into species and subspecies.

Your Re-Creation

Post your DNA fingerprint "photographs" alongside those of others in the class. Compare and search for matches. Discuss the significance of finding matches or no matches.

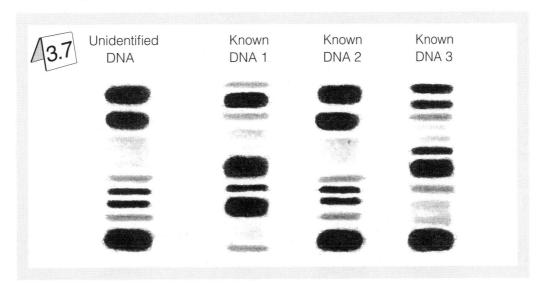

3.7   Unidentified DNA   Known DNA 1   Known DNA 2   Known DNA 3

Handout 3-A
Creating a DNA Fingerprint: Student Lab Investigation

What Did You Discover About Creating a DNA Fingerprint?

1. Why is DNA considered the golden key of forensic evidence?

2. If 96% of a chimpanzee's DNA is the same as human DNA, how much human DNA could determine individual characteristics?

3. Which DNA fingerprint image would look more similar:

   a. That of an Asian elephant and red-tailed hawk or an Asian elephant and African elephant? Explain.

   b. That of a child and his mother, or a child and a neighbor? Explain.

4. Read your comments on DNA fingerprints in your Investigator Notebook (*What do I know.... What do I want to know...*). Now answer this question: *What have I learned about DNA fingerprints?*

STUDENTS: TAKE A CLOSER LOOK

- How can DNA from blood be unique to an individual, while blood type is only unique to a large group of people?
- If the banding pattern of a DNA fingerprint can identify a species, how can it also identify an individual?
- Why do scientists only look at certain sections of DNA and not all of it?
- DNA is commonly taken from blood, but a red blood cell does not have a nucleus. Where is the DNA in blood?
- How is the restriction enzyme responsible for making the individualized banding pattern of a DNA fingerprint?
- How has the ability to create a DNA fingerprint changed criminal investigations from the 1980s and before?

National Science Teachers Association

Handout 3-B

Your DNA Strand

Name _____ Date _____

DO NOT CROSS - CRIME SCENE - DO NOT CROSS - CRIME SCENE - DO NOT CROSS - CRIME SCENE - DO NOT CROSS - CRIME SCENE - DO NOT CROSS - CRIME SCENE - DO NOT CROSS - CRIME SCENE - DO NOT CRO

TA	AT	GC	CG	GC	AT
GC	CG	AT	AT	AT	CG
AT	CG	CG	CG	TA	CG
CG	GC	TA	AT	TA	CG
TA	AT	CG	TA	TA	CG
AT	TA	CG	GC	AT	CG
TA	TA	CG	TA	CG	AT
CG	AT	TA	TA	GC	GC
CG	AT	GC	AT	CG	CG
GC	AT	AT	AT	CG	TA
AT	CG	AT	AT	AT	CG
TA	TA	TA	TA	CG	TA
GC	CG	AT	AT	GC	AT
AT	CG	CG	CG	CG	TA
CG	TA	AT	CG	TA	CG
AT	AT	TA	CG	AT	CG
TA	AT	GC	TA	AT	CG
TA	GC	TA	AT	AT	AT
AT	TA	CG	TA	CG	CG
CG	TA	GC	CG	AT	CG
AT	CG	AT	GC	TA	GC
TA	AT	CG	CG	TA	TA
CG	TA	TA	TA	TA	TA
CG	TA	AT	AT	TA	TA
CG	CG	AT	CG	AT	AT
TA	CG	CG	TA	AT	AT
TA	GC	CG	TA	CG	TA
AT	AT	CG	TA	CG	CG
CG	AT	TA	AT	TA	TA
GC	AT	AT	AT	CG	AT
AT	TA	TA	CG	CG	AT
AT	CG	TA	CG	GC	AT
CG	CG	CG	GC	CG	CG
CG	AT	AT	AT	TA	TA
TA	TA	TA	AT	CG	TA
AT	TA	CG	AT	TA	AT
TA	TA	AT	TA	AT	CG

Handout 3-C
DNA: The Golden Key of Forensic Evidence

Name _____ Date _____

CRIME SCENE - DO NOT CROSS - CRIME SCENE - DO NOT CROSS - CRIME SCENE - DO NOT CROSS - CRIME SCENE - DO NOT CROSS - CRIME SCENE - DO NOT CROSS -

DNA (deoxyribonucleic acid) can be taken from hair, bones, blood plasma, skin, saliva, and other cellular tissue or body fluids. Since the mid-1980s, DNA fingerprinting has become the strongest evidence used to connect a person to a crime scene, to trace family relationships, and to identify species and relationships among species.

What Do Forensic Scientists Need to Know?

Scientists complete the lab procedures for making a clear DNA fingerprint from DNA evidence. Because they have a thorough understanding of the structure of DNA and its unique features among species and individuals, they can interpret the fingerprints. When scientists match DNA fingerprints from evidence with those obtained from the suspect's DNA, this evidence often becomes the pivotal proof of a person's guilt. In contrast, a lack of a DNA match has reversed court decisions by supporting a person's innocence.

What Is DNA Fingerprinting?

DNA holds the genetic instructions for all traits of an individual, from eye color to disease susceptibility.

Found in the cells of every living organism, it is unique for each species and for each individual. Most DNA is the same in individuals of the same species, including humans. This lets forensic scientists who are investigating wildlife crimes match DNA evidence to a particular species or related species. In contrast, other sections of DNA are different for each individual. Scientists examine these unique sections to find a one-to-one match between evidence and a suspect, victim, or witness.

Scientists can take the DNA from evidence and make a picture, or "fingerprint," of the individual it belongs to. Then they can compare it to DNA fingerprints of suspects, victims, or witnesses (Figure 3.8).

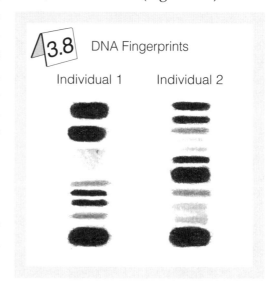

3.8 DNA Fingerprints

Individual 1   Individual 2

Handout 3-C
DNA: The Golden Key of Forensic Evidence

Why Is a Person's DNA Unique?

DNA is a unique sequence of nucleotides that come from mom and dad. The sequence of the nucleotides carries messages, or codes, for the traits of a particular species and individual. A DNA sequence has a four-letter alphabet of nucleotide bases—guanine, thymine, cytosine, adenine—that is written like this: AATCGTTTGACCTCTAGG. When in the double helix shape, the nucleotide bases are organized in a string of nucleotide base pairs: A-T, T-A, G-C, C-G (Figure 3.9). Adenine only pairs with thymine, and cytosine only pairs with guanine.

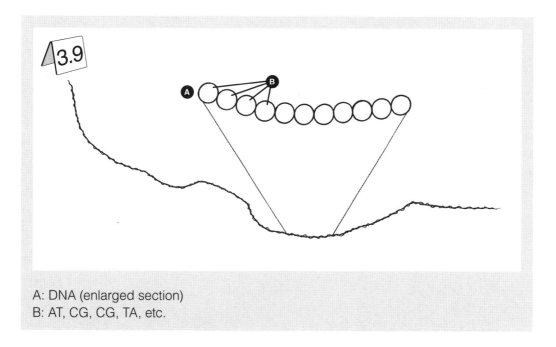

3.9

A: DNA (enlarged section)
B: AT, CG, CG, TA, etc.

The Latest in DNA Fingerprinting Methods

The method you have demonstrated in this lesson is the original lab technique for creating a DNA fingerprint. The problem with using this method on crime evidence is that it requires a large amount of high-quality DNA. If there is too little evidence, or the evidence is damaged or contaminated, this method may not work well.

(Continued on p. 82)

Handout 3-C
DNA: The Golden Key of Forensic Evidence

This problem was solved by the development of PCR (Polymerase Chain Reaction), a method using an enzyme that will make many copies of one small section of DNA.

Scientists focus on a locus (location) of DNA that they know varies greatly among individuals. These sections do not code for a trait, but repeat a pattern of 2–10 nucleotide base pairs. If the number of repeats in two DNA samples is different, the scientists can conclude that the samples came from two different people.

<u>Person 1</u>

——— CACACACA ———

OR

<u>Person 2</u>

CACACACACACACA ———

After using PCR to make enough copies of this section to make a visible image, scientists put the DNA in a gel electrophoresis box (as you did in the lab) to separate and identify it.

Many copies of the section made:

CACACACA
CACACACA
CACACACA
CACACACA
CACACACA, etc.

Gel image may be only one or two bands. The width and location of the band in the box determines a match.

REFERENCE

Schefter, J. 1994. DNA fingerprints on trial. *Popular Science* (Nov.): 60–64.

National Science Teachers Association

Lesson 4: Fingerprints

The Crime: "DNR Offers Reward for Information in Wolf Poaching Case"

"The Department of Natural Resources [DNR] is offering a $1,000 reward for information that leads to an arrest and conviction in a suspected poaching of a gray wolf in the eastern Upper Peninsula [UP] this winter.

"On Dec. 14, a mortality signal from a radio collar was picked up from a DNR airplane doing a wildlife surveillance flight in the eastern UP. The signal was picked up around the Pickford area, according to DNR Law Enforcement Division reports. The wolf wearing the radio collar had last been seen on Nov. 29.

"The following day, DNR personnel tracked the radio collar to the Munuscong River in Chippewa County. The collar was located under the ice, but not retrieved due to poor ice. No human tracks were spotted in the snow from the air, but fairly recent wolf tracks had crossed the river downstream. There was an elevated deer blind in the vicinity with a clear view of the location, DNR reports noted.

"On March 7, a Michigan State Police search and dive rescue team recovered the radio collar from the river during a training exercise. The collar showed evidence of being cut off of the animal, law enforcement officials said...."

Source: State of Michigan, Department of Natural Resources. April 20, 2006. www.michigan.gov/dnr/0,1607,7-153-10371_10402-141386--M_2006_4,00.html

Topic: fingerprint
Go to: *www.scilinks.org*
Code: UF06

Investigator Questions

1. What is the crime?

2. How could fingerprints be used as evidence connecting the suspect(s) to the crime?

Lesson 4: Fingerprints

Teacher Guidelines

Overview

Fingerprints have been used for over 100 years to match suspects to evidence. The evolution of lab techniques from dusting with brushes, to chemical fuming, to computerized digital scanning has made prints clearer and more reliable for forensic scientists to "read."

In this lesson, students practice scientific inquiry strategies as they make a set of ink fingerprints and use reference papers to help distinguish between patterns. After learning the anatomy of fingerprints, student groups will make a set of unidentified fingerprints on a variety of surfaces. This evidence, along with each group's set of fingerprint cards, will be exchanged for another group to examine and identify.

Connections to the National Science Education Standards

Standard	Category	Lesson Connection
Content Standard A— Abilities necessary to do scientific inquiry (grades 5–12)	Science as Inquiry	Students independently make fingerprints, distinguish among fingerprint patterns by using reference papers, and compare and match fingerprint evidence. They demonstrate one or more lab procedures to make latent fingerprints visible.
Content Standard C— Structure and function in living systems (grades 5–8)	Life Science	Students explain the physical structure of fingertips and how fingerprints are made.
Content Standard E— Abilities of technological design (grades 5–12)	Science and Technology	Students use and compare several lab procedures to identify visual and latent fingerprints. They explain how technology has improved the clarity of fingerprints.

Standard	Category	Lesson Connection
Content Standard F— Science and technology in society (grades 5–8)	Science in Personal and Social Perspectives	Students explain how improved lab procedures for identifying fingerprints have affected criminal investigations.

Time Required

2 50-minute class periods

Materials

For each student: "Leave Only Fingerprints: Student Lab Investigation" (Handout 4-A, p. 89)

Part 1: "Make and Identify Your Fingerprints" from Handout 4-A
- Fingerprint cards (Handout 4-B) (one for each student)
- Ink pads
- Magnifying lenses
- 3" × 5" white paper
- "Identifying Fingerprints" (Handout 4-C)

Part 2: "Prepare Mystery Fingerprint Evidence" from Handout 4-A:
- Completed fingerprint card (completed in Part 1)
- 1 lab tray, tub, or box per four students
- Rubber surgical gloves (one per student)
- Small fingerprint-free objects (beakers, baby food jars, glasses, microscope slides, paper, cardboard, plastic)
- 3" × 5" white and colored paper

Part 3: "Identify the Mystery Fingerprint Evidence" from Handout 4-A

There are three different possible techniques for carrying out this part of the student investigation (the dusting powder technique, the superglue [cynanoacrylate] technique, and the iodine crystals technique). The teacher may use one, two, or all three! Here are the materials needed for each technique.

Dusting Powder Technique
- Butcher paper to cover table
- Fingerprint powder or baby powder

SAFETY ////

Dusting Powder Technique
- Wear latex first aid gloves.
- If swallowed, drink 1–2 glasses of water and call a physician.
- If the dusting powder comes in contact with skin, wash with warm water and soap. If skin is irritated from contact, wash with water for 15 minutes and call a physician.
- If the dusting powder comes in contact with eyes, wash thoroughly with water for 15 minutes. If irritation continues, call a physician.

Using Forensics: Wildlife Crime Scene!

- Fine, soft, and thick cosmetic powder brushes
- Clear 1"–2" cellophane tape or packing tape
- 3" × 5" paper (contrasting color to powder)
- Evidence: Glass jar or plastic object (contrasting color to dust)

Superglue (Cynanoacrylate) Technique
- Superglue tube
- Aluminum foil
- Airtight glass jars
- Tweezers or surgical gloves
- Weak heating source (lamp, coffee cup warmer, hot plate)
- Surgical gloves
- Evidence: Glass or plastic microscope slides OR paper or cardboard pieces that can fit into fuming jar

Iodine Crystals Technique
- Airtight jar with small amount of iodine crystals
- Tweezers or surgical gloves
- Evidence: Glass or plastic microscope slides OR paper or cardboard pieces that can fit into fuming jar

Teaching Plan

Introduction

1. Read aloud and discuss "The Crime: 'DNR Offers Reward for Information in Wolf Poaching Case'" (p. 83).

2. Use the K-W-L format. Have students respond to the following questions in their Investigator Notebooks:

   - *What do I <u>know</u> about fingerprints? (Put a star by information you are not sure is accurate.)*
   - *What do I <u>want to know</u> about fingerprints?*

3. Introduce the lab (Handout 4-A, p. 89) by explaining that students will learn to identify their own fingerprints, practice making fingerprints on different surfaces, and identify mystery fingerprints of classmates using a variety of forensics lab techniques.

Making and Identifying Student Fingerprints

4. Give each student a copy of the lab (Handout 4-A). Guide students in the procedure for making their own sets of fingerprints (Part 1 of the lab) at individual tables, group tables, or a teacher-monitored table.

    Note: Students can also use the technique of law enforcement officers. Working with partners, have one person ink a fingertip. The partner then presses the finger onto the paper or rolls the fingertip across the paper. Be aware that many students have difficulty figuring out how much pressure to put on a partner's finger to get a clear print.

5. Have students read "Identifying Fingerprints" (Handout 4-B) and answer the "What Does It Mean?" questions at the end of the handout. Students can refer to their own prints while reading.

6. After completing the reading, have students identify the patterns of their own prints on their fingerprint cards.

Making Mystery Prints

7. Introduce Part 2 of the lab. Demonstrate the lab technique(s) the student will use to make latent prints visible. These techniques—dusting powder, superglue, and iodine crystals—are given in the student lab.

8. Put students in investigative teams of four. Have them put their fingerprint cards in their lab tray and follow the lab directions. If they are using the dusting powder technique, give them glass or plastic objects to make their fingerprints. If they are using the superglue technique or the iodine crystals technique, they can use glass or plastic microscope slides or paper or cardboard pieces that fit into their fuming jars. Follow the safety procedures for the technique(s) you choose.

Identifying the Mystery Fingerprint Evidence

9. Introduce Part 3 of the lab. Demonstrate one or more lab techniques (powder dusting, iodine crystals, superglue) for making the latent prints visible. Then allow the students to finish the lab.

10. Revisit "The Crime: 'DNR Offers Reward for Information in Wolf Poaching Case'" as a class to see if students have new insights.

Extensions

- Research other fingerprinting techniques used today by law enforcement.
- Research other ways fingerprint identification is being used in our country and around the world that is not a part of law enforcement.
- Invite a division of wildlife officer, law enforcement officer, or attorney to speak to your class about how fingerprint evidence is used in criminal cases.
- Visit a law enforcement fingerprinting lab.

WEB LINKS

Brazoria County Sheriff's Department: Identification Division. n.d. *www.brazoria-county.com/sheriff/id/fingerprints/index.htm*

Fingerprints. Forensic Medicine, University of Dundee. *www.dundee. ac.uk/forensicmedicine/nurse/notes/fingerprints.htm*

Latent fingerprints experiment. n.d. Oracle ThinkQuest Library. *http:// library.thinkquest.org/04oct/00206/p_fing.htm*

Taking legitimate fingerprints. n.d. Federal Bureau of Investigations. *www.fbi.gov/hq/cjisd/takingfps.html*

Wertheim, P. A. n.d. Atmospheric superglue method. Crime and Clues: The Art and Science of Criminal Investigation. *www.crime-andclues.com/superglue.htm*

Handout 4-A
Leave Only Fingerprints:
Student Lab Investigation

Name _____ Date_____

Your Job

Make an ink copy of your fingerprints and identify patterns. In teams, make latent (invisible) and visible fingerprints on paper, plastic, or glass. After exchanging mystery prints, use several forensics lab procedures to identify the owners of the prints.

Part 1: Make and Identify Your Fingerprints

1. Using scrap paper and a dark-colored ink pad, practice making a fingerprint with a clear pattern. Here's how to do it:

    a. Line up the edge of a piece of scrap paper with the top edge of the table in front of you. Place the entire first joint of each finger flat on the paper with the rest of your hand hanging off the edge of the table.

    b. Lightly press the first joint of your thumb on the ink pad.

    c. Transfer the print by either pressing your thumb straight down onto the paper using two fingers of your other hand and then lifting straight up OR rolling your thumb from the left edge to the right edge using your other hand for guidance. You can also work in pairs to assist each other.

2. Get a fingerprint card (Handout 4-B) from your teacher. You will make a set of clear fingerprints of both hands. Here's how to do it:

    a. Fold the paper under the top row of fingerprint boxes. These boxes now sit at the bottom of the visible page. Place this row of boxes on the edge of the table in front of you.

    b. Use the ink pad to make a set of fingerprints on the fingerprint card for one hand. After getting teacher approval of your prints, wash your hand.

    c. Refold the fingerprint card under the second row of boxes.

    d. Make a set of fingerprints for the second hand. After getting teacher-approval of your prints, wash your hand.

3. Read "Identifying Fingerprints" (Handout 4-C) and answer the "What Does It Mean?" questions at the end. Look at your own prints while reading. Use the "Fingerprint Pattern Key" in Handout 4-C, pp. 96–99, and magnifying lens to identify the patterns for each finger. Write the pattern below each print on your card.

Using Forensics: Wildlife Crime Scene!

Handout 4-A
Leave Only Fingerprints: Student Lab Investigation

Part 2: Prepare Mystery Fingerprint Evidence

1. Get a tray of required materials (rubber surgical gloves; 3" × 5" white and colored paper; and small, fingerprint-free objects that your teacher will provide) for your group of four.

2. Place the fingerprint cards for all your group members in the bottom of the tray.

3. Pick two group members to create visible ink print evidence on paper (#4 below) and two members to create latent oil print evidence on glass, plastic, or cardboard (#5 below).

4. To create *visible ink* fingerprint evidence:

    a. One person make ink prints of your thumb and pointer finger from either hand on a piece of 3" × 5" paper. Label it "Evidence 1."

    b. The second person makes ink prints of your thumb and pointer finger from either hand on a second 3" × 5" paper. Label it "Evidence 2."

    c. Place the mystery prints in the tray.

5. To create *latent oil* fingerprint evidence:

    a. Your teacher will tell you which forensic lab techniques (dusting powder, superglue, or iodine crystals) you will be using. If you will be using the dusting power technique, make your prints on a glass jar or plastic piece. If you will be using the superglue technique or the iodine crystals technique, you can use glass or plastic microscope slides OR paper or cardboard pieces that fit into the fuming jars.

    b. Put a latex glove on one hand before touching the objects. Pick up a clean object with your gloved hand. Hold only the edge. Mark each object as "Evidence #3" or "Evidence #4."

    c. Wipe the fingers of your other hand across your forehead or along the sides of your nose to coat them with body oil.

    d. Carefully press the first joints of your thumb and first two fingers straight down onto the object. Then lift them straight up.

    e. Place the object in the tray using only your gloved hand.

    f. On a separate piece of paper, record whose prints are on Evidence #1, #2, #3, and #4. Give your key to the teacher.

National Science Teachers Association

Handout 4-A
Leave Only Fingerprints:
Student Lab Investigation

Part 3: Identify the Mystery Fingerprint Evidence

Your teacher will let you know which forensic lab techniques (dusting powder, superglue, or iodine crystals) you will be using to make the latent prints visible.

1. Exchange your tray of evidence with another group and form two pairs within your group.

2. Each pair chooses a visible ink print and a latent oil print to identify.

3. Use a magnifying lens to compare the visible ink prints to the fingerprint cards.

4. Identify the owner of the print.

5. Follow the technique, specified by your teacher, for making prints visible with dusting powder, superglue, or iodine crystals.

6. Use a magnifying lens to compare the print to the fingerprint cards.

7. Identify the owner of the print.

8. Check the accuracy of your results by getting the group's key from the teacher.

If You Are Using the Dusting Powder Technique, You Will Need:
- Butcher paper to cover table
- Fingerprint powder or baby powder
- Fine, soft, and thick cosmetic powder brushes
- Clear 1"–2" cellophane tape or packing tape
- 3" × 5" paper (contrasting color to powder)
- Evidence: glass jar or plastic object (contrasting color to dust)

Procedure

1. Working in pairs, have one person put on a plastic glove and pick up the glass or plastic evidence. Tear off a piece of clear tape that is long enough to hold onto the edges and still cover the print. Be careful to not

Handout 4-A
Leave Only Fingerprints: Student Lab Investigation

add your fingerprints to the center of tape. Hang tape from the edge of the table to use later.

2. Lightly touch the tips of the brush in the powder and tap off the excess.

3. Lightly dust the glass item in a circular motion until the print becomes visible. The powder will stick to the oily grooves of the print. Be careful not to drown the print with too much powder.

4. While one person holds the evidence, the partner needs to attach one edge of the tape beyond one side of the print and roll the tape over the print, being careful not to make creases or air bubbles. Then he or she slowly pulls off the tape with the transferred print.

5. Tape the lifted prints onto paper that is different from the powder color. Identify the print pattern and owner.

If You Are Using the Superglue (Cynanoacrylate) Technique, You Will Need:
- Superglue tube
- Aluminum foil
- Airtight glass jars
- Tweezers or surgical gloves
- Weak heating source (lamp, coffee cup warmer, hot plate)
- Surgical gloves
- Evidence: Glass or plastic microscope slides OR paper or cardboard pieces that can fit into fuming jar.

Procedure

1. Blow into the empty fuming jar to add humidity to the air.

2. Work under a fume hood or in a ventilated area. Put a drop of superglue on a small piece of aluminum foil. Use tweezers or surgical gloves to put the foil in the bottom of the fuming jar.

3. Carefully put the fingerprinted evidence in the jar so that it does not touch the superglue.

National Science Teachers Association

Handout 4-A
Leave Only Fingerprints:
Student Lab Investigation

4. Close the lid tightly and place the jar by a warm lamp or on a hot plate set on "low."

5. Let the fumes from the superglue react with the print for 5–10 minutes. If the print is not visible, add either more heat or another drop of superglue and let sit for another 5 minutes. If you use too much superglue or leave the print for too long, a layer of white will hide the fingerprint.

6. When the print is visible, remove the evidence from the fuming jar and identify the owner.

If You Are Using the Iodine Crystals Technique, You Will Need:

- Airtight jar with small amount of iodine crystals
- Tweezers or surgical gloves
- Evidence: Glass or plastic microscope slides OR paper or cardboard pieces that can fit into fuming jar.

Procedure

1. Pick up the fingerprinted evidence with tweezers or surgical gloves. If the evidence is flat paper or plastic and will be hard to get out of the fuming jar, attach it to a paper clip on a string.

2. Work under the fume hood or in a ventilated area. Quickly open the fuming jar containing a few iodine crystals and put the prints in the jar. Let the string hang over the opening onto the outside of the jar. Close the jar tightly.

3. Let the iodine fumes develop the prints for about 15 minutes.

4. Under the fume hood or in a ventilated area, open the jar, remove the print, and immediately close the jar tightly. Identify the owner.

Handout 4-B
Fingerprint Card

Name _____ Date _____

Right Hand

Thumb	1st Finger	2nd Finger	3rd Finger	4th Finger

Classification of Print Patterns:

_____ _____ _____ _____ _____

Left Hand

Thumb	1st Finger	2nd Finger	3rd Finger	4th Finger

Classification of Print Patterns:

_____ _____ _____ _____ _____

Prints taken by: _____

National Science Teachers Association

Handout 4-C
Identifying Fingerprints

Name_____ Date_____

Why is the search for fingerprints at the scene of a crime so important? It's because each person on the planet has a unique set of prints, different from that of the other billions of people. Even identical twins have different fingerprint patterns. A fingerprint can prove that a certain person was at the place of the crime or touched something that was used in a crime.

Juan Vucetich, a Coatian-born Argentine anthropologist and police official, pioneered the use of fingerprinting in criminal investigations over 100 years ago. In 1891 Vucetich began the first filing of fingerprints based on ideas of Francis Galton, ideas that he expanded significantly. In 1892, Vucetich made the first positive identification of a criminal through the use of fingerprints. Two children had been murdered and their mother had received several knife wounds, but survived. She accused a male acquaintance of the crime, but a bloody fingerprint discovered at the scene proved to be a match to the mother. Faced with the evidence, she confessed and was convicted of the crime (NLB 2006). Argentine police adopted Vucetich's method of fingerprinting, and it spread to police forces all over the world.

In 1902, Dr. Henry P. DeForrest pioneered the use of fingerprinting in the United States. DeForrest led the campaign to systematically fingerprint all candidates taking the civil service exam for the New York Civil Service Commission. This action ended the practice of paying someone to take the exam in the real candidate's place. The following year, the New York State Prison System began fingerprinting all of its inmates, and in 1904 the International Association of Chiefs of Police created the first national fingerprint collection site, the National Bureau of Criminal Identification (Sellin 1971). Today the FBI keeps a computerized database of over 49 million sets of fingerprints for criminals, civilians, military personnel, and government employees.

What Does the Forensic Scientist Need to Know?

To analyze fingerprint evidence, a forensic scientist must understand the anatomy of fingerprints and be able to distinguish among the many fingerprint patterns. He or she must also able to choose and conduct the most appropriate lab technique to make a latent (invisible) print visible.

Handout 4-C
Identifying Fingerprints

What Is a Fingerprint?

A fingertip has small ridges and grooves that create a unique pattern. The purpose of the ridges is to create friction between the fingertips and the object being touched.

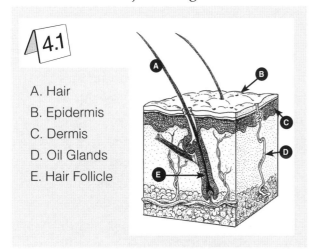

4.1

A. Hair
B. Epidermis
C. Dermis
D. Oil Glands
E. Hair Follicle

The skin is made of two layers (see Figure 4.1). The outer epidermis is worn off and replaced throughout a lifetime. The inner dermis holds oil and sweat glands that keep the skin moist. This oil pools in the grooves between the friction ridges. When a finger touches an object, the oil transfers the pattern onto the object. This oil print can be matched to a finger, and to the person who made it.

The ridge pattern forms during early fetal development and never changes. In the past, people have tried unsuccessfully to remove their fingerprints, but because the ridges are in deep layers of the skin, permanent removal of them would deform and damage the use of the hands.

Fingerprint Pattern Key

There are eight fingerprint patterns: plain arch, tented arch, radial loops, ulnar loops, plain whorl, central pocket whorl, double loop whorl, and accidental whorl. These patterns fall into three groups: arches, loops, and whorls (Figure 4.2).

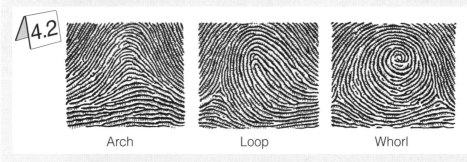

4.2

Arch   Loop   Whorl

Each group has a different number of *deltas*, the place where ridges converge from three sides to form a triangle shape. Arches have no deltas, loops have one, and whorls have two (Figure 4.3).

National Science Teachers Association

Handout 4-C
Identifying Fingerprints

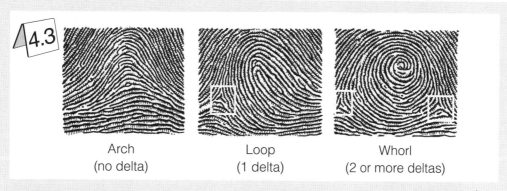

Arch
(no delta)

Loop
(1 delta)

Whorl
(2 or more deltas)

Arches

Arches are the simplest patterns and have no deltas. The ridges enter from one side of the finger and exit on the opposite side (Figure 4.4).

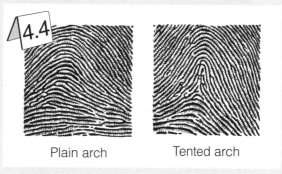

Plain arch

Tented arch

- Plain Arch—A plain arch moves across the finger with no center point (core) or intersecting ridges.

- Tented Arch—The center core of the tented arch looks like a vertical pole holding up a tent, sometimes mistaken for a delta.

Loops

Loops are the most common print pattern. A loop has ridges that enter and exit from the same side of the finger. It has one delta on the other side.

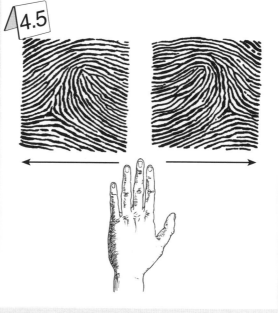

If you know which hand the print was taken from, you can classify it as a *radial loop* or an *ulnar loop*. Place your right hand palm-down next to the loops in Figure 4.5. If the loop goes toward your little

Handout 4-C
Identifying Fingerprints

finger (and ulnar bone), it is an ulnar loop. If the loop goes toward your thumb (and radial bone), it is a radial loop. Now place your left hand on the paper. The ulnar loop becomes a radial loop, and vice versa.

Whorls

The center of a whorl looks like a circle, or the ridges move in a circular direction. Most whorls have two deltas, though some may have more. There are four different types of whorls (Figure 4.6).

- Plain Whorl—The center ridges form a circle, with larger circles moving out from it like rings on a lake after a rock breaks the surface of water. If an imaginary line were drawn between the two deltas, it would cut across those rings.

- Central Pocket Whorl—The center circle of ridges is there, but very small. The outer ridges move to one side of the pattern, causing it to look like a loop. It has two deltas, but the imaginary connecting line does not cross the center circles.

- Double Loop Whorl—This whorl is actually two separate loops wrapped together in the center of the print. They have separate shoulders and two deltas.

- Accidental Whorl—This uncommon whorl is a combination of different loop and whorl patterns. It usually has more than two deltas.

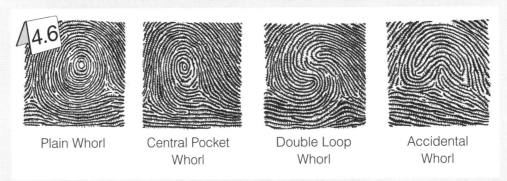

4.6

Plain Whorl   Central Pocket Whorl   Double Loop Whorl   Accidental Whorl

What Types of Fingerprint Evidence Are There?

There are three types of fingerprint evidence: latent prints, visible prints, and plastic impressions. These types describe the surface the print was made on and how the print was made.

- A *latent print* is a mark left on a surface from the finger's natural oil. This type of print is not clearly visible until another material touches

National Science Teachers Association

Handout 4-C
Identifying Fingerprints

or reacts with the oils. The most common method to make a latent print visible is to dust it with powder that attaches to the oils left on the surface. Iodine crystals and superglue both cause chemical reactions with the oils that make the latent print visible. Law enforcement agencies can now use computers to digitally scan a hand or fingertips.

- A *visible print* can be seen without any additional help from other materials. It is made when a fingertip—covered with paint, ink, oil, dirt, cream, or other colored substance—touches another surface and leaves a mark.

- *Plastic impressions* are three-dimensional prints made when a finger is pressed into a soft material that holds its shape. Impressions can be made in clay, putty, grease, wet paint, or soft wax.

What Did You Discover About Fingerprinting?

1. Explain one of several reasons people began collecting and identifying fingerprints.

2. Describe or draw the anatomy of a fingerprint using the following terminology: *ridge, groove, oil, dermis, sweat gland.*

3. What makes a fingerprint unique?

4. How do deltas help identify a print?

5. What is the most common fingerprint pattern?

6. What are the differences among latent, visible, and three-dimensional fingerprints?

7. What lab technique(s) did you use to make latent prints visible? What worked well and what would you do differently next time?

8. Read your comments on fingerprints in your Investigator Notebook *(What do I know about fingerprints? What do I want to know about fingerprints?).* Respond to the following question: *What have I learned about fingerprints?*

Handout 4-C
Identifying Fingerprints

STUDENTS: TAKE A CLOSER LOOK

- Will waxing fingertips or fingertip surgery remove or mask a person's fingerprints? Justify your answer.
- What can investigators conclude when fingerprints at a crime scene are matched to a specific individual?
- Why are fingerprints more effective than many other types of evidence at supporting a person's innocence or guilt in a crime?

REFERENCES

Sellin, J. T. 1971. *The police and the crime problem.* New York: Arno Press.

Wikipedia. n.s. *http://en.wikipedia.org/wiki/Juan_Vucetich*

Lesson 5: Hair Identification

The Crime: "Bangkok Luxury Stores Raided for Wildlife Trafficking"

"*July 18, 2006, Bangkok, Thailand.* Thai authorities are pursuing a wildlife-related investigation following yesterday's simultaneous raids on three downtown Bangkok locations suspected of trafficking in products made from the highly endangered Tibetan Antelope. Police detained four dealers for questioning and confiscated over 250 purported "shahtoosh" shawls, which can cost between $1,200–$12,000 a piece. The shops targeted in the raid are located in high-end commercial areas of Bangkok, catering to wealthy tourists buyers from Europe and Japan—underscoring the market for the illegal, costly wool. Thai authorities await the results of tests to determine the authenticity of the confiscated shawls....

"Unlike other wools that can be harvested by shearing or combing, shahtoosh can only be obtained by killing Tibetan Antelopes (*Pantholops hodgsonii*), which live almost exclusively in the remote Qinghai-Tibetan Plateau. A single shawl requires wool from three to five dead antelopes.

"Since 1979, the antelope has been listed in Appendix I of the Convention on International Trade in Endangered Species of Wild Fauna and Flora (CITES), prohibiting all trade in shahtoosh. IUCN (The World Conservation Union) classifies the Tibetan Antelope as Vulnerable to extinction in its Red List of Threatened Species.

"Despite being illegal, shahtoosh, which means "the king of wools" in Persian, is still highly sought-after because of its exceptionally fine quality. Shahtoosh shawls can command prices of up to $12,000 on the black market. Driven by this fashion craze, poaching has drastically slashed the Tibetan Antelope population. In 1900, around one million antelopes lived in the wild; today, there may be as few as 50,000."

Source: Bangkok Luxury Stores Raided for Wildlife Trafficking. July 18, 2006. TRAFFIC News Room. www.traffic.org/RenderPage.action?CategoryId=1047

Investigator Questions

1. What was the crime?

2. How can a forensic scientist show that the shawl's wool is from the endangered Tibetan antelopes?

3. How is using Tibetan antelope wool different from using wool of other animals?

National Science Teachers Association

Lesson 5: Hair Identification

Teacher Guidelines

Overview

Crime scene evidence can include strands of human hair, an unidentified animal pelt, or animal hair on the ground near a suspected poaching. Hairs that look alike with the naked eye can become distinctly different when viewed under the microscope. For example, human hair anatomy is different from that of nonhuman mammal hair. Hair from other mammal groups can also be distinguished microscopically.

In this lesson, students will use the microscope to draw and describe the structure of hair from classmates and other mammal species. Based on observations, they will use reference materials to compare similarities and differences in the hair. Finally, they will determine how hair can be used as evidence for a crime.

Connections to the National Science Education Standards

Standard	Category	Lesson Connection
Content Standard A— Abilities necessary to do scientific inquiry (grades 5–12)	Science as Inquiry	Students use a microscope and reference papers to independently discover and document differences in human and nonhuman hair.
Content Standard A— Understandings about scientific inquiry (grades 5–12)	Science as Inquiry	Students observe and record how hair can be identified by mammal group microscopically when differences are not visual with the naked eye.
Content Standard C— Structure and function in living systems (grades 5–8)	Life Science	Students identify the parts of hair and their functions.

Time Required

2 50-minute class periods

Materials

- Handouts (one for each student):
  - "Knowing Hair Inside Out: Student Lab Investigation" (Handout 5-A, p. 107)
  - "Identified by a Hair" (Handout 5-B, p. 112)
- Light microscope
- Microscope slides and cover slips
- Cups of water
- Droppers
- Ruler
- Prepared slides (see "Teaching Plan/Getting Ready," below) of a variety of North American mammals: deer, mountain lion, elk, rabbit, black bear, sheep, goats, any others available. Can include domesticated mammals.

Teaching Plan

Getting Ready

- Collect strands of hair from a variety of North American mammals. Native mammal hair can be obtained from the state division of wildlife, a state park, a local nature center, a taxidermist, or a hunter.
- Make prepared microscope slides.
  - a. Label blank slides with the name of the mammal.
  - b. Place one hair on the slide and seal it with thick layer of clear fingernail polish.

Guiding Students

1. Read aloud and discuss "The Crime: 'Bangkok Luxury Stores Raided for Wildlife Trafficking'."

2. Use the K-W-L format. Have students respond to the following questions in their Investigator Notebooks:

   - *What do I <u>know</u> about hair? (Put a star by information you are not sure is accurate.)*
   - *What do I <u>want to know</u> about hair?*

3. Give students "Knowing Hair Inside Out: Student Lab Investigation" (Handout 5-A) and "Identified by a Hair" (Handout 5-B). Introduce students to identification of hair as a forensic technique by having them complete steps 1–4 in Handout 5-A. Make sure everyone gets to see a hair medulla of a classmate's since many people do not have medullas.

4. Have students read and discuss "Identified by a Hair" (Handout 5–B) and answer the "What Does It Mean?" questions on page 115.

5. Have students complete step 5 in Handout 5-A.

6. Revisit "'The Crime: 'Bangkok Luxury Stores Raided for Wildlife Trafficking'" as a class to see if students have new insights.

SAFETY ///////

- Hair allergies: Any students with allergies to certain animal hair should not touch hair samples. Hair on microscope slides should not cause a reaction because it is sealed.

Extensions

- Make microscope slides of outer scale patterns of hairs from people and other mammals to identify. To make microscope slides of hair scales, paint a thick layer of clear fingernail polish onto a slide. Immediately lay part of the hair on top of the polish. After the polish dries, carefully lift and remove the hair. An imprint will be left in the dried polish. Look at the scales under the microscope.
- Invite a division of wildlife officer, police investigator, or attorney to talk about how hair evidence is used in criminal cases.

WEB LINKS

Deedrick, D. W. July 2000. Hairs, fibers, crime, and evidence. Forensic Science Communications 2:3. *www.fbi.gov/hq/lab/fsc/backissu/jul2000/deedric1.htm*

Hair identification. *www.labessentials.com/microscopes_experiments.htm*

Hairs, fibers, crime, and evidence. *www.fbi.gov/hq/lab/fsc/backissu/jul2000/deedric1.htm*

Koch, S. Jan. 2004. Microscopy of hair part 1: A practical guide and manual for human hairs. *Forensic Science Communication 6:1. www.fbi.gov/hq/lab/fsc/backissu/jan2004/research/2004_01_research01b.hum#structure*

Microscopy of hair part 1: A practical guide and manual for human hairs. *www.fbi.gov/hq/lab/fsc/backissu/jan2004/research/2004_01_research01b.hum#structure*

Handout 5-A
Knowing Hair Inside Out: Student Lab Investigation

Name_____ Date_____

CRIME SCENE - DO NOT CROSS - CRIME SCENE - DO NOT CROSS - CRIME SCENE - DO NOT CROSS - CRIME SCENE - DO NOT CROSS - CRIME SCENE - DO NOT CROSS -

Your Job

Use the microscope to examine, compare, and identify human and nonhuman mammal hair.

Your Steps

1. Pull one hair from your head and measure its length. Record the length and color in the table "Comparing Human and Nonhuman Hair." (For now, just do the human hair. You will be coming back to the table to fill in the information on "Other mammals.")

2. Make a wet mount of the hair.

   a. Put several drops of water in the center of the microscope slide.

   b. Lay the hair on the microscope slide so that the root and tip are both in the water.

   c. Place a cover slip over the hair and water by setting it on edge in the water and gently dropping it over the hair.

3. Look at your hair under the microscope. Describe and draw it in the table. Then look at the hair of *other* students and record your observations. Answer questions 1–4 of "What Did I Discover?" on page 110.

4. Read "Identified by a Hair" (Handout 5-B). Answer the "What Does It Mean?" questions at the end of the handout.

5. Look at prepared microscope slides of two nonhuman mammals and record your observations in the table "Comparing Human and Nonhuman Hair" and the table "Identifying Nonhuman Mammal Hair." Answer questions 5–8 of "What Did I Discover?" on pages 110–111.

Handout 5-A
Knowing Hair Inside Out: Student Lab Investigation

Comparing Human and Nonhuman Hair

Name	Hair length (cm)	Draw and describe hair and color without using the microscope.	Draw and describe hair color as seen through the microscope.	Medulla width* is: -Greater than 1/3 hair width -1/3 or less of hair width -Absent
Student				
Student				
Other mammal				
Other mammal				

*The medulla appears like a dark line or broken line down the middle of a person's hair. Not everyone's hair has a medulla.

National Science Teachers Association

Handout 5-A
Knowing Hair Inside Out:
Student Lab Investigation

Identifying Nonhuman Mammal Hair

Animal	Draw microscopic appearance of hair	*Medulla pattern: (Uni- or multiserial, vacuolated, amorphous, lattice)	Medullary Index = Width of medulla / Width of hair (estimate at ¼, ½, ¾, 1)

*Use "Anatomy of a Hair" (Handout 5-B, pp. 112–115) to classify medulla patterns.

Handout 5-A
Knowing Hair Inside Out: Student Lab Investigation

What Did I Discover?

1. What is one way to tell the difference between hairs from two people without the microscope?

2. What is one way to microscopically tell the difference between hairs from two people?

3. What was a difference between your hair and your classmate's hair?

4. Some people have hair with a dark core called a *medulla*. What type of medulla do you have? Look at hairs from other students and classify them below.

    Absent   _____   : STUDENT(S) _____
    medulla   _____

    Broken   _____   : STUDENT(S) _____
    medulla   - - - -
                    _____

    Continuous   _____   : STUDENT(S) _____
    medulla   _____

5. How are medulla patterns of human hairs different from those of other mammal hairs?

    Write "human" or "nonhuman mammal" beside each description of medullary indexes.

    a. _____   Absent
    b. _____   Less than 1/3 of hair diameter
    c. _____   More than 1/3 of hair diameter

    Compare the visible colors of a hair with its color(s) under the microscope.

National Science Teachers Association

Handout 5-A
Knowing Hair Inside Out:
Student Lab Investigation

6. Explain how to tell the difference between hairs of several nonhuman mammals.

7. You are investigating a mammal poaching crime and find three different types of hair. The medullary indexes are 1/4, 3/4, and 0. How many hairs are from people and how are many from other mammals? Justify your answer.

   The human hair evidence has no medulla. The suspect's hair has no medulla.

   a. Which is true?

   _____ The hair belongs to the suspect.

   _____ The hair is in the same category as the suspect's hair.

   _____ The hair does not belong to the suspect.

   b. Explain your choice.

8. Read your comments on hair in your Investigator Notebook (*What do I know about hair? What do I want to know about hair?*). Then respond to the following question: *What have I learned about hair?*

Handout 5-B
Identified by a Hair

Name _____ Date _____

Humans shed about 100 strands of hair each day. As a result, hair evidence is often found at crime scenes. A single strand of hair can tell investigators about the person from whom it was shed (possible ethnicity of the person, where on the body it came from), but the hair itself cannot point to one suspect. At this level of forensic examination, it is considered indirect or circumstantial evidence, meaning investigators can classify a suspect with a larger group of people having similar types of hair, but they cannot make a one-on-one match.

To make hair a more powerful piece of direct evidence, DNA can be extracted to create a DNA fingerprint. So where is DNA in hair? Hair is made of keratin, a protein also found in human fingernails and toenails and in animal claws, horns, and hooves. Keratin itself does not have DNA, but the follicle at the base of the hair, with thousands of cells rich in DNA, is a scientist's treasure chest.

What Do Forensic Scientists Need To Know?

Even without testing DNA, forensic scientists can learn much from a single hair. By knowing hair structure, they can determine if the hair is from a human or another mammal. Once that distinction is made, scientists can narrow it down further, matching the hair to a particular species. This process is essential for identifying victims in crimes against wildlife.

Anatomy of a Hair

Visible Structure of Hair

Hair, made of the protein keratin, is an outgrowth of skin in mammals. It can be described visually by length, color, root/follicle and tip appearance, and amount of curl (Figure 5.1).

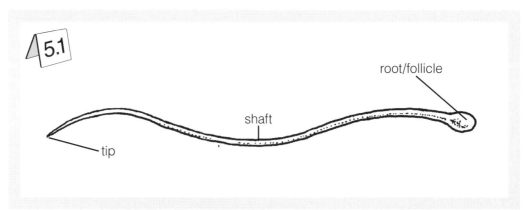

5.1

root/follicle

shaft

tip

National Science Teachers Association

Handout 5-B
Identified by a Hair

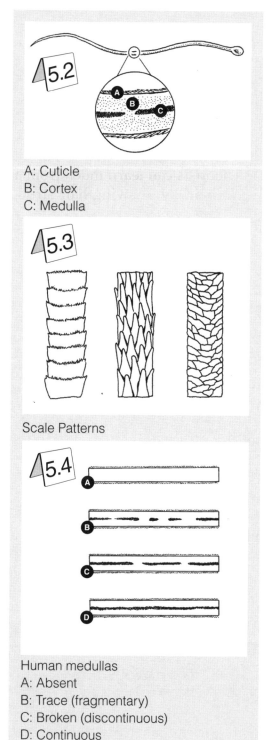

5.2

A: Cuticle
B: Cortex
C: Medulla

5.3

Scale Patterns

5.4

Human medullas
A: Absent
B: Trace (fragmentary)
C: Broken (discontinuous)
D: Continuous

Microscopic Structure of Hair

When examined microscopically, the three distinct parts of hair can be seen: the cuticle, the cortex, and the medulla (Figure 5.2).

The *cuticle* is the transparent outer covering of hair that acts as a protective barrier to hold in moisture. It is seen under the microscope as a layer of scales pointing toward the tip of the hair (Figure 5.3). The shape of the scales varies among mammal species.

The *cortex* is the main body of the hair that gives it shape. It contains the pigment for hair color.

The *medulla* is a core of cells that runs down the center of the cortex through the length of the hair. Made of soft keratin and air, the medulla's unique features help match the hair to the mammal species. In humans the medulla has no clear shape (i.e., it is amorphous) and is often absent. It is categorized into four groups: absent, trace (fragmentary), broken (discontinuous), and continuous (Figure 5.4).

The medullas of other mammals are more prominent and have distinct shapes. Some are shown in Figure 5.5.

Handout 5-B
Identified by a Hair

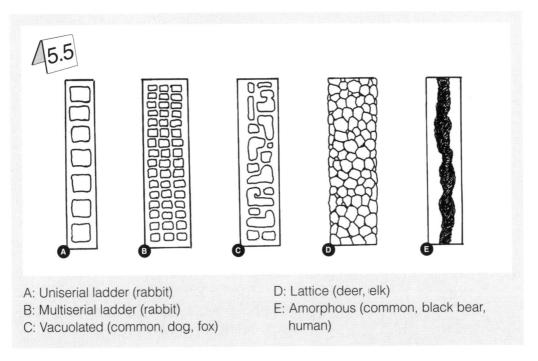

A: Uniserial ladder (rabbit)
B: Multiserial ladder (rabbit)
C: Vacuolated (common, dog, fox)

D: Lattice (deer, elk)
E: Amorphous (common, black bear, human)

Medullary Index

The medullary index gives a number to the size ratio between the width (diameter) of the medulla and the width (diameter) of the entire hair.

Medullary Index = $\dfrac{\text{width of medulla}}{\text{width of hair}}$

For example, if the width of the medulla under the microscope is 2 mm and the width of the hair is 8 mm then the medullary index = 2/8 = 1/4.

The medullary index can identify whether the hair is from a human or other mammal. In humans the medulla is narrow or absent, with its medullary index between 0 and 1/3. In other mammals, the medulla fills much of the hair's diameter with a medullary index between 1/3 and 1.

National Science Teachers Association

Handout 5-B
Identified by a Hair

What Does It Mean?

1. Why is hair considered indirect or circumstantial evidence in court?

2. What is the difference between the hair shaft and the hair follicle?

3. For Figure 5.6, label the following parts of a hair: cuticle, cortex, medulla. Give their function.

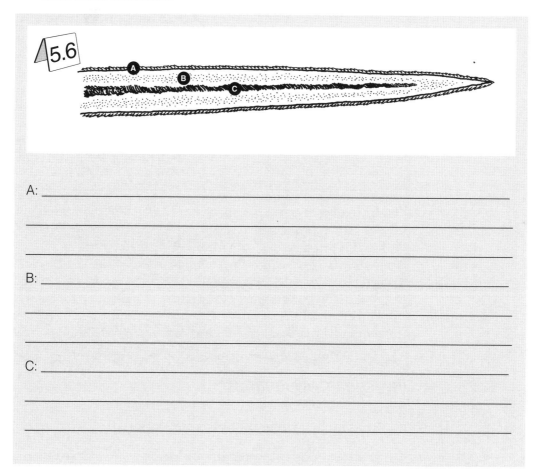

5.6

A: _____

_____

_____

B: _____

_____

_____

C: _____

_____

_____

4. How does the medullary index help determine if the hair is from a human or other mammal?

Lesson 6: pH and pH Indicators

The Crime: "Dead in the Water"

"Early this month a cry of alarm came over e-mail from my friend Zoltan Lontay in Hungary. The Hungarian news had just announced an enormous fish kill in the Szamos river on that country's eastern border. A wave of cyanide was moving down the Szamos and into the Tisza, Hungary's second largest river. No one knew what had happened, but there was talk of a mine, operated by an Australian company, across the border in Romania—a mine that uses cyanide....

"It was indeed a gold mine, of the modern sort that allows even very dilute gold deposits to be extracted from tons of rock economically. The rock is dug, crushed, and piled in heaps, through which cyanide drips to leach out the gold. The tricky part is what then to do with the cyanide. In Romania it was dumped into an above-ground pool held by an earth dam....

"[The] poison in the pool was enough to kill a million people.... On January 30 the dam collapsed. Within half a day cyanide concentrations in the Szamos reached 150–300 times the safe level. Life in the river was exterminated, from fish to plankton.

"Several hundred thousand people live in the danger zone. No drinking, fishing, or water extraction from the river or from wells along the river is allowed. The city of Szolnok on River Tisza is distributing bottled water, five liters per family per day. Food industries and paper mills have shut down...."

Source: Meadows, D. H. Feb. 14, 2000. "Dead in the Water." Daily Grist (Environmental News & Commentary). www.grist.org/comments/citizen/2000/02/14/in/index.html

Investigator Questions

1. What is the crime, though unintentional?

2. The dam breaks and people living along the river notice dead fish in the water. They contact you. You take samples of the water from the dead zone and water from an unaffected area to a forensic scientist. What kinds of chemical tests could be done on these samples to figure out why the fish are dying?

3. What would the pH tell you about the health of the water?

National Science Teachers Association

Lesson 6: pH and pH Indicators

Teacher Guidelines

Overview

Topic: pH
Go to: www.scilinks.org
Code: UF07

Topic: pH scale
Go to: www.scilinks.org
Code: UF08

All solutions have a pH, and pH can be an important clue to chemical composition. Any solution taken as evidence can be tested for pH to learn about the solution. Investigators can also take the pH of any liquids or powders on a suspect's or a victim's body to determine if the liquids or powders are factors in the crime.

In this lesson, students learn the basic chemistry of pH by physically demonstrating, as a class, the relationship between H^+ and OH^- that creates acidic, basic, and neutral solutions. Then they will use tokens or beans to show how the logarithmic ratios of ions change as a pH changes. Finally, the students will apply this knowledge using pH indicators to determine the pH of household solutions.

Connections to the National Science Education Standards

Standard	Category	Lesson Connection
Content Standard A—Abilities necessary to do scientific inquiry (grades 5–12)	Science as Inquiry	Students discover and demonstrate understanding of ion relationships in pH levels through guided manipulative lab activities. After conducting a predesigned lab, they interpret the results from a variety of pH indicators to determine the pH range of tested solutions. They explain the benefits of using more than one pH indicator to test for pH.

Standard	Category	Lesson Connection
Content Standard B—Properties and changes of properties in matter (grades 5–8) Chemical reactions (grades 9–12)	Physical Science	Students use models, manipulatives, and a lab to show the relationship between H^+ and OH^- in solutions as pH levels change. They explain why strong acids and bases are more reactive than neutral or weak solutions.

Time Required

1½–2 class periods

Materials

- Handouts (one for each student):
  - "The Ion Balancing Act of pH" (Handout 6-A, p. 123)
  - "Testing pH With pH Indicators: Student Lab Investigation" (Handout 6-B, p. 129)
  - "More Practice With Ph Indicators" (Handout 6-C, p. 132)
- Cards for each student: H^+ (side 1), OH^- (side 2) written in big letters
- pH scale (on board or overhead):

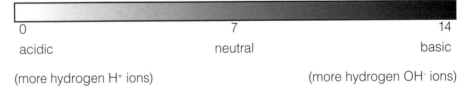

0   7   14
acidic   neutral   basic

(more hydrogen H^+ ions)   (more hydrogen OH^- ions)

- 200 tokens (beans or beads) for *each pair* of students: 100 of one color or type; 100 of another color or type
- Ziplock plastic bags to hold the tokens for each pair of students
- Samples of diluted shampoo, lemon juice, lye, and baking soda solution
- Droppers
- Spot plates
- Paper towels
- Three or more pH indicators:
  - bromthymol blue (BTB)
  - Congo red (CR)
  - phenolphthalein (PHT)
- (Alternative nontoxic pH indicators: Liquid from boiled red cabbage, beets, and/or tea)

Teaching Plan

Getting Ready

1. Make an ion card for each student with H^+ written on one side and OH^- on the other (making H_2O). Make the H^+ and OH^- large enough that students can read them across the room.

2. Choose tokens (beans, beads) of two colors. Count out 100 of each color or type for each pair (or larger group) of students, or let students do this as the first step of the lab activity.

3. Choose three pH indicators to be used in the demonstration and lab. Bromthymol blue (full range indicator), Congo red (acid indicator), and phenolphthalein (base indicator) can be used in combination. The natural indicators from solutions of red cabbage, beets, tea, or black beans can replace any or all of these.

Guiding Students

Introduction

1. Read aloud and discuss "The Crime: 'Dead in the Water'."

2. Use the K-W-L format. Have students respond to the following questions in their Investigator Notebooks:

   • *What do I <u>know</u> about pH and pH indicators? (Put a star by information you are not sure is accurate.)*
   • *What do I <u>want to know</u> about pH and pH indicators?*

Activity 1: Making a Classroom pH Solution

1. Give each student an ion card, and ask students what molecule is made when the two ions are combined (H_2O). Explain that periodically the H^+ (proton) separates from OH^-. As long as there are the same amounts of H^+ and OH^- in a solution, the pH is neutral.

2. Set students up for the class activity by telling them they are the ions in a container (classroom) of pure water. Each person can only be one ion. Have them stand up and work together to form a neutral solution by holding the correct ratio of H^+

and OH⁻ ion cards (1:1).

3. Explain that acids have more H^+ than OH^-, and bases have more OH^- than H^+. The greater the difference, the stronger the acid (lower number on the pH scale) or base (higher number on the pH scale). Tell the class to form the pH solutions below by deciding what combination of ions are needed. (Each student holds up his or her sign to show his or her contribution to the solution. You can point to the pH scale (see "Materials" list) to reinforce the connection between your words, their actions, and the pH scale.)

pH Solutions:
- Neutral solution (point to pH 7)
- Acid (any level)
- Base (any level)
- Weak base
- Strong base
- Strong acid
- Weak acid solution

4. Have students summarize the activity in their Investigator Notebooks using words and/or pictures.

Activity 2: Neutralizing the Classroom's pH Solution

1. Divide the class in half to represent two different solutions. Using their ion cards, students demonstrate what happens to the pH when two solutions of different pHs are mixed. Using their ion signs, have one group make a strongly basic solution and the other make a strongly acidic solution.

2. After forming two lines that face each other, have the groups mix (keeping the same ions on their cards) and form a circle. Have them explain what happened to the ion ratio and pH when the two solutions mixed. You can repeat this with other combinations of solutions.

3. Collect the ion cards and have students sit down with a partner for the next pH activity.

4. Have students summarize the activity in their Investigator

Notebooks using words and/or pictures.

5. Read and discuss "The Ion Balancing Act of pH" (Handout 6-A) from the beginning up to the section "What's the Difference Between pH Levels?"

Activity 3: The Real Meaning of a Difference in pH Levels

1. Give each pair of students tokens of two colors (or types). Designate one color as H^+ and the other as OH^-. Tell them to make a neutral solution with 100 tokens of each color.

2. Explain that if a solution changes from pH 7 to pH 6, the number of ions does not change by 1, but by a power of 10. This is called a logarithmic scale. So a decrease of one number on the pH scale (from 7 to 6) represents a 10-fold increase in H^+ amounts in relation to OH^-.

3. Ask students to show each of these pH levels by changing the ratio of the OH^- to H^+. They can record these ratios in their Investigator Notebooks by drawing a table showing pH level and its ratio of OH^- to H^+ shown with the tokens.

   - pH 6 (more acidic than pH 7, so 10 OH^- to 100 H^+)
   - pH 5 (acid: 1 OH^- to 100 H^+)
   - pH 8 (more basic than pH 7, so 100 OH^- to 10 H^+)
   - pH 9 (base: 100 OH^- to 1 H^+)
   - Predict pH 4 and 3, etc., or show by having each token represent 10 ions.

4. From the student handout "The Ion Balancing Act of pH" (Handout 6-A) have students read and discuss "What's the Difference Between pH Levels?"

Teacher Lab Demonstration of pH Indicators

1. Introduce students to pH indicators, explaining each step, but not interpreting results.

   a. Fill three test tubes one quarter full of tap water in front of the students.

   b. Put 1–2 drops of a different pH indicator into each test tube. Choose three indicators that will turn different colors (e.g., bromthymol blue, Congo red, phenolphthalein, red cabbage).

c. Ask students to write down what happened and give a possible explanation for the results based on their knowledge of pH.

2. From the student handout "The Ion Balancing Act of pH," read "How Do pH Indicators Work?" and discuss the "What Did I Discover?" questions with students.

3. Give the students "Testing pH With pH Indicators" (Handout 6-B). Go over the students' procedure ("Your Steps") and have them conduct the lab in pairs or threes.

4. If students need more practice, give them "More Practice With pH Indicators" (Handout 6-C).

5. Have students complete and discuss "What Did I Discover?" questions in "Testing pH With pH Indicators" (Handout 6-B).

6. Revisit "The Crime: 'Dead in the Water'" as a class to see if students have new insights.

SAFETY ////

- Consider using nontoxic pH indicators: Red cabbage juice, beet juice, or tea.
- Wear safety goggles.

For chemical indicators:

- If swallowed, drink 1–2 glasses of water and call a physician.
- If indicator comes in contact with skin, wash with water. If skin is irritated from contact, wash with water for 15 minutes.
- If indicator comes in contact with eyes, wash thoroughly with water for 15 minutes. If irritation continues, call a physician.
- If spilled, wipe up immediately with water.

WEB LINKS

Acid/base indicators. *www.chemistry.about.com/library/weekly/aa112201a.htm*

How to make red cabbage indicator. *www.chemistry.about.com/library/weekly/aa012803a.htm*

Handout 6-A
The Ion Balancing Act of pH

Name _____ Date _____

`- CRIME SCENE - DO NOT CROSS - CRIME SCENE - DO NOT CROSS - CRIME SCENE - DO NOT CROSS - CRIME SCENE - DO NOT CROSS - CRIME SCENE - DO NOT CROSS -`

We are affected every day by the pH of liquids in and around us. The food we eat and liquids we drink have pH levels, and our body organs require specific pHs to keep us healthy. Some people's bodies are sensitive to acids, so they may choose to not drink colas, orange and apple juices, coffee, and beer. Doctors sometimes suggest that women not drink cola (pH 2.5) because its phosphoric acid removes essential calcium from their bones. But strong acids are perfectly normal in the stomach, where gastric acids (pH 1.5–2.0) are essential for digesting foods.

The cleaning power of certain products is related to pH. Cleaners like ammonia and bleach are strong bases (pH over 11.5) while milder hand soaps have lower pHs (9.0 and 10.0). But these strong basic cleaners can also destroy the clothes or objects they are meant to clean if not used properly. When is a neutral or nearly neutral pH preferred?

Even water is not the same, in terms of pH values. Acid rain (pH 5.0 or less) from industrial air pollution harms plants and wildlife, but we can swim in seawater with a basic pH of 8.0. If chemicals with strong pHs are spilled into an unpolluted (pH 5.0–8.0) lake or river, the dramatic pH rise or drop could change a healthy water ecosystem into a dead zone by killing all life. Only after the water's pH returns to a healthier, more neutral, pH level would animals and plants return.

Representative pH Values

Substance	pH	Substance	pH
Hydrochloric acid, IOM	-1.0	Tea or healthy skin	5.5
Battery acid	0.5	Milk	6.5
Gastric acid	1.5–2.0	Pure water	7.0
Lemon juice	2.4	Healthy human saliva	6.5–7.4
Cola	2.5	Blood	7.34–7.45
Vinegar	2.9	Seawater	7.7–8.3
Orange or apple juice	3.5	Hand soap	9.0–10.0
Beer	4.5	Household ammonia	11.5
Acid rain	<5.0	Bleach	12.5
Coffee	5.0	Household lye	13.5

Retrieved July 18, 2007 from *en.wikipedia.org/wiki/PH*

Handout 6-A
The Ion Blancing Act of pH

What Does the Forensic Scientist Need to Know?

Forensic scientists must be able to choose and run appropriate lab tests to identify the pH of a solution collected as evidence. If pH indicators are used, scientists will select several different indicators to narrow down the pH range. Since all solutions have a pH, any taken as evidence could be tested to help solve a crime. Investigators can also take the pH of liquids or powders on a suspect's or victim's body to determine if they are factors in a crime.

Scientists must know the meaning of the pH scale and values, how to identify acids and bases, how acids and bases are formed chemically, and how they react when mixed. Scientists can then use this knowledge to relate the pH of the solution to possible effects it would have on living things and the natural habitat at the crime scene.

What's the Difference Between Acids and Bases?

The term *pH* was coined long after scientists categorized acids and bases. For hundreds of years scientists observed that some solutions had common characteristics. If something tasted sour, corroded metals, and turned blue litmus paper red, it was called an acid (*acidus* is Latin for "sour"). If something tasted bitter, felt slippery, and changed red litmus paper to blue, it was called a base.

It was later discovered that acids, such as lemon juice, vinegar, and carbonated drinks, all release hydrogen ions (H^+) when mixed with water. Hydrogen ions are protons (positively charged atomic particles), so acids are also called proton donors. Bases, like ammonia and soap, release hydroxyl ions (OH^-) when mixed with water and are called proton acceptors because OH^- attracts H^+ (proton). A hydroxyl ion is really just an H_2O molecule that lost a proton.

What Is pH?

pH Scale

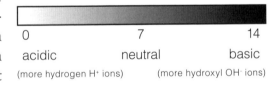

0	7	14
acidic	neutral	basic
(more hydrogen H^+ ions)		(more hydroxyl OH^- ions)

Neutral Scale

The strength of an acid or base is measured on a pH scale. A pH ("power of hydrogen" or the "potential of hydrogen") level indicates the amount of hydrogen

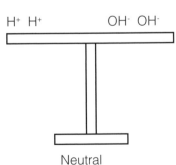

Neutral

124

Handout 6-A
The Ion Balancing Act of pH

ions (H^+) in a solution in relation to the amount of hydroxyl ions (OH^-). Pure water has equal amounts of H^+ and OH^-, putting it in the neutral middle of the pH scale with a pH of 7.

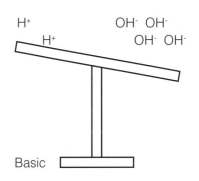

Acid Scale

If an acid is mixed with water or another liquid, it will release H^+ (protons). As acids get stronger, the difference between H^+ and OH^- gets larger, with more H^+ in solution. Acid levels span from 0 (strongest) to 6 (weakest).

Basic Scale

If a base is mixed with water or another liquid, it will attach to H^+. As bases get stronger, the difference between OH^- and H^+ gets larger, with more OH^- in solution. Base levels span from 8 (weakest) to 14 (strongest).

What's the Difference Between pH Levels?

The pH scale is a logarithmic scale, which means that each step represents a 10-fold change. What is changing? Remember that pH is measuring the ratios of H^+ and OH^-. So a decrease of one number on the pH scale represents a 10-fold increase in H^+ concentration in relation to OH^-. For example, a pH of 2 has 10 times more H^+ than a pH of 3; a pH of 13 has 100 times less H^+ than a pH of 11.

Strong acids (battery acid, stomach acid) and strong bases (bleach, lye, ammonia) have the highest amounts of H^+ and OH^- respectively. When these very reactive ions contact objects, the chemical changes can burn holes in clothes and other materials, corrode metals, and harm skin. Diluting the strong acid or base with water, or mixing it with a contrasting pH solution, will bring the new solution closer to neutral and make it less reactive.

Handout 6-A
The Ion Blancing Act of pH

Name _____ Date _____

How Do pH Indicators Work?

In the lab, pH can be determined with pH paper, electronic probes, or pH indicators. pH indicators are chemicals that, when mixed with a solution, will change colors according to the pH of the solution. Each color indicates a pH range. For instance, bromthymol blue turns yellow for pH 0 to 6, green for pH 6 to 7.8, and blue for pH 7.8 to 14. Phenolphthalein only changes colors for bases (base indicator), while Congo red only changes colors for acids (acid indicator). Below are four common pH indicators and the colors they show.

Bromthymol blue (BTB):
- yellow for a pH of 0 to 6
- green for a pH of 6 to 7.8
- blue for a pH of 7.8 to 14

1	2	3	4	5	6	7	8	9	10	11	12	13	14

Yellow   Green   Blue

Congo red (CR):
- blue for a pH of 1 to 3
- purple for a pH of 3 to 4.9
- red for a pH of 4.9 to 14

1	2	3	4	5	6	7	8	9	10	11	12	13	14

Blue   Purple   Red

Phenolphthalein (PHT):
- colorless for a pH of 1 to 8
- light pink for a pH of 8 to 10
- hot pink for a pH of 10 to 14

1	2	3	4	5	6	7	8	9	10	11	12	13	14

Clear   Light pink   Hot pink

National Science Teachers Association

Handout 6-A
The Ion Balancing Act of pH

Red cabbage:
- red for a pH of 1 to 3
- purple for a pH of 4 to 5
- violet for a pH of 6 to 7
- blue for a pH of 8 to 9
- blue-green for a pH of 10 to 11
- greenish-yellow for a pH of 12 to 14

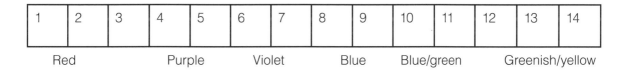

1	2	3	4	5	6	7	8	9	10	11	12	13	14

Red   Purple   Violet   Blue   Blue/green   Greenish/yellow

Since each pH indicator changes colors for different pH ranges, a solution can be tested with several indicators to narrow its possible pH range. For example in the diagram below, a hypothetical solution was tested with three pH indicators. By finding the pH overlap among them, the pH range becomes narrower.

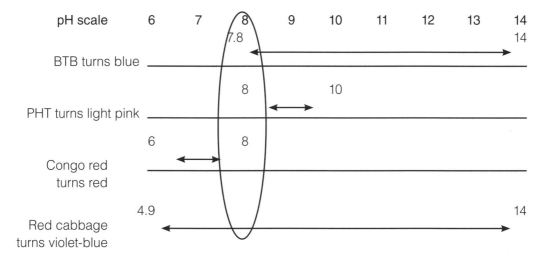

The overlap of pH ranges is 7.8 – 8.

- Blue for a pH of 1 to 3
- Purple for a pH of 3 to 4.9
- Red for a pH of 4.9 to 14

Handout 6-A
The Ion Blancing Act of pH

Name _____ Date _____

What Did You Discover About the Ion Balancing Act of pH?

1. What are three ways pH is a part of our daily lives?

2. How can the pH of evidence be useful to a wildlife crime investigator?

3. What ions are formed in pure water and how do they affect the pH of a solution?

4. If the solution is neutral (pH 7), what color would the indicators turn?

    a. BTB _____
    b. PHT _____
    c. CR   _____
    d. RC   _____

STUDENTS: TAKE A CLOSER LOOK

- Does pure water have a higher concentration of H^+ or OH^-? Justify your answer.
- Why are both strong acids and strong bases dangerous?
- All pH indicators test the same pH levels. Agree or disagree, and justify your answer.
- pH levels change as H^+ amounts change. Agree or disagree, and justify your answer.

National Science Teachers Association

Handout 6-B
Testing pH With pH Indicators: Student Lab Investigation

Name _____ Date _____

Your Job

Use a combination of pH indicators to determine the pH of household solutions.

Your Steps

1. Work in pairs.

2. Set the spot plate on a paper towel and label the rows and columns as shown below. Leave your spot plate on the paper towel during the lab.

	BTB	CR	PHT
Shampoo	◯	◯	◯
Lemon juice	◯	◯	◯
Lye	◯	◯	◯
Baking soda	◯	◯	◯

3. Fill out columns 1 and 2 (Solution and Indicators) of your data table, "My Findings" (p. 131).

4. Put 2–3 drops of the solutions into the labeled cups.

5. Add 1 drop of the pH indicator to the labeled cups.

6. Complete the data table:

   a. Record the indicator and color change, if any, for each sample.

   b. Write the solution's pH range that the color indicates. Refer to page 126 for the pH ranges for each indicator.

Handout 6-B
Testing pH With pH Indicators: Student Lab Investigation

c. Compare the pH ranges shown by the three indicators. Where do the ranges overlap? For example, if Indicator 1 pH range is 2–7 and Indicator 2 pH range is 6–8, then the overlap range is 6–7. Record this range in the data table.

d. Record the pH category for this range: acid, base, or neutral. In the previous example, the solution is neutral or a very weak acid.

What Did You Discover About pH Indicators?

1. a. Which is a base indicator? (*Hint:* Acids and neutrals were the same color.)

   b. Which is an acid indicator? (*Hint:* Neutrals and bases were the same color.)

   c. Which indicator identified the full pH scale (acids, neutral solutions, and bases)?

2. Why was each solution tested with three indicators instead of just one?

3. What should you do if two indicators show the solution is a strong base, and another indicator shows the same solution is neutral?

4. Read your comments about pH and pH indicators in your Investigator Notebook (*What do I* know *about pH and pH indicators? What do I* want to know *about pH and pH indicators?*). Then respond to the following question: *What have I* learned *about pH and pH indicators?*

National Science Teachers Association

Handout 6-B
Testing pH With pH Indicators: Student Lab Investigation

- CRIME SCENE - DO NOT CROSS - CRIME SCENE - DO NOT CROSS - CRIME SCENE - DO NOT CROSS - CRIME SCENE - DO NOT CROSS - CRIME SCENE - DO NOT CROSS -

My Findings (Data Table)

Instructions:

Record the results of your three pH indicator tests for each of the four solutions. Then find the pH range indicated by each color change. Finally, compare the pH ranges for all three indicators for each solution to determine the overlapping range. Use the pH scale to match that range with the category of acid, neutral, or base. Record the solution's pH category.

Solution	Indicator	Color change from indicator	Color's pH range (1–14)	pH Range Acid, Base, Neutral

Handout 6-C
More Practice With pH Indicators

Name _____ Date _____

- CRIME SCENE - DO NOT CROSS - CRIME SCENE - DO NOT CROSS - CRIME SCENE - DO NOT CROSS - CRIME SCENE - DO NOT CROSS - CRIME SCENE - DO NOT CROSS -

Instructions: Use your notes on pH and pH indicator ranges to answer the following questions.

1. Solution A turns blue when bromthymol blue (BTB) is added. What range of pH can you say the solution is?

2. Solution A turns light pink when phenolphthalein (PHT) is added. What range of pH can you say the solution is, based on this test?

3. Congo red (CR) is added to Solution B. It turns purple. What range does this indicate?

4. If PHT is added to Solution B, what color would you predict it to turn? Why?

5. The following results were reported for Solution C.

    Results   What pH range
                                           does this result indicate?

    BTB—Solution turns green   _____

    CR—Solution turns red   _____

    PHT—Solution turns hot pink   _____

Which test does not support the results of the other two tests? Why?

6. a. If you want to find out if an unknown solution has a pH greater than 10, which indicator would you use?

    b. What color would indicate this pH?

7. a. If you want to find out if an unknown solution has a pH of less than 3, which indicator would you use?

    b. What color would indicate this pH?

8. a. If you want to find out if an unknown solution has a pH of 8, what TWO indicators would you need to use?

    b. What color would each indicator need to become?

    Indicator 1: _____

    Indicator 2: _____

National Science Teachers Association

Lesson 7: Mammal Skulls

The Crime: "Massive Tiger Bone Seizure in Taiwan Highlights Continued Poaching Threat"

"A massive seizure of tiger bone in Taiwan last month has clearly shown that there is little evidence of a major reduction in poaching of tigers in the wild and signals the urgent need for strong enforcement action by both tiger range states and potential consumer countries. In the largest ever single seizure of tiger bone in Taiwan, and one of the largest ever in Asia since 2000, Kaohsiung Customs authorities in Taiwan on July 4th confiscated over 140 kg of tiger bones, including 24 skulls, in a shipment from Jakarta, Indonesia. The contraband was hidden in a container of deer antlers being exported to Taiwan for use in traditional medicines....

"The Convention on International Trade in Endangered Species of Wild Fauna and Flora (CITES) prohibits the international trade in parts and derivatives from tigers, elephants and pangolins and all three are totally protected species in Indonesia. However, a TRAFFIC [TRAFFIC is a wildlife trade monitoring network] Southeast Asia report released last year found that despite full protection, poaching of and trade in Indonesia's tigers continues unabated. According to TRAFFIC Southeast Asia regional program officer Chris Shepherd, the report estimated that at least 50 tigers were killed or removed from the wild in Indonesia per year between 1998 and 2002. 'This single shipment intercepted in Taiwan last month represents nearly half that annual figure,' Shepherd said. 'Assuming that all these tiger parts were sourced from Sumatra, Indonesia is in real danger of losing its last remaining Tiger sub-species—the Sumatran tiger—if the widespread illegal trade in tiger parts is not stopped....'"

Excerpts taken from "Massive tiger bone seizure in Taiwan highlights continued poaching threat." (August 8, 2005) TRAFFIC NewsRoom. www. traffic.org/news/Tiger_poaching. htm

Investigator Questions

1. What was the crime?

2. How could forensic scientists identify the animal species of the skulls?

3. How were the skulls used as evidence of a crime?

Lesson 7: Mammal Skulls

Teacher Guidelines

Overview

Animal skulls provide a wealth of information to the scientist. Besides identifying the species, the skull can show the animal's eating preferences, size, gender, brain development, health, cause of death, classification levels, and much more. Investigators of wildlife crimes who need proof that a particular animal or species has been harmed can also run DNA tests from the cells of the skull. In this lab students will examine the teeth in mammal skulls and categorize them by eating preferences. Then they will use a dichotomous key to identify the animal species for each skull.

Connections to the National Science Education Standards

Standard	Category	Lesson Connection
Content Standard A— Abilities necessary to do scientific inquiry (grades 5–12)	Science as Inquiry	Students compare and record teeth types in various unidentified mammal skulls. Using this data and reference papers, they classify the mammals as herbivores, carnivores, omnivores, and insectivores. Students also identify skull structure and species by using a dichotomous key.
Content Standard C— Populations and ecosystems (grades 5–8)	Life Science	Students categorize animals (skulls) as herbivores, carnivores, or omnivores based on their teeth.
Content Standard C— Diversity and adaptations of organisms (grades 5–8) Biological evolution (grades 9–12)	Life Science	Students show how tooth type and size tell what an animal is adapted to eat. They recognize the differences and similarities of skulls and tooth combinations in related species.

Time Required

1–2 50-minute classes

Materials

- Handouts (one for each student):
  - "Teeth Tell All" (Handout 7-A, p. 140)
  - "Check Out Those Teeth! Student Lab Investigation" (Handout 7-B, p. 144)
  - "Key to Skulls of North American Mammals: Student Lab Investigation" (Handout 7-C, p. 146)
  - "What Did I Discover About Animal Skulls?" (Handout 7-D, p. 155)
- Actual or plastic molds of mammal skulls (e.g., deer, elk, bear, coyote, fox, bobcat, weasel, squirrel, mouse, raccoon, opossum, skunk, rabbit, porcupine, beaver, prairie dog, shrew)
- Rulers or tape measures

Teaching Plan

Getting Ready

1. It is best to use actual skulls or skull models, but if that is not possible, copy photos of skulls from print or online resources (see "Web Links," p. 139). You need a minimum of four North American mammal skulls of different species (herbivore, gnawing herbivore, carnivore, omnivore), with an ideal number being eight to twelve skulls. A shrew or bat skull could be added to show insectivore teeth patterns. Actual or plastic molds of skulls can be borrowed or purchased from

   - State wildlife or conservation agency
   - U.S. Fish and Wildlife Service
   - Natural history museum
   - State or national park
   - Local nature center or wildlife refuge
   - Taxidermist or hunters
   - Skulls Unlimited (1-800-695-SKULL, *www.skullsunlimited.com*)
   - Acorn Naturalists (*www.acornnaturalists.com/store*)

Online photos of skulls can be found at the "Web Links" addresses for "Animal Skull Collection," "Spinning Skulls," or "Skulls Unlimited International."

2. Mark each skull with a number or letter.

3. Decide if students will do one or both lab investigations ("Check Out Those Teeth!" [Handout 7-B] and "Key to Skulls of North American Mammals" [Handout 7-C]). The skull evidence in the final crime investigation (Section 3 in this book) needs to be identified using the dichotomous key in Handout 7-C.

Guiding the Students

Introduction

1. Read aloud and discuss "The Crime: 'Massive Tiger Bone Seizure in Taiwan Highlights Continued Poaching Threat.'"

2. Use the K-W-L format. Have students respond in their Investigator Notebooks.

    • *What do I know about skulls? (Put a star by information you are not sure is accurate.)*
    • *What do I want to know about skulls?*

3. Show the class skulls from two different species. Ask:

    • How are they the same? How are they different?
    • What can you learn from examining a skull?

Readings and Activities

4. Read and discuss "Teeth Tell All" (Handout 7-A). Have students make a chart or two-column notes describing the different types of eaters and the differences in teeth. *Hint*: To show your class examples of tooth types, lay a skull on its side on the overhead projector.

5. Give each student a copy of "Check Out Those Teeth! Student Lab Investigation" (Handout 7-B).

6. Set one numbered skull at each station around the room. Students complete the data table in Handout 7-B by referring to

the handout "Teeth Tell All" (Handout 7-A). Make sure students examine at least one of each type of eater as they rotate through the stations. When they are done, you can show them a list of possible animals for them to try to match to the skulls based on their observations.

7. Give each student a copy of "Key to Skulls of North American Mammals: Student Lab Investigation" (Handout 7-C, pp. 146–152) or another listed in "Web Links." Explain that scientists often identify a skull by using a dichotomous key that describes distinct skull characteristics of the animal species or genus. Scientists must know the parts of the skull and be able to distinguish between skulls based on the key's descriptions.

8. Practice using the key by working as a class to identify one skull.

9. Then have students work in small groups to identify a minimum of two skulls (a herbivore skull and a carnivore or omnivore skull) with the key. Students should record the number and characteristic for each step on the data sheet on page xxx to show the logic used to get to their animal choice.

10. Have students fill out "What Did I Discover About Animal Skulls?" (Handout 7-D) and discuss their answers as a class.

11. Revisit "The Crime: 'Massive Tiger Bone Seizure in Taiwan Highlights Continued Poaching Threat'" as a class to see if students have new insights.

Extensions

Make other observations and comparisons of skulls:

- Compare orbital position and relative size (eye socket) in relationship to over-all skull size. In general, the larger the orbital in comparison to the skull, the sharper the animal's eyesight. More forward-facing orbitals suggest binocular vision of predator species (felines); more side-facing orbitals suggest monocular vision of prey species (elk).
- Compare the size of nasal passages. Most animals with larger, longer nasal passages (canines, deer family) have a better sense of smell than animals with smaller, shorter nasal passages (felines).
- Compare the size of the skull bones that protect the middle and inner ear (ear bullae). Animals with larger inflated ear bullae (bear) tend to have much better hearing than those with smaller deflated ear bullae (horse).
- Have students research the strength of the animals' senses and compare what they find to skull observations of the orbitals, nasal passage, and ear bullae.
- Compare nonhuman skulls with human skulls.
- Compare measurements of different parts of one skull or the same parts in different skulls.

WEB LINKS

Animal bites, lesson plan. Skullduggery, Inc. *http://skullduggery.com/Lessons/0960.pdf*

Animal skull collection. *www.d91.k12.id.us/skyline/teachers/robertsd/skulls.htm*

Dichotomous key to mammals of Southwest Ohio. *www.environmentaleducationohio.org/VirtualTour/TeachingTools/AnimalClassification/skullkey.pdf*

Skulls Unlimited International. *www.skullsunlimited.com*

Spinning skulls. Animal Diversity Website. University of Michigan Museum of Zoology. *www.animaldiversity.ummz.umich.edu/site/topics/skullpromo.html*

Handout 7-A
Teeth Tell All

Name _____ Date _____

Animal skulls provide a wealth of information to the scientist. Besides the important identification of the species, the skull can show the animal's eating preferences, size, gender, brain development, health, cause of death, classification levels, and much more. Investigators of wildlife crimes who need to match a particular animal or species victim to the evidence can also run DNA tests from the cells of the skull.

What Does the Forensic Scientist Need to Know?

The forensic scientist must know the parts of the skull and the differences among skulls of animal groups. Using dichotomous keys and other resources to examine and measure, they look for distinguishing characteristics to identify the species of the skull.

How Can a Skull Be Identified?

The types, shapes, and patterns of teeth give the quickest clues about the owner, but if the teeth are missing, scientists can identify the skull from other characteristics. For instance, the shape of a feline skull is always round when viewed from the top compared to the shape of a canine skull, which is oblong. Other clues about the species of the skull are found in the size and position of the eye sockets and nasal passage, the shape of ear bullae or tubes, and the size of the brain case. Some species are identified by distinct suture patterns on the skull.

Types of Teeth

Incisors—Located across the front of the mouth; used for cutting (Figure 7.1).

Canines—One canine can be located behind each side of the incisors (four at the most). They work like daggers and are used to grab and hold onto prey. Clues to what an animal eats are given by the presence or absence of the canine, as well as its length.

Molars and premolars—These cheek teeth are located behind the canines and continue to the back of the jaw. They are wide teeth used for grinding, crushing, or cutting.

National Science Teachers Association

Handout 7-A
Teeth Tell All

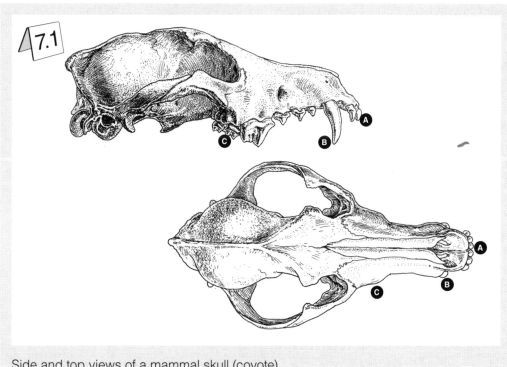

Side and top views of a mammal skull (coyote)
A: Incisors   B: Canines   C: Molars

Teeth Patterns Tell Eating Tales

Herbivores

Examples of herbivores are deer, elk, bison, moose, goats, sheep, peccaries, musk ox, horses, and cattle. These plant-eating animals have wavy-topped cheek teeth (molars and premolars) to grind apart tough plant parts. In some herbivores, these teeth look like a geologic cut through a mountainside because they show alternating layers of hard white enamel and softer darker dentine. As the animal eats, the dentine wears away faster than the enamel to create a sharp edge good for grinding tough plant parts (Figure 7.2).

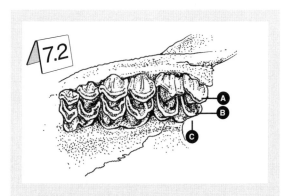

Herbivore molars and premolars
 (white-tailed deer)
A: Enamel
B: Dentine
C: Sharp ridges

Handout 7-A
Teeth Tell All

Most herbivores do not have canines. Exceptions are male horses, with small canines used for defense, and animals in the pig family with tusks. One group of herbivores, the North American artiodactyls, are missing both top incisors and canines. These animals—deer, goats, sheep, cattle, and musk ox—chew with only cheek teeth (peccaries are the exception).

Gnawing Herbivores

Examples of gnawing herbivores are prairie dogs, beavers, porcupines, squirrels, and rabbits. These rodents and rabbits are also plant eaters, but they have specialized, long, curved incisors to crack nuts, rip apart tough plant parts, or chew through wood (Figure 7.3). These teeth are quickly worn down from gnawing, so they must grow continually throughout the animal's lifetime.

These incisors must stay sharp to cut through tough plant parts. What's the trick? It's all in the enamel. The outer face of the incisors has an extra layer of enamel that strengthens and protects the teeth, but the inner face is covered with softer dentine. When the animal gnaws, it is constantly sharpening its teeth by shaving off layers of the inner dentine faster than the outer enamel.

The other teeth of gnawing herbivores are like those of other herbivores— wavy-topped cheek teeth for grinding, and no canines.

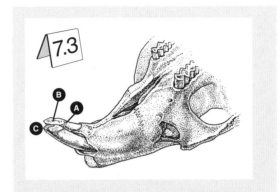

Gnawing herbivore incisor (hoary marmot)
A: Enamel
B: Dentine
C: Constantly sharpened point

Carnivores

Examples of carnivores are the cat family, wolves, ferrets, mink, badgers, and river otters. Since carnivores hunt and eat other animals, their teeth are completely sealed and protected by hard white enamel. Carnivores have

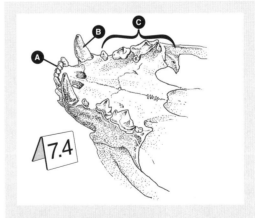

Carnivore teeth (bobcat)
A: Incisor
B: Canine
C: Molars/premolars

Handout 7-A
Teeth Tell All

long pointed canines to grab and hold onto prey, and sharp-edged incisors to cut through the tough muscle and body parts (Figure 7.4). The cheek teeth are different sizes and shapes, with most having deep grooves and sharp points that resemble a cluster of tiny canines. This shape is best for crushing and cutting prey.

Omnivores

Examples of omnivores are foxes, coyotes, raccoons, bears, and skunks. Omnivore teeth are a mix of herbivore and carnivore teeth since omnivores eat both plants and animals. Their sharp-edged incisors and long canines look like those of carnivores, though the canines are not as sharp (Figure 7.5). The cheek teeth are a blend of herbivore and carnivore cheek teeth—they do not have the tall, sharp points of the carnivore, but do have more grooves and blunt points (e.g., see human molars) than the flatter herbivore teeth. All teeth are sealed in hard white enamel.

Insectivores

Examples of insectivores are bats and shrews. These animals look like they have a mouthful of canines (Figure 7.6). All teeth (incisors, canines, and cheek teeth) are small, sharp daggers. In bats, the incisors are smaller than the canines. All teeth are sealed with hard enamel for protection as the insectivores catch and crush hard-shelled insects, other arthropods, and small animals.

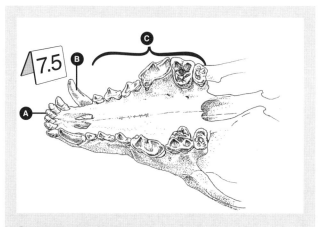

Omnivore teeth (coyote)
A: Incisor
B: Canine
C: Molars/premolars

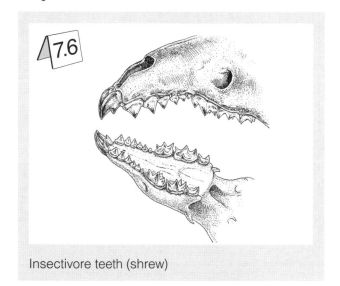

Insectivore teeth (shrew)

STUDENTS: TAKE A CLOSER LOOK

- What information can an animal skull tell about the animal?
- Can an animal skull be identified if all the teeth are missing?

Handout 7-B

Check Out Those Teeth!
Student Lab Investigation

Name _____ Date _____

- CRIME SCENE - DO NOT CROSS - CRIME SCENE - DO NOT CROSS - CRIME SCENE - DO NOT CROSS - CRIME SCENE - DO NOT CROSS - CRIME SCENE - DO NOT CROSS -

1. Examine 3–4 skulls at lab stations. Describe the shape and structure of the different types of teeth, comparing them to the information in "Teeth Tell All" (Handout 7-A).

Data Table: Skull Observations

	Incisors	Canines	Molars, premolars (cheek teeth)
Skull 1			
Skull 2			
Skull 3			
Skull 4			

Handout 7-B
Check Out Those Teeth!
Student Lab Investigation

2. Based on your observations, predict if each animals ate plants, animals, or both. Write an "I think… because..." statement for each skull.

    Skull 1:

    Skull 2:

    Skull 3:

    Skull 4:

3. Based on your observations, what animal do you think each skull belongs to?

    Skull 1:

    Skull 2:

    Skull 3:

    Skull 4:

Handout 7-C

Key to Skulls of North American Mammals: Student Lab Investigation

Name _____ Date _____

Use the dichotomous key on pages 148–152 to identify the skull. In the data table that follows the key, record the key number and characteristics for each step you choose.

Key to Skulls of North American Mammals

This key is intended as a first step in identifying skulls of some representative North American mammals.

This is a "dichotomous key"; that is, you identify a specimen by working through the key and making a series of "either/or" (dichotomous) choices. Choices are arranged in "couplets," or pairs of statements. From each couplet, choose the statement that best describes your specimen. This will lead you to the name of a mammal or group of mammals or it will lead you to another couplet farther down the key. Simply work through the steps in sequence until you have a tentative identification.

Check your tentative identification against published pictures or other descriptions. Suggestions for further reading are provided on page 154. There are excellent resources on the Web. For example, the University of Michigan's Museum of Zoology maintains an excellent site that provides photographs of skulls of most of the mammals listed here: *http://animaldiversity.ummz.umich.edu/site/accounts/specimens/Mammalia.html*

This key uses features of the skulls and teeth only. That is because such cranial and dental remains are the remains that are usually found in the field, in owl pellets, and the like. Some basic vocabulary is needed to use this key. Terms that are likely to be unfamiliar are defined in parentheses or labeled on the accompanying diagrams.

A dental formula is a shorthand method to indicate the number and variety of teeth in a particular mammal. Dental formulas frequently appear in keys. Here is the dental formula for the genus *Canis*: I = 3/3, C = 1/1, P = 4/4, M = 2/3, Total = 42.

- Note that the formula describes one side of the skull. The total number of teeth is calculated by adding together all the numbers given in the dental formula and multiplying by 2, for the two sides of the jaw.

- Teeth are described per "quadrant"—upper left, lower right, etc. The number above each "slash" mark represents the number of teeth in one quadrant of the upper jaw; the lower

Handout 7-C

Key to Skulls of North American Mammals: Student Lab Investigation

numeral represents the teeth of one quadrant of the lower jaw.

• Abbreviations: I = incisors, C = canines, P = premolars, and M = molars. A dental formula can be further abbreviated by deleting initials for the various types of teeth, for example: 3/3, 1/1, 4/4, 2/3 = 42.

If a particular kind of tooth is not present in a species, a zero appears in the formula. For example, rodents lack canines and many species (such as the Norway rat, *Rattus norvegicus*) lack premolars. The dental formula of the rat is therefore:

1/1, 0/0, 0/0, 3/3 = 16.

Handout 7-C

Key to Skulls of North American Mammals: Student Lab Investigation

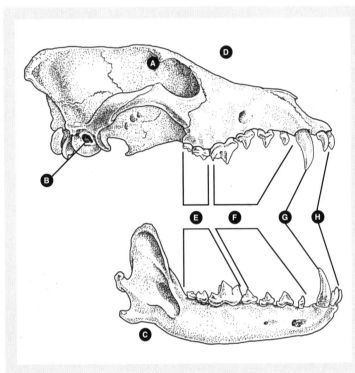

Coyote top and bottom teeth

A: Postorbital process
B: Auditory bulla
   = ear capsule
C: Mandible
D: Skull
E: Molars (cheek teeth)
F: Premolars (cheek
   teeth)
G: Canine
H: Incisors

1   Cheek teeth all about the same shape: simple, peg-like, widely spaced;
    no incisor teeth ....**Armadillos**

    Cheek teeth different in shape from front to back in the tooth-row,
    or if all similar in shape, then incisors absent 2

2   Incisors 5/4 on each side of the jaw; posterior of mandible with
    prominent, inward-directed shelf .... **Opossums**

    Incisors 3/3 or fewer on each side of the jaw;
    posterior of mandible without inward-directed shelf 3

3   Upper incisors present..4

    Upper incisors absent...21

4   Canine tooth absent 5

    Canine teeth present 13

National Science Teachers Association

Handout 7-C

Key to Skulls of North American Mammals: Student Lab Investigation

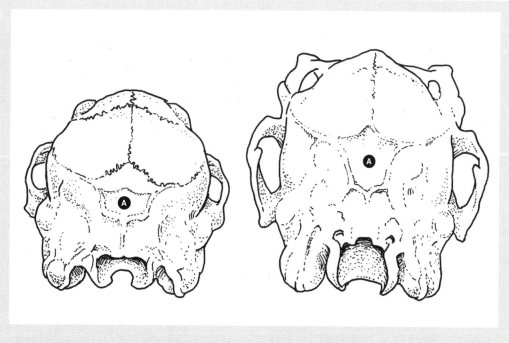

Backs of hare and rabbit skulls showing interparietal bone (A).

5 Incisors 2/1...Lagomorphs: pika, rabbits, hares, 6

   Incisors 1/1 .... Rodents, 7

6 Interparietal bone distinct;
   skull usually less than 75 mm long...............................**Cottontail Rabbits**

   Interparietal bone fused to parietal in adult, indistinct; skull greater
   than 75 mm long..**Jackrabbits**

7 Infraorbital foramen (opening below eye socket) oval, larger than foramen magnum (canal for spinal cord at back of skull). ....**Porcupines**

   Infraorbital foramen (opening below eye socket) smaller than foramen
   magnum (canal for spinal cord at back of skull).......................................8

8 Size large, greatest length of skull > 125 mm.................................. **Beavers**

   Size smaller, greatest length of skull < 125 mm 9

Handout 7-C

Key to Skulls of North American Mammals: Student Lab Investigation

9   Opening beneath eye socket (infraorbital foramen) small, rounded to triangular in shape; lower premolars present, total teeth 20 or more ....Squirrels, 10

Opening beneath eye socket (infraorbital foramen) of moderate size, a vertical slit, no lower premolars, total teeth 18 or fewer..Rats and mice, 12

10   Cheekbones angled toward midline of skull, so cheek region narrower in front, broader in the rear (look at shape from top)..............11

Cheekbones roughly parallel, not strongly angled toward midline of skull (look at shape from top)............................**Tree squirrels**

11   Skull greater than 63 mm long, cheekbones relatively heavy ....Prairie dogs

Skull less than 63 mm long, cheekbones not particularly robust ....Ground squirrels

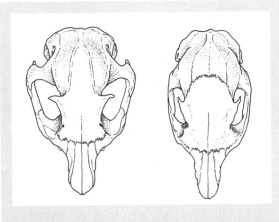

12   Skull less than 30 mm long........Native mice

Skull more than 40 mm long ....Native rats: woodrat = "packrat"

Tree squirrel and prairie dog skulls (top views).

13   Canine not markedly longer than adjacent teeth; size small, skull less than 25 mm long..**Shrews**

Canine markedly longer than adjacent teeth; size medium to large, skull greater than 30 mm long...Carnivores, 14

14   Shearing teeth (carnassials, last upper premolar over first lower molar) poorly developed; skull greater than 250 mm long .... **Bears**

Shearing teeth (carnassials, last upper premolar over first lower molar) well developed, skull less than 250 mm long ....Other carnivores, 15

Handout 7-C
Key to Skulls of North American Mammals: Student Lab Investigation

15 Molars 2/2, total teeth 40..**Raccoons**

   Molars 1/,1 1/2, or 2/3 on each side of jaw 16

16 Molars 2/3 on each side of jaw ....Dog Family, 17

   Molars 1/1 or 1/2 on each side of jaw..18

17 Postorbital process thick, convex (bulged outward) on top; skull greater
   than 160 mm long..**Coyotes**

   Postorbital process thin, concave (dished in) on top; skull less than
   150 mm long...**Foxes**

18 Molars 1/1, total teeth 28 or 30 ....Cat Family, 19

   Molars 1/2, on each side of jaw 20

19 Skull greater than 150 mm long ....**Mountain lions**

   Skull less than 125 mm long ....**Bobcats, lynx**

20 Auditory bullae (ear capsules) small and flattened....................... **Skunks**

   Auditory bullae (ear capsules) not conspicuously flattened, but larger
   and rounded..**Weasels**

21 Males (less well-developed in females) with horns over permanent
   bony core ....Cow Family, 22

   Males (but not females) with antlers (branching structures of bone);
   if antler shed, then "stump" ("pedicel") still obvious........Deer Family, 24

22 Horns branched; horn sheath shed annually ....**Pronghorn**

   Horns not branched 23

23 Horns of males robust (increasingly heavy with age), yellowish brown
   in color, strongly curved backwards...................................**Bighorn Sheep**

   Horns of moderate size, black in color, only slightly curved
   backwards ....**Mountain Goats**

Using Forensics: Wildlife Crime Scene!

Handout 7-C

Key to Skulls of North American Mammals: Student Lab Investigation

24 Antlers with prominent branch over eye (brow tine); upper canines present; length of skull from sockets of incisors to foramen magnum (canal for spinal cord) greater than 350 mm .... **Wapiti, or Elk**

Antlers without prominent brow tine; upper canine absent; length of skull from sockets of incisors to foramen magnum (canal for spinal cord) less than 300 mm 25

25 Antlers with Y-shaped (dichotomous) branches........................**Mule Deer**

Antlers with one long anterior beam bearing secondary tines ....**White-tailed Deer**

National Science Teachers Association

Handout 7-C

Key to Skulls of North American Mammals: Student Lab Investigation

Key #	Characteristics

Species Identification: _____

Handout 7-C

Key to Skulls of North American Mammals: Student Lab Investigation

REFERENCES

Burt, W. H., and R. P. Grossenheider. 1976 *Field guide to the mammals: Field marks of all North American species found north of Mexico.* Peterson Field Guide Series. Boston: Houghton Mifflin.

Fitzgerald, J. P., C. A Meaney, and D. M. Armstrong. 1994. *Mammals of Colorado.* Denver, CO: Denver Museum of Natural History and Boulder, CO: University Press of Colorado.

Glass, B. P., and M. L. Thies. 1997. *A key to the skulls of North American mammals*, 3rd ed. Privately printed. See the "classifieds" in a recent number of the *Journal of Mammalogy* for availability. This differs from Jones and Manning (1992) in that illustrations are line drawings rather than photographs.

Hall, E. R. 1946. *Mammals of Nevada.* Berkeley: University of California Press. This classic reference has been re-issued by the University of Nevada Press (1995); it is particularly valuable for its illustrated glossary.

Jones, J. K., Jr., and R. W. Manning. 1992. *Illustrated key to skulls of genera of North American land mammals.* Lubbock, TX: Texas Tech University Press.

Martin, R. E., R. H. Pine, and A. F. DeBlase. 2001. *A manual of mammalogy with keys to families of the world*, 3rd ed. Dubuque, IA: W. C. Brown.

Roest, A. I. 1991. *A key-guide to mammal skulls and lower jaws. A nontechnical introduction for beginners.* Eureka, CA: Mad River Press.

Handout 7-D
What Did I Discover About Mammal Skulls?

Name _____ Date _____

- CRIME SCENE - DO NOT CROSS - CRIME SCENE - DO NOT CROSS - CRIME SCENE - DO NOT CROSS - CRIME SCENE - DO NOT CROSS - CRIME SCENE - DO NOT CROSS -

Answer these questions after completing the lab investigation "Check Out Those Teeth!" and/or "Key to Skulls of North American Mammals."

1. An animal skull was found at the scene of a wildlife crime. What kind of information would investigators want to learn about the skull from the forensic lab?

2. What can you conclude about this animal's eating preferences?

   a. A skull with no canines or incisors.

   b. A skull with long canine teeth, incisors, and sharp high-crowned (deep grooved) molars.

   c. A skull that has no canines but has pairs of long, curved, sharp incisors.

3. The soft and hard layers of teeth are seen in some animals like deer and elk.

   a. What are these two layers called?

   b. How do these layers create the grinding structure of the tooth?

4. Read your comments on skulls in your Investigator Notebook *(What do I <u>know</u> about skulls? What do I <u>want to know</u> about skulls?)*. Then respond to the following question: *What have I <u>learned</u> about skulls?*

Lesson 8: Tracks and Trace Fossils

The Crime: "West African Black Rhino Extinct, Group Says"

"The West African black rhinoceros has likely gone extinct, the World Conservation Union (IUCN) announced last week…. Extensive surveys in northern Cameroon, the animals' last known refuge, found no trace of the rhino subspecies….

"Richard Emslie of IUCN's Species Survival Commission told BBC News that a trio of experts systematically scoured 1,200 miles (2,500 kilometers) of habitat in northern Cameroon. The survey failed to find any sign of the West African black rhino. 'They looked for spoor [droppings], they looked for the rhino's characteristic way of feeding, which has an effect like a pruning shear,' Emslie, a rhino expert based in KwaZulu-Natal Province, South Africa, told the news service. 'But they didn't find anything to indicate a continued presence in the area…. They did, however, come across lots of evidence of poaching, and that's the disconcerting thing."

"Poachers have hunted the animals for decades for their horns to supply markets in Yemen and Asia. Rhino horn is used in traditional Asian medicine to fight malaria, epilepsy, fevers, and other ailments. In Yemen the horns are in demand as carved handles on traditional daggers…. According to some estimates, there were 14,000 black rhinos as recently as 1980 and more than 100,000 in 1960."

Excerpts taken from Markey, S. July 12, 2006. "West African Black Rhino Extinct, Group Says," National Geographic News: Animals and Nature. http://news.nationalgeographic.com/news/2006/07/060712-black-rhino.html. *For a related article, see Appel, A. December 12, 2005. "Footprints May Be Key to Protecting Rare Rhinos." National Geographic News.* news.nationalgeographic.com/news/2005/12/1212_051212_wildtrack.html

Investigator Questions

1. What is the suspected crime?

2. What kinds of evidence of rhinos were experts looking for?

3. What trace (temporary) fossil evidence from poachers might have been found?

Lesson 8: Tracks and Trace Fossils

Teacher Guidelines

Overview

Animal and human tracks are one of many types of trace (temporary) fossils that leave clues about who was at a crime scene or other location and about what happened there. In this lesson, students discover what can be learned from tracks and other trace fossils by telling the stories hidden in clues of mystery track patterns. Taking on the role of wildlife biologists, they will identify animal tracks found in a new wilderness area and make a field guide for visitors. An extension activity has students report on the predicted predator/prey balance in the area based on their findings.

Connections to the National Science Education Standards

Standard	Category	Lesson Connection
Content Standard A— Abilities necessary to do scientific inquiry (grades 5–12)	Science as Inquiry	Students examine a variety of track evidence, identify who made each, and describe the animal's behavior when possible.
Content Standard C— Diversity and adaptations of organisms (grades 5–8) Interdependence of organisms (grades 9–12)	Life Science	Students identify and compare tracks of species living in the same ecosystem. They use references to create a field guide describing tracks, other trace fossils, and animal interactions in the ecosystem.

Time Required

1 or 2 50-minute classes

Materials

- Handouts (one for each student):
  - "Mystery Track Pattern Cards" (Handout 8-A, pp. 161–165)

- "Tracking Trace Fossils" (Handout 8-B, p. 166)
- "Making Tracks to Protect Land: Student Lab Investigation" (Handout 8-C, p. 168)
- "Tracks Found in a New Protected Wilderness Area" (Handout 8-D, p. 170)
- "Field Guide to Mammal Tracks" (Handout 8-E, p. 175)

Teaching Plan

Getting Ready

1. Copy the "Mystery Track Pattern Cards" (Handout 8-A). (Make enough for half of the class—students will work in pairs—to have one of each.) Cut apart the track pattern cards and sort them by number to make a set of 1s, a set of 2s, etc. (*Optional:* Use life-size rubber or plaster track replicas to enhance the "Mystery Track Pattern Cards." These can be purchased from science supply and nature education supply stores or borrowed from a local nature center, state division of wildlife, or state park.)

Guiding Students

1. Read aloud and discuss "The Crime: 'West African Black Rhino Extinct, Group Says.'"

2. Use the K-W-L format. Have students respond in their Investigator Notebooks:

   - *What do I <u>know</u> about tracks and trace fossils? (Put a star by information you are not sure is accurate.)*
   - *What do I <u>want to know</u> about tracks and trace fossils?*

3. Make a class list of what can be learned from looking at tracks.

"Mystery Track Pattern" Activity

1. Place copies of Mystery Track Pattern Card #1 face down in front of students (one card for each pair of students). After every pair has a pattern card, tell them to turn the card over, look at it, and quietly discuss what the tracks suggest was happening. Then have students explain their proposed "track stories" to the class. Repeat Step 1 with pattern cards #2–8. (The answers are on the sheet "Answers to Mystery Track Patterns" on p. 165.)

2. Explain trace fossils (i.e., temporary pieces of evidence), with

Extension

Students can create their own mystery track patterns. Have them use the "Field Guide to Mammal Tracks" (Handout 8-E) to design a mystery track pattern that tells a story about one or more animals. The animal story can relate to the wilderness area or can be about any animals in the field guide. Post or share the drawings and have students figure out their classmates' track stories.

tracks being one example. Note that all animals leave trace fossils that can be identified. In some cases, this is the only evidence people find of a rare or shy animal. Have students brainstorm trace fossils (e.g., feathers, nests, burrows, bones, scat) and discuss what can be learned from trace fossils.

3. Have students read "Tracking Trace Fossils" (Handout 8-B) and answer the "What Does It Mean?" questions at the end.

4. Pass out "Making Tracks to Protect Land: Student Lab Investigation" (Handout 8-C). Read "Your Job" aloud and give students options for the design of their field guides. Pass out "Tracks Found in a New Protected Wilderness Area" (Handout 8-D). After students measure the tracks in "Tracks Found in a New Protected Wilderness Area," they can get the "Field Guide to Mammal Tracks" (Handout 8-E) to identify the tracks and begin research for their own field guides.

5. Students make their own field guides.

   Note:

   ▪ Before beginning, decide how you want students to design their field guides. They can be done on the computer or by hand on full, half, or three-fold papers.

   ▪ You may alter the information you want students to pull from the "Field Guide to Mammal Tracks" depending on your time and course focus.

6. Have students read their comments on tracks and trace fossils in their Investigator Notebooks (*What do I know about traks and trace fossils? What do I want to know about tracks and trace fossils?*) and write a response to the following question: *What have I learned about tracks and trace fossils?*

7. Revisit "The Crime: 'West African Black Rhino, Group Says'" as a class to see if students have new insights.

Extensions

- Invite a member of a search-and-rescue team to speak about tracking people who are lost.
- Give students a piece of shoe-size foil. Have them set the foil on carpeted floor or a folded towel and gently step on it to make a track of their shoe print. Show the tracks to the class and ask what the differences are between the tracks. Explain that search-and-rescue teams encourage hikers to make foil tracks before leaving their camps or vehicles. They are invaluable if someone gets lost.
- Invite a hunter to talk with students about how he uses tracks and other trace fossils to locate animals he is hunting.
- Invite a division of wildlife officer to talk with students about how she uses animal tracks and other trace fossils to locate and identify animals or criminal suspects.
- Measure students' stride and straddle (stride = the distance from where a part of one foot touches the ground to where the same part of the other foot touches the ground; straddle = the width between the outer edges of two feet—perpendicular to travel.). Use pedometers to determine how many strides it takes to travel a mile and how that number differs among individuals. Find stride information for different-size animals and determine the number of strides they take in a mile.

WEB LINKS

Get a tracks field guide for your zip code at National Wildlife Federation. *eNature.com/zipguides*

Tracking, Tracks, and Sign: Mammal Tracks and Sign. *www.wildwood-survival.com/tracking/mammals/index.html*

REFERENCES

Burt, W. H., and R. P. Grossenheider. 1976. *Field guide to the mammals: Field marks of all North American species found north of Mexico.* Peterson Field Guide Series. Boston: Houghton Mifflin.

Halfpenny, J. C. 1986. *A field guide to mammal tracking in North America.* Boulder, CO: Johnson Books.

Halfpenny, J. C. 1998. *Scats and tracks of the Rocky Mountains.* Helena, MT: Falcon.

Handout 8-A
Mystery Track Pattern Cards

1

2

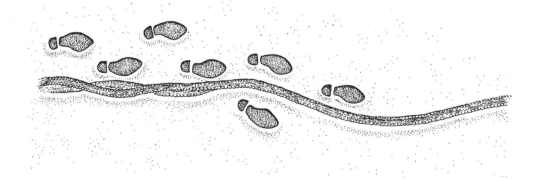

Handout 8-A

Mystery Track Pattern Cards

3

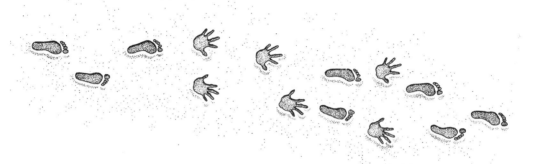

4

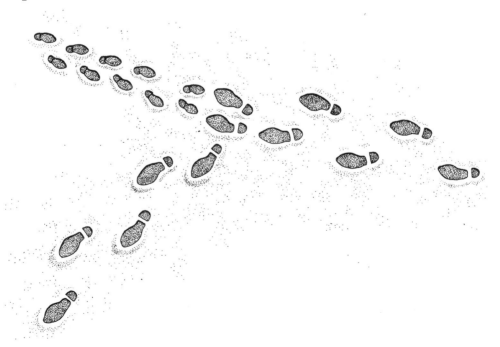

Handout 8-A
Mystery Track Pattern Cards

5

6

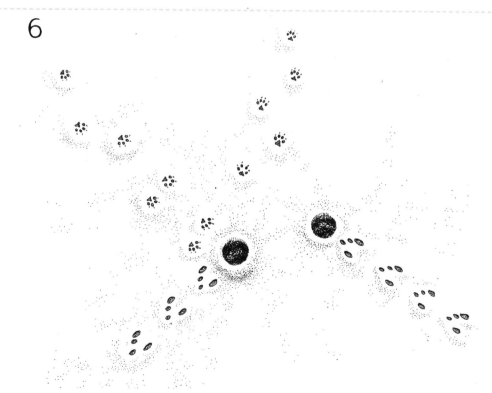

Handout 8-A
Mystery Track Pattern Cards

7

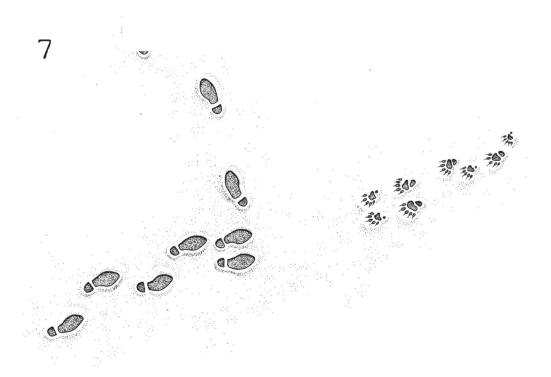

8

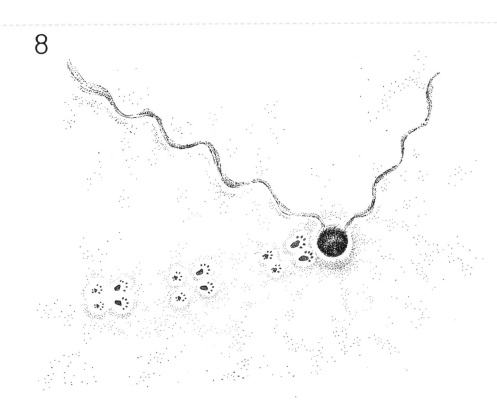

National Science Teachers Association

Handout 8-A

Mystery Track Pattern Cards

Answers to "Mystery Track Pattern Cards"

Below are the stories told by the track patterns:

1. A person walks, sits down, takes off shoes, stands up, and walks away.

2. A person is walking a bike, swings her leg over the bike, pushes off, and rides away.

3. A barefooted person walks into a handstand, walks on his hands, comes back down onto his feet, and walks away.

4. A child and adult walk toward each other and stop. The adult picks up the child and walks away.

5. A mouse is running. A raptor (hawk, owl) flies down and carries away the mouse, leaving only wing prints in the snow.

6. A rabbit runs down a hole. A fox follows, stops at the hole, then walks away. The rabbit escapes out another hole.

7. A person is walking and stops when she sees a skunk walking toward her. The skunk also stops. The person runs in another direction.

8. A ground squirrel runs into a hole. A snake follows the squirrel into the hole. The snake comes back out. The squirrel is either hiding in the hole or has been eaten.

Handout 8-B
Tracking Trace Fossils

Name _____ Date _____

All of the following people must be observers of the fleeting, subtle signs left by the animals they are tracking:

- A wildlife officer trying to find a bear that has been raiding garbage cans and bird feeders in a neighborhood
- A hunter searching for a deer in a forested area
- A wildlife biologist tracking the movement of wolves that have been reintroduced into an area to bring balance back to the ecosystem
- A park ranger walking a trail trying to confirm a visitor's report of a mountain lion
- A search-and-rescue team looking for a lost hiker

The most familiar indicator, footprints, is only one of many types of temporary animal signs, called trace fossils.

What Does a Forensic Scientist Need to Know?

There is an art to finding tracks and other trace fossils in nature or a crime scene. Investigators and scientists need to recognize subtle impressions from tracks and know where to look for other trace (temporary) fossils that an animal has left behind. Knowledge of the animals that naturally live in the ecosystem is essential. Once the evidence is collected, the scientist can make measurements and look for distinguishing characteristics to identify the animal. Telling the "story" behind the trace fossils is helped by the scientist's knowledge of the animal's natural behaviors.

What Is a Track?

A track usually refers to a footprint, but it can also be a mark on the ground left from an animal's tail, wing, hand, or other body part. People leave other unique tracks from objects like tires, skis, or snowmobiles.

What Are Trace Fossils?

Trace fossils are temporary pieces of evidence, including tracks, bones, shells, feathers, impressions, trails, burrows, nests, borings, and scat. Each can give clues about who was where and what happened.

Why Are Animal Tracks Important?

Human and other animal tracks are studied for many different reasons. Besides the situations listed at the beginning of this handout, law enforcement officers can follow the tracks of a suspect or victim and use tracks or other trace fossils to identify someone involved in a crime.

Handout 8-B
Tracking Trace Fossils

A single animal footprint can tell the tracker the species, the animal's age and gender, the direction of travel, and the approximate time or day the animal was there. A more detailed story of the animal becomes clear when a series of tracks is found. This group of footprints and other signs could show how the animal was moving (running, walking, trotting), as well as its speed, health, or behavior.

Are All Trace Fossils Useful Evidence?

Not all trace fossils are equal in a wildlife crime investigator's eye. The most powerful evidence comes from the body of the animal victim or human suspect. Feathers, hair, blood, and bones all contain cells with DNA that, when tested, can be matched to a single individual. Body cells, and DNA, can often be collected from clothes, blankets, and other materials that touched the body of the animal or person.

Other trace fossils like burrows, nests, and tree scrapings are helpful in identifying a species of ani-

mal, but unless DNA is found, the evidence would describe a group instead of an individual. Another type of indirect, or circumstantial, evidence is from tracks. Footprints, shoe prints, and tire tracks again narrow the focus and can eliminate animal species or human individuals, but they are not a direct link to an individual. It is possible to convict a suspect with a large body of indirect evidence, though DNA is evidence of choice.

What Did You Discover About Tracks and Trace Fossils?

1. What is the difference between a track and a trace fossil?

2. What additional information could you gather from a series of tracks that you could not get from a single track?

3. Name an animal that lives in your community. Describe several kinds of trace evidence it might leave and where you would look to find that trace evidence.

STUDENTS: TAKE A CLOSER LOOK

- Which trace fossil evidence would crime investigators prefer to find at a crime scene: hair or a footprint? A nest or a feather? Justify your answers.
- Can you identify an individual from a shoeprint? Defend your answer.

Handout 8-C
Making Tracks to Protect Land:
Student Lab Investigation

Name_____ Date_____

- CRIME SCENE - DO NOT CROSS - CRIME SCENE - DO NOT CROSS - CRIME SCENE - DO NOT CROSS - CRIME SCENE - DO NOT CROSS - CRIME SCENE - DO NOT CROSS -

Your Job

As a wildlife biologist, you have been asked to identify the tracks of wildlife species living in a new protected wilderness area. After identifying these tracks, you will research and design a visitors' field guide to the area, giving information about each species.

Your Steps

1. Your teacher will give you "Tracks Found in a New Protected Wilderness" (Handout 8-D). Measure and record the length and width of each track. (Do not include claws/nails in measurement.) Then use the "Field Guide to Mammal Tracks" (Handout 8-E) to identify them.

2. Design a field guide that includes all of the following parts or selected parts (as specified by your teacher):

   - Cover: Title of field guide
   - Introduction:
     - title of field guide and the name you are giving to the wilderness area
     - an overall and specific explanation of what visitors can expect to see when they visit the wilderness area
     - an explanation of possible reasons why this area is now protected from development
   - Animal Pages (include the following information for each animal):
     - name of animal and drawing of animal track (*Optional:* picture of animal)
     - measurements of track
     - written description of (a) how the track can be distinguished from other similar tracks, (b) what other trace fossils (signs) the animal might leave, and (c) where visitors should look for these trace fossils
   - Predator/Prey Table: Make a table that lists the animals and what they eat. Are there any predator/prey relationships among the animals you are researching?
   - Food Relationships Table: Use the "Field Guide to Mammal Tracks" to make a table explaining the food relationships among all the animals in the area. The column headings in your table should be "Animal name," "Type of eater (herbivore/carnivore/omnivore)," and "What the animal eats."

National Science Teachers Association

Handout 8-C
Making Tracks to Protect Land: Student Lab Investigation

3. Animal Inventory and Management Plan: Write an animal inventory and management plan in which you include the following information:

   a. Diversity of wildlife species in the area (number and names of species)

   b. Number of species that are herbivores, carnivores, and omnivores

   c. Why it is important to know the eating behavior of the species before deciding how to improve the balance and health of the ecosystem

   d. Suggestions for improving the health and balance of the wilderness area

   e. Suggestions for other types of information that should be examined to learn more about the health of the ecosystem

Optional Activities for the Student-Designed Field Guide

Option 1: Wilderness Area Food Web

Create a food web showing the connections among the animals in the wilderness area you have chosen for your field guide and make predictions of what other animals or plants must also be in the area to support these identified animals.

Option 2: Is This a Balanced Ecosystem?

Write a report in which you advise the conservation organizations and government agencies that are managing the wilderness area about ways to keep balance in the ecosystem. Use information gathered for your Animal Inventory and Management Plan (step 3 above) in your report.

Handout 8-D
Tracks Found in a New Protected Wilderness Area

Name _____ Date _____

- CRIME SCENE - DO NOT CROSS - CRIME SCENE - DO NOT CROSS - CRIME SCENE - DO NOT CROSS - CRIME SCENE - DO NOT CROSS - CRIME SCENE - DO NOT CROSS -

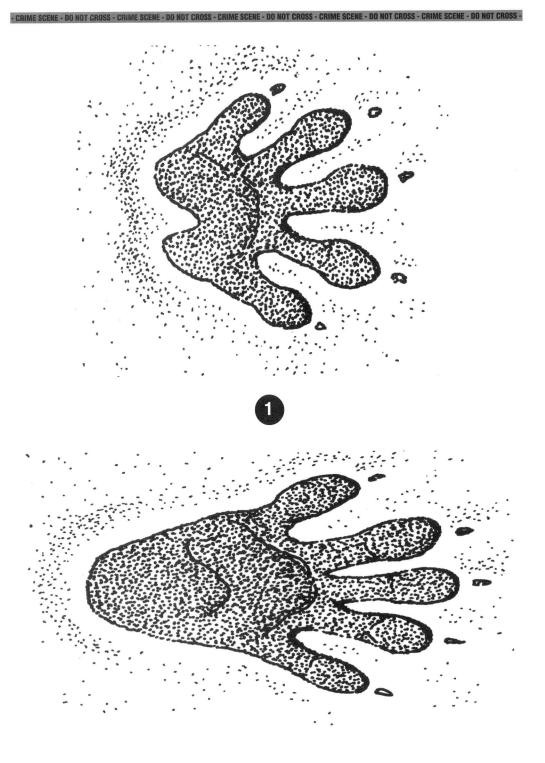

1

National Science Teachers Association

Handout 8-D
Tracks Found in a New
Protected Wilderness Area

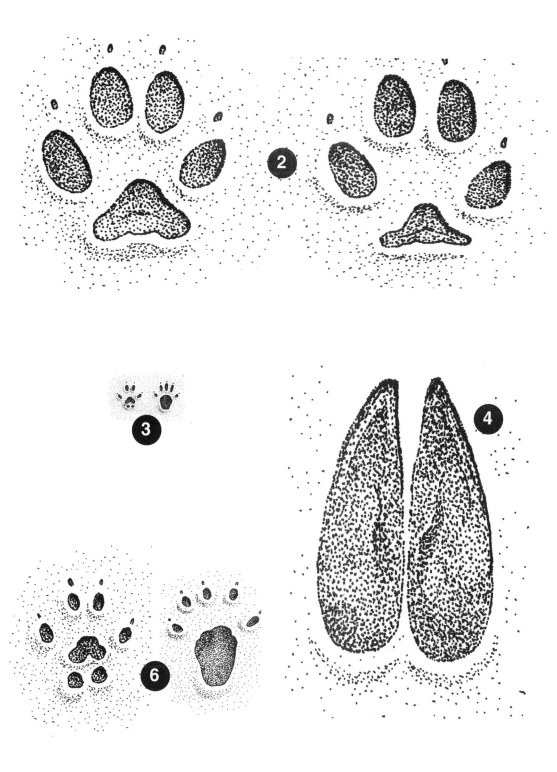

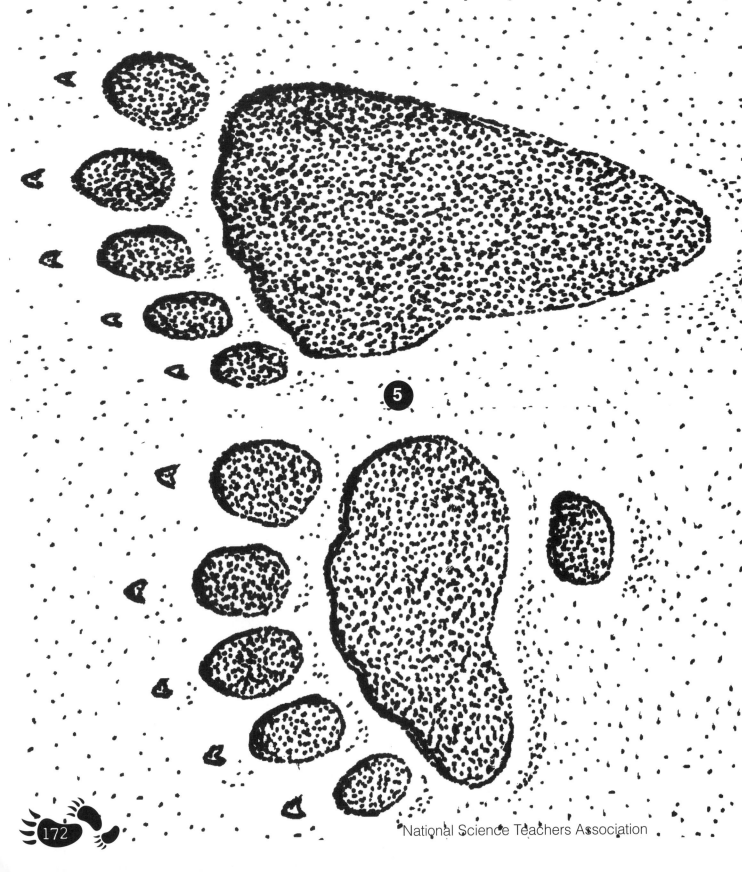

5

National Science Teachers Association

Handout 8-D
Tracks Found in a New Protected Wilderness Area

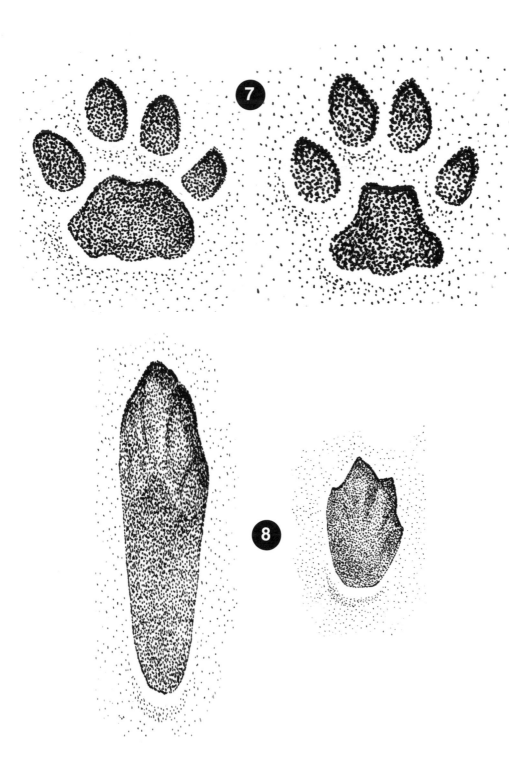

Handout 8-D
Tracks Found in a New Protected Wilderness Area

Name _____ Date _____

Answers to Tracks Found in New Protected Wilderness Area

(Give this answer sheet to students **after** they have identified the tracks in Handout 8-D by using the "Field Guide to Mammal Tracks" [Handout 8-E]).

1 Raccoon

2 Fox

3 Mouse

4 Deer

5 Black bear

6 Squirrel

7 Bobcat

8 Rabbit

National Science Teachers Association

Handout 8-E

Field Guide to Mammal Tracks

Name _____ Date _____

- CRIME SCENE - DO NOT CROSS - CRIME SCENE - DO NOT CROSS - CRIME SCENE - DO NOT CROSS - CRIME SCENE - DO NOT CROSS - CRIME SCENE - DO NOT CROSS -

1. Black bear
2. Bobcat
3. Cottontail rabbit
4. Coyote
5. Deer
6. Elk (Wapiti)
7. Fox
8. Mountain lion
9. Mouse
10. Porcupine
11. Raccoon
12. Squirrel
13. Striped skunk

All track measurements are average sizes as reported in James C. Halfpenny. 2001. *Scat and Tracks of the Rocky Mountains*, 2nd ed. Guilford, CT: The Globe Pequot Press.

1. Black Bear (Ursus americanus)

Front	Hind
4.5 × 4 in	7 × 3.5 in
(11.3 × 10 cm)	(17.8 × 8.8 cm)

Track: Five toes. Claws on front foot. Hind foot looks like human print because of distinct heel.

Other animals with similar tracks: Grizzly bear and Alaskan brown bear are larger.

Habitat: Forests and swamps in eastern United States; mountains and foothills of the western United States.

Habits: Usually active at night, but can be seen during the day. Eats berries, nuts, insects, small mammals, eggs, and honey. Also scavenges dead animals, human garbage, and birdseed from feeders. Adaptable to living around people and towns. Climbs trees.

Other Signs (trace fossils): Claw marks on trees to mark territory, signs of digging into ant mounds and open logs, large scat piles often full of seed pits from native berry bushes and sunflower-seed shells from bird feeders.

Handout 8-E
Field Guide to Mammal Tracks

2. Bobcat (Lynx rufus)

Front	Hind
2 × 2.1 in	2.1 × 1.9 in
(5 × 5.3 cm)	(5.3 × 4.8 cm)

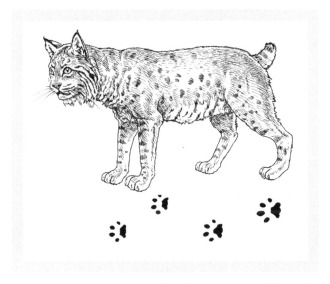

Track: Round. Four toes. Usually does not show claws.

Other animals with similar tracks: Lynx and mountain lion are larger. Coyote more oval and shows claws.

Habitat: Rock ledges, forests, swamps, and caves.

Habits: Mostly active at night. Solitary. Eats small mammals and birds. Dens found in hollow logs and rock crevices.

Other Signs (trace fossils): Covers scat with dirt. Food covered to return to later.

3. Cottontail Rabbit (Sylvilagus ssp.)

Front	Hind
1.25 × 1 in	3.5 × 1 in
(3.2 × 2.5 cm)	(8.8 × 2.5 cm)

Track: Hind foot about more than twice as long as front foot. Toes hard to distinguish because the foot is covered with fur. Track pattern when hopping has the larger hind feet prints in front of the smaller front feet prints.

Other animals with similar tracks: Jackrabbit and snowshoe hare have larger feet.

Habitat: Very adaptable. Lives wherever there is grass and cover.

Habits: Dens in the ground or in a brush pile. Active day and evening all year round.

Handout 8-E
Field Guide to Mammal Tracks

Other Signs (trace fossils): Tops of grasses and other green-stemmed plants bitten off. Tips of new growth on plants bitten off. Hole in ground leads to burrow.

4. Coyote (Canis latrans)

Front	Hind
2.5 × 2.35 in	2.25 × 1.9 in
(6.3 × 5.8 cm)	(5.7 × 4.8 cm)

Track: Oval-shaped, claws usually show.

Other animals with similar tracks: Wolves are larger. Foxes are smaller.

Habitat: Prairies, open woodlands. Very adaptable—has been seen in cities, deserts, and alpine areas.

Habits: Often nocturnal, but can be seen at any time. Omnivore scavenger (eats almost anything). Eats mostly small rodents, rabbits, and berries. Lives in a ground den.

Other Signs (trace fossils): Territory marked with scat piles. Hole in ground or hillside leads to den.

5. Deer

5a. Mule deer
(Odocoileus hemionus)

Front	Hind
3.25 × 2.6 in	3.1 × 2.5 in
(8.2 × 6.5 cm)	(7.8 × 6.3 cm)

Handout 8-E
Field Guide to Mammal Tracks

5b. White-tail deer (*Odocoileus virginianus*)

Front	Hind
3 × 1.9 in	2.6 × 1.5 in
(7.5 × 4.8 cm)	(6.5 × 3.8 cm)

Habits: Most active in the early mornings and evenings. Eats mostly twigs and shrubs (browser). Will eat grasses and other green-stemmed plants.

Other Signs (trace fossils): Creates a flattened bowl-shaped area the size of the animal when it beds down. Antlers may leave imprints in the snow when feeding. Males shed antlers in January and February. Mule deer antlers are branched in pairs. Whitetail deer antlers have prongs that extend singly from a main beam.

6. Elk (Wapiti) (*Cervus canadensis*)

Front	Hind
4.75 × 3 in	4.25 × 2.9 in
(11.8 × 7.5 cm)	(10.7 × 7.3 cm)

Track: Heart-shaped with slightly convex sides. Pointed tip of the "heart" points in the direction of travel, like an arrow.

Other animals with similar tracks: Pronghorns, goats, and sheep have concave sides. Elk is larger and wider.

Habitat: Wooded areas for cover. Moves into meadows to feed at twilight. Found in all types of habitat except arctic and desert.

National Science Teachers Association

Handout 8-E
Field Guide to Mammal Tracks

Track: Blocky heart shape with front tip split and wider. Rounded, convex sides. The narrower tip points in the direction of travel.

Other animals with similar tracks: Deer and pronghorn have narrower, smaller pads with tips coming to more of a point. The outer edge curves outward and is rounder than moose, sheep, deer, and pronghorn.

Habitat: Forests, mountain meadows, and high plains.

Habits: Active in early mornings and evenings. Beds down in trees during the day. Eats grasses, herb, twigs, and bark. Usually seen in groups of 25 or more.

Other Signs (trace fossils): Chew marks on trunks of trees. Males shed antlers from February through March. Creates a flattened bowl-shaped area the size of the animal where it beds down.

7. Fox

7a. Red fox *(Vulpes vulpes)*

Front	Hind
2 × 1.8 in	1.9 × 1.7 in
(5 × 4.5 cm)	(4.8 × 4.3 cm)

7b. Gray fox *(Urocyon cinereoargenteus)*

Front	Hind
1.8 × 1.6 in	1.7 × 1.6 in
(4.5 × 4.0 cm)	(4.3 × 4.0 cm)

Red fox

Track: Usually shows claws. Slightly oval print. Large spaces between toe pads.

Other animals with similar tracks: Coyote and wolf larger; dog toes more splayed versus forward pointing

Habitat: Variety of habitats—brush, farm crops, combination of forest and open areas, cities.

Habits: Most active at night and early morning but seen at all times of day. Omnivore that eats insects, rabbits, mice, berries, and fruits.

Other Signs (trace fossils): Holes in ground leading to den, small bones around den entrance, musky-smelling scat.

Handout 8-E
Field Guide to Mammal Tracks

8. Mountain Lion (Puma concolor)

Front	Hind
3.5 × 3.6 in	3.25 × 3 in
(8.8 × 9.0 cm)	(8.2 × 7.5 cm)

Track: Size of baseball. Four toes. Track appears round. Claws are usually not seen. Large toe marks.

Other animals with similar tracks: Wolves have claw marks and their track is more oval. Bears have five toes.

Habitat: Open woodland, riparian areas with trees, and rocky cliffs and ledges with good cover.

Habits: Follow the deer they prey upon, even into neighborhoods. They also eat porcupines. Solitary animals. Most active at night, but can be seen anytime.

Other Signs (trace fossils): Often covers scat with dirt. Hides food. Marks territory with scrapes (piles of plant parts and dirt).

9. Mouse

Deer mouse (P. maniculatus)

Front	Hind
0.3 × 0.3 in	0.4 × 0.3 in
(0.8 × 0.8 cm)	(1 × 0.8 cm)

Track: Track is smaller than a fingerprint. Four toes are in the front foot; five toes are on the back foot. Hopping track patterns show the larger back feet immediately in front of the smaller front feet. Leaping distances are 3–17". A tail drag may be visible.

Other animals with similar tracks: Shrew tracks are larger and have

National Science Teachers Association

Handout 8-E
Field Guide to Mammal Tracks

five toes on the front feet. The vole does not show a tail drag mark. Usually trots instead of jumping.

Habitat: Different species of mice are found in almost any habitat.

Habits: Active at night. Lives in burrows or sheltered ground nests of grass, sometimes around houses. Stashes seeds in different locations near nest.

Other Signs (trace fossils): Nests of grass and leaves are found in burrows, wood piles, and tree cavities. Piles of nuts, seeds, and empty shells. Tiny, oval-shaped scat pellets.

10. Porcupine
(Erethozon dorsatum)

Front	Hind
1.7 × 1.3 in	2.7 × 1.7 in
(4.3 × 3.3 cm)	(6.8 × 4.3 cm)

Track: Track leaves a rough texture because the sole is covered with small nubs. The front foot has four toes; the hind foot has five. The track pattern often shows a pigeon-toed walk, with the toes turned slightly inward. The tail drag may be continuous between feet. Belly drag marks may be visible in the snow.

Other animals with similar tracks: Rough texture of tracks make them unique.

Habitat: Lives in forested areas or places with shrubs.

Habits: Most active at night. Spends most of its time in the tops of trees chewing bark. Awkward on the ground. Eats small twigs, inside of bark, and leaf buds. Likes salt. Does not hibernate. Dens found in rock caves and hollow trees.

Other Signs (trace fossils): Pieces of chewed-off green twigs scattered around the base of a tree. Patches of bark missing from the trunk and branches.

11. Raccoon (Procyon lotor)

Front	Hind
2.5 × 2.5 in	4 × 2.3 in
(6.3 × 6.3 cm)	(10 × 5.8 cm)

Track: Five slender toes, larger rounded tips, long slender heel. Looks like small human hands and feet.

Other animals with similar tracks: River otter has toe webbing. Mink is smaller.

Habitat: Banks of lakes and streams, storm drains in cities.

Habits: Common visitor to trash cans and bird feeders. Nocturnal omnivore that eats many types of plants, seeds, and animals—fruits, nuts, insects, crayfish, eggs, and frogs. Lives in dens made in dead trees, hollow logs, and the ground.

Other Signs (trace fossils): Scrape marks and holes beside streams from digging for crayfish. Piles of crayfish exoskeletons. Holes in dirt from digging for worms.

12. Squirrel

**12a. Red squirrel
(Tamiasciurus hudsonicus)**

**12b. Eastern gray squirrel
(Sciurus carolinensis)**

Front	Hind
1 × 1 in	0.9 × 1 in
(2.5 × 2.5 cm)	(2.3 × 2.5 cm)

Track: Track is the size of a thumbprint. The front foot has four toes; the back foot has five toes. Can leap up to three feet. Track patterns show the larger back feet in front of the smaller back feet between leaps.

Other animals with similar tracks: Chipmunks have smaller tracks; marmots have larger tracks. The prairie dog and ground squirrel have long claws.

National Science Teachers Association

Handout 8-E
Field Guide to Mammal Tracks

Habitat: Red squirrels live in coniferous forests of the United States, Canada, and Alaska. Eastern gray squirrels live in deciduous forests, parks, and communities in the eastern and southern United States.

Habits: Active during the day all year. Makes nests of grass, sticks, and leaves in trees or under stumps or logs. Feeds on a wide variety of plant parts (seeds, nuts, conifer cones), eggs, and fungi.

Other Signs (trace fossils): Tunnel runways under the snow. Nut stashes. Leave piles of pinecone scales and partially eaten cones at the base of trees.

13. Striped Skunk (Mephitis mephitis)

Front	Hind
1.5 × 1.25 in	1.9 × 1.4 in
(3.8 × 3.1 cm)	(4.8 × 3.5 cm)

Track: This track is about the size of a teaspoon. Each foot has five long toes, with the front having long claws.

Other animals with similar tracks: Badgers have bigger tracks.

Habitat: Found in many different habitats, including grasslands and deserts. Lives in abandoned dens or hollow logs. Can live next to and under buildings.

Habits: Mostly active at night and early in the morning. Can dig out small rodents. Eats insects as well as small mammal and bird eggs. Does not hibernate.

Other Signs (trace fossils): Musky odor carried long distances and easy to identify. Remains of insects, a torn up nest, or punctured eggs. Up to 8" diameter conical holes left after digging for insects.

Section 3

Investigating
and Solving
a Wildlife
Crime

Investigating and Solving a Wildlife Crime

Overview

> *Teacher:* **Before you do anything else, read the "Crime Summary" (Handout a, pp. 190–191) to learn the background details of the wildlife crime.**

In this section, students investigate a wildlife crime involving bears. They work in teams to review crime scene reports, conduct interviews of crime suspects and witnesses (played by volunteer school staff and parents), analyze evidence in the lab, and bring charges against the criminal(s).

Using Investigator Notebooks During the Crime Investigation

Solving a crime is like putting together the pieces of a very large jigsaw puzzle. Crime investigators gather hundreds, sometimes thousands of pieces of information from interviews, evidence, examination of the crime scene, and much more.

To help put together this crime puzzle, investigators often keep a personal notebook to record information about everything they do on a case. This information may include

- notes from interviews,
- sketches of the crime scene,
- evidence seen and collected,
- questions that need to be answered,
- witness lists, and
- ideas about connections among crime puzzle pieces.

They use these notes to write formal reports that can be used in the court of law.

In this wildlife crime investigation, students can keep an Investigator Notebook to help organize their actions, discoveries, questions, and ideas. At the beginning of each class period, students write what they plan to do that day and what questions they hope to answer. At the end of each class period, students summarize what they did and learned. Teachers should encourage students to write at least one question they would like answered in coming days and to note any problems or successes.

If desired, students can add much more to their notebooks. The information from the forensic lab papers (Day 4) and other worksheets can be recorded directly in their notebooks. When students prepare their case for the prosecuting attorney, they can transfer their Investigator Notebook notes into their Final Case Reports.

As they work their way through the investigation, student should be sure to answer all of the following questions in their Investigator Notebooks and their Final Case Reports:

- What was the crime?
- Who is the suspect?
- Who is the victim?
- What laws were broken?
- What evidence proves this?
- What evidence is irrelevant to the case?

Preparing for the Wildlife Crime Investigation

Teacher Guidelines

**Before students can begin investigating the wildlife crime, you have to prepare the stage by organizing a cast of characters and compiling essential papers for student investigative teams.

About a week before the investigation begins, select a cast of eight suspects and witnesses, distribute their handouts, and review interview procedures. In addition, papers for Investigative Team Envelopes must be copied. Once the investigation begins on Day 1, you want everything in place for the student investigative teams to progress smoothly. (To look over what students will do on Investigation Day 1, see Handout e, p. 199.)**

Preparing Cast Members (Suspects and Witnesses):

1. **Read the following handouts so you understand what the crime investigation is all about.** Then give a copy of each handout to each of the eight cast members (staff or parents who play the roles of suspects and witnesses).

    - "Crime Summary" (Handout a, p. 190)
    - "Cast of Characters (Suspects and Witnesses) and Character Statements" (Handout b, p. 192)
    - "Suspects and Witnesses Time and Location for Wildlife Crime Interviews" (Handout c, p. 196)
    - "Logistics for Wildlife Crime Investigation Interviews" (Handout d, p. 197)

    (Also needed: Name tag or desk name plate for each cast member)

2. Explain the task of the cast members: An interview group of student investigators will go to each cast member on ____ [day] between ____ and ____ [times] to ask questions about each cast member's knowledge of various details pertaining to the crime. The cast members should answer their questions based on the information available in "Cast of Characters (Suspects and Witnesses) and Character Statements." In addition, four cast mem-

bers (Cory and Eliza Lucero and Meagan and Ryan Dixon) will be fingerprinted by the student interview groups.

3. More details for the cast members are given in the teacher guidelines for "Day 2: Interviewing Suspects and Witnesses."

Preparing for Students' Investigation Day 1:

1. Put the following materials in a large (10″ × 13″) envelope (Investigative Team Envelope), one envelope for each group of students (the groups are also called "investigative teams"). Number each envelope.

    • "Investigation Day 1: Has a Wildlife Crime Been Committed? Student Instructions" (Handout e, p. 199)

    • "Initial Crime Reports" (Handout f, p. 201)

    • "Big Game Hunting Season for Colorado: Rifle Seasons" (Handout g, p. 205)

    • "Hunting Laws and Regulations for Colorado" (Handout h, p. 206)

    • MailExpress receipt (Handout i, p. 208)

    • "Timeline of Wildlife Crime in Ward, Colorado" (Handout j, p. 209) (one for each team member)

    • One folder for each student (to hold students' individual papers)

2. Each student will also need an Investigator Notebook. If you did not use the notebooks in Section 2, Lessons 1–8, now is the time to introduce the notebooks (for background see pp. xxv–xxvi).

3. Get a map of Colorado (use your own source; be sure it includes Denver, Boulder, and Ward—a mountain town, northwest of Boulder).

Handout a
Crime Summary

This summary is to be given to cast members but NOT to students. The summary reveals details of the crime and the guilty persons—all of which the students will try to determine on their own.

- CRIME SCENE - DO NOT CROSS - CRIME SCENE - DO NOT CROSS - CRIME SCENE - DO NOT CROSS - CRIME SCENE - DO NOT CROSS - CRIME SCENE - DO NOT CROSS -

October 10:

Ryan Dixon left his home in Boulder, Colorado, and drove to his cabin in Ward. Later that day he went to the town market to buy day-old donuts, cantaloupe, and apples to use as bear bait. He set up the bear bait station in the forest behind the cabin. He set up a motion-detector camera at the bait station. The camera took a photo when any animal walked into the baited area. This is how he found out when bears were visiting the site at night and how many were visiting.

October 11:

Cory Lucero arrived at the cabin. Both men had hunting licenses for October 12–16. Cory had licenses for one elk and one mule deer. Ryan had licenses for one elk and one black bear.

October 12–15:

Cory legally killed a deer. Ryan legally killed an elk.

October 12–14:

Without Cory's knowledge, Ryan staked out the bait station on the nights of October 12 and 14. He killed one bear legally and removed the gall bladder and paws before taking the bear back to the cabin on the morning of October 15.

October 16:

Ryan and Cory left the cabin. Cory went home. Ryan said he was stopping by Shane Potter's cabin on the way to the airport. He said he was to fly to St. Louis, Missouri, on business that week. Actually, Ryan did not visit Shane or fly to St. Louis. Instead, he returned to the cabin.

October 16–21:

Ryan shot four more bears at the bait station. Each time a bear was shot, Ryan used his ATV to drag the body a short distance from the bait station. Then he skinned it, cut off its paws, and took out the gall bladder. At one point, he cut his hand while taking the bear parts, used a rag to stop the bleeding, and dropped it on the ground. He drove his ATV back to the cabin with these body parts and left the bodies in the forest for scavengers.

National Science Teachers Association

Handout a
Crime Summary

October 20:

Ryan called his sister Eliza Lucero. She left her home in Boulder with a cooler of dry ice. As she was packing her car, neighbor Erika Crocker came over to give her a letter that had been delivered to the wrong address. Erika noticed the smoke coming from the cooler when Eliza's drink spilled in it. Eliza took the dry ice to the cabin where she helped package the bear paws and gall bladders in dry ice to be mailed to Ed Lee in San Francisco. She filled out the MailExpress package slip.

October 21:

MailExpress courier Linda Klemp picked up the package from the cabin. It was sent to Ed Lee. Ryan and Eliza returned home.

October 22:

The package arrived, along with a note from Ryan, at Ed and Becky Lee's house. Ed Lee had already paid Ryan $500 for each gall bladder. The package was taken to a room where the Lees prepared traditional Asian medicines for their store. Ed dried the gall bladders and ground them into powder. Becky then sold the powder in their Traditional Asian Medicine store for liver, eye, asthma, and heart problems.

A note from Ryan told Ed Lee to send Ryan payment for the bear paws. After a search, the San Francisco police didn't find the paws and believe they had been sent overseas to a restaurant to make gourmet bear-paw soup. There is no bear-paw evidence.

Handout b
Cast of Characters (Suspects and Witnesses) and Character Statements

This summary is to be given to cast members but NOT to students. The summary reveals details of the crime and the guilty persons—all of which the students will try to determine on their own.

- CRIME SCENE - DO NOT CROSS - CRIME SCENE - DO NOT CROSS - CRIME SCENE - DO NOT CROSS - CRIME SCENE - DO NOT CROSS - CRIME SCENE - DO NOT CROSS -

Suspects and Witnesses

1. Cory Lucero—cabin co-owner, husband of Eliza Lucero

   (played by _____)

2. Eliza Lucero—cabin co-owner, wife of Cory Lucero, and sister of Ryan Dixon. Guilty of selling black bear gall bladders and paws.

   (played by _____)

3. Ryan Dixon—cabin co-owner, husband of Meagan Dixon, and brother of Eliza Lucero. Guilty of poaching black bears to sell gall bladders and paws.

   (played by _____)

4. Meagan Dixon—cabin co-owner, wife of Ryan Dixon

   (played by _____)

5. Erika Crocker—Colorado Springs neighbor of Luceros

   (played by _____)

6. Linda Klemp—MailExpress courier

   (played by _____)

7. Jack(ie) Wilmore—San Francisco police officer

   (played by _____)

8. Becky Lee—wife of Ed Lee and co-owner of Traditional Asian Medicines store

   (played by _____)

Character Statements

1. Cory Lucero, Cabin owner

My wife and I live in Boulder, Colorado, and own the Ward cabin with Meagan and Ryan Dixon. We've had the cabin for eight years. I go hunting alone and with Ryan Dixon.

I was there just there a week ago. It was great! I went to the cabin after work on October 11 and got home on October 16. My wife Eliza stayed home because she had other plans. Ryan drove to the cabin early on the 11th. We left at the same time on the 16th. He stopped at the cabin of a friend, Shane Potter, before going on his business trip to St. Louis, Missouri.

Ryan couldn't sleep well on several nights, so he went for a long walk. He

Handout b
Cast of Characters (Suspects and Witnesses) and Character Statements

came back long after I had gone to bed. He took some long afternoon naps.

I did not notice a cut on Ryan's hand while at the cabin. The tractor in the shed is mine. The Dixons own the ATV.

I had licenses to hunt deer and elk. I got a deer this month.

[Cory will give permission for the interview groups to get his fingerprints. The groups also will get copies of his hunting licenses.]

- Mule deer. 1st season, October 12–16. Filled. Carcass tag torn off.
- Elk. 1st season, October 12–16. Not filled.

2. Eliza Lucero, Cabin owner

My husband and I live in Boulder, Colorado, and own the Ward cabin with Meagan and Ryan Dixon. Ryan is my brother. We bought the cabin eight years ago. I did not go to the cabin this fall. Sometimes I go for a day or so while Cory and Ryan are there hunting, but this year I already had other plans.

Cory left for the cabin after work on October 11. He hunted with Ryan and came home on October 16.

[Eliza will give permission for the interview groups to fingerprint her.]

3. Ryan Dixon, Cabin owner

My wife and I live in Boulder, Colorado. We own the cabin in Ward with

Cory and Eliza Lucero. Eliza is my sister. We've had the cabin for seven or eight years. I go hunting alone and with Cory Lucero. I got to the cabin on October 11 and left at the same time as Cory on October 16. I cut my hand when hunting with Cory. [Ryan has a large Band-Aid on his left hand.]

My wife Meagan likes to come to the cabin with me, but was teaching during my hunting week. She's a high school science teacher.

On my way to the airport I stopped at the cabin of my friend, Shane Potter. He was hunting this week, too. Then I went directly to the Denver International Airport to catch a plane to St. Louis, Missouri. I design computer software and had meetings in St. Louis all week. I got home on the evening of October 21.

I own the ATV in the cabin's shed. The Luceros own the tractor.

I got a bear and an elk.

[Ryan will give permission for the interview groups to get his fingerprints. The teams will get copies of his hunting licenses.]

- Black Bear. 1st season, October 12–16. Filled. Carcass tag torn off.
- Elk. 1st season, October 12–16. Filled. Carcass tag torn off.

4. Meagan Dixon, Cabin owner

My husband and I live in Boulder, Colorado, and own the Ward cabin

Handout b
Cast of Characters (Suspects and Witnesses) and Character Statements

with Cory and Eliza Lucero. I am a high school science teacher. I go to the cabin with my husband and the Luceros whenever we can get away. I haven't been to the cabin since August. I was teaching during the week Cory and Ryan were hunting.

Ryan went to work on Monday, October 10, and then left for the cabin. He called me on the 16th to say he was leaving the cabin and heading for the Denver airport. He had to go to a business meeting in St. Louis. He got home on the night of October 21. He cut his hand while gutting one of the animals he killed.

[Meagan gave permission for the interview groups to fingerprint her.]

5. Erika Crocker, Luceros' neighbor in Boulder

I walk my dog every day. I remember seeing Eliza Lucero packing up her car with food and a small suitcase like she was going somewhere for awhile. This was on October 20, my day off. I went over to give her a letter that accidentally came to my house. I must have surprised her. She was arranging something in a large red cooler (she had on gloves) and her cup fell off the trunk of the car and spilled inside the cooler. Lots of steam came out. She said she was taking some food to a sick friend. I did not see her for a few days. Maybe she was staying with the friend. Cory was home.

6. Linda Klemp, MailExpress courier

I am new on the job. This was my first visit to that cabin in Ward. Usually people come to town to mail a package. I got a call from a woman asking for a pick-up on the morning of October 21. The package was about $3' \times 2' \times 2'$.

I arrived about 15 minutes before the time they requested. A man answered the door. He wasn't happy that I was there early. He had gloves on but no jacket. He told me to wait. Before he closed the door I saw a large red cooler inside the cabin. I could hear a woman talking while I was waiting, but I could not understand what was being said. It was too muffled. When I got the box from the man, the packing slip said the contents were elk. I checked past MailExpress records for any packages sent from this address. They show that the Dixons and Luceros have sent packages of similar weight to Ed Lee in San Francisco for several years.

7. Jack(ie) Wilmore, San Francisco Police Officer

My police department has conducted an undercover investigation of Ed and Becky Lee. Here is what we know. They have lived at their current address for 10 years. They own a store called Traditional Asian Medicines. They receive packages from

Handout b
Cast of Characters (Suspects and Witnesses) and Character Statements

around the country containing products for the store, though many senders seem to be individuals who are not a part of any company. For several years the Lees have been receiving packages from Ward, Colorado. They mail packages regularly to locations in China, Korea, Japan, Australia, and Singapore.

An undercover officer met Ed Lee in his house to try to sell him some items for the store. He reported that the Lees have a lab in their house, where they prepare much of the medicines for their store. Lee's record book was opened to the most recent entries. These medicines were prepared after the date the package was sent from Colorado: Asthma Treatment, Liver Treatment, Eye Treatment, and Heart Treatment. He also got a photograph of a letter sitting on a table from "Ryan Dixon" to Lee. [A copy of the letter has been made for each investigative team.]

There was no sign of the bear paws, but a package was sent to Singapore a day after the Colorado package arrived.

We recommend that the Colorado wildlife investigators go undercover as customers to the Lees' Traditional Asian Medicines store. The un-dercover investigators should buy these medicines: Asthma Treatment, Liver Treatment, Eye Treatment, and Heart Treatment. Then they should take the medicines to their forensic lab and compare the contents to the animals recently poached in Ward.

8. Becky Lee, Co-owner, Traditional Asian Medicines store

I helped a group of customers that came into my store together. They needed medicines for their health problems. I sold one person Eye Treatment for her red itchy eyes. Another person had a relative who was recently diagnosed with liver failure. I am sure the Liver Treatment will help. Two others in the group bought Asthma Treatment and Heart Treatment for their own health problems.

Several people in the group wanted to see rare gifts I sell from around the world. I told them that if they returned this evening I could show them anything they wanted: skins of big cats, trinkets made from elephant tusks and sea turtle shells, even a live monkey they could buy as a pet. One person asked where I got them. I told them not to worry, that all the paperwork looks legal.

Handout c

Suspects and Witnesses Time and Location for Wildlife Crime Interviews

- CRIME SCENE - DO NOT CROSS - CRIME SCENE - DO NOT CROSS - CRIME SCENE - DO NOT CROSS - CRIME SCENE - DO NOT CROSS - CRIME SCENE - DO NOT CROSS -

Dear Suspects and Witnesses:

Thank you for agreeing to take part in this unique educational opportunity for my students. I have filled in the date and times of your interviews in the form below. Student investigators from a class will be assigned to interview you. They will come to your location and talk with you as a group.

Suspect or witness name _____

Your (real) name _____

Interview date _____

Interview time _____

Your location _____

Handout d
Logistics for Wildlife Crime Investigation Interviews

CRIME SCENE · DO NOT CROSS · CRIME SCENE · DO NOT CROSS · CRIME SCENE · DO NOT CROSS · CRIME SCENE · DO NOT CROSS · CRIME SCENE · DO NOT CROSS ·

Before the Interviews(s)

Location—Please fill in the "Your Location" line in "Suspects and Witnesses Time and Location for Wildlife Crime Interviews" (Handout c) and return to me so I can tell the investigators where to find you for your interview. Tell other staff in your work area your character's name. They may need to guide students to you.

"Cast of Characters (Suspects and Witnesses) and Character Statements" (Handout b)—Read through the statement of your character and the other seven characters so you are ready to answer investigators' questions.

Personal props—You may choose to add any props to your attire or office on the day of the interviews.

Required props will be given to several of you before the interviews.

- Cory Lucero—Copies of two hunting licenses
- Ryan Dixon—Copies of two hunting licenses
- Jack(ie) Wilmore—A handwritten letter to Ed Lee from Ryan Dixon
- Becky Lee—Four small containers of different powdered "medicines."

During the Interview(s)

"Cast of Characters (Suspects and Witnesses) and Character Statements" (Handout b)—This handout has information that is important for you to convey to the interview teams. You can choose your personality, either offering information to student investigators or being more difficult and only answering questions that are asked. (This may mean they will need to interview you again later.) Please avoid making up details to answer questions. Such additional information may be contradictory to information other suspects and witnesses give and can send students on wild goose chases in a case that already holds many challenges to solve!

"Permission for an Interview" (Handout m)—Investigators will introduce themselves and ask you to sign the form "Permission for an Interview." (You will keep this, add comments, and return it to me later.) Investigators will begin asking you questions they have prepared in class.

Questioning—If the answer to a question is not in the script, tell the investigators, "I don't know." Then

Handout d
Logistics for Wildlife Crime Investigation Interviews

the investigators will know that either you have not been given the information OR you are not allowed to share the information with them.

Fingerprinting—Cory and Eliza Lucero and Meagan and Ryan Dixon. Before the interviews(s).

After the Interview(s)

Return the "Permission for an Interview" handouts and props to me. Thanks again.

National Science Teachers Association

Handout e
Investigation Day 1:
Has a Wildlife Crime Been Committed?

- CRIME SCENE - DO NOT CROSS - CRIME SCENE - DO NOT CROSS - CRIME SCENE - DO NOT CROSS - CRIME SCENE - DO NOT CROSS - CRIME SCENE - DO NOT CROSS -

Student Instructions

Your Job

You are wildlife investigators of a crime committed in the forested mountains of Ward, Colorado. With your team, read the "Initial Crime Reports" and other documents in your Investigative Team Envelope. Each person in your team records information in his or her own Investigator Notebook and on his or her timeline (Handout j).

Your Steps

1. Your team has received an Investigative Team Envelope. Write team members' names on your envelope. All team papers, including evidence your team collects during the investigation, must be kept here. Write your name on a folder for your individual papers. All papers and Investigator Notebooks must stay in the classroom throughout the investigation.

2. As a class, brainstorm what types of information would be important to record in your notebooks. Read "Initial Crime Reports" aloud in teams and write information in your Investigator Notebooks (e.g., when and where the crime occurred, who was there, who should be interviewed, what was found and seen).

3. On your timeline (Handout j), write key words for what happened each day.

4. Look at "Big Game Hunting Season for Colorado: Rifle Seasons." On your timeline, write hunting seasons that were in effect near the time of the crime.

5. Read through "Hunting Laws and Regulations for Colorado." Underline the key words that define poaching. Underline the key words in each description of an offense against wildlife.

Handout 9

Investigation Day 1: Has a Wildlife Crime Been Committed?

6. Look over the MailExpress receipt and record any useful information in your notebooks.

7. If there is enough time, make a list of people you think should be interviewed tomorrow.

Handout f
Initial Crime Reports

`- CRIME SCENE - DO NOT CROSS - CRIME SCENE - DO NOT CROSS - CRIME SCENE - DO NOT CROSS - CRIME SCENE - DO NOT CROSS - CRIME SCENE - DO NOT CROSS -`

1. Interview of Adam Tweed, with wife, Patricia, and children, Luke and Wendy

Interviewed by: Wildlife Officer Mark Rucks

Location: Cabin owned by Adam Tweed, located in Ward, Colorado (west of Boulder)

Date: October 22

We are on vacation at our cabin this week. Today our family was getting ready to go for a hike. We saw some ravens circling an area about 1/2 mile from the cabin. We decided to walk in that direction. When we got close we found what looked like a trashed campsite with scraps of food all over the ground. There was a camera set up on the edge of the clearing. It was hidden under a tarp. The grass was trampled down. Close to the food scraps was a place with lots of blood and hair. It looked like whatever had been there was big and was dragged away through the trees. My wife, Patricia, stayed there with the kids —Luke and Wendy—while I (Adam) followed the drag marks for several hundred yards. The smell was horrible! I found a bunch of large partially gutted, skinned animal bodies that were decomposing and being scavenged by the ravens. We imme-

diately went back to the cabin and called 911.

2. Wildlife Officer Report After Inspection of Crime Scene

Submitted by: Wildlife Officer Mark Rucks

Location: Ward, Colorado

Date: October 22

Habitat of crime scene:

Ward, Colorado, is located about 20 miles west of Boulder in Roosevelt National Forest. The crime scene is in montane forest (ponderosa pine, aspen, blue spruce), approximately 1/2 mile from the nearest cabin.

Findings:

The crime scene is a probable wildlife bait station set along a wildlife trail. Scraps of donuts, cantaloupe, and apples were scattered in a small clearing in the trees. A motion-detector camera, covered by a waterproof tarp, was hidden on the edge of the clearing. These cameras are often used to find out what wildlife are in the area and when they pass through. Blood was found 10 feet from the food scraps. The plants were trampled in the area around the blood. Drag marks and tire tracks

Handout f
Initial Crime Reports

went from the blood site through the trees about 100 yards. Blood and hair were found along this trail.

The drag marks end at a dumping site for animal carcasses. The skinned bodies of four animals were found. One was a recent kill. All have been scavenged and are at different stages of decomposition. All feet have been cut off. It appears that the abdomens had been cut open instead of torn open by scavengers. A bloody rag was found near the carcasses.

The tire tracks went from the alleged bait site to the carcasses and finally to the Lucero/Dixon cabin's shed. The owners are neighbors of the Tweeds (reporting party).

Evidence collected from the scene:

- Bloody rag
- Skull
- Animal track
- Hairs from the carcasses, from ground near the carcasses, and from the tarp over motion detector camera
- Tire tracks in forest

3. Second Interview of Adam and Patricia Tweed

Interviewed by: Wildlife Officer Mark Rucks

Location: Ward, Colorado

Date: October 23

QUESTION: What do you know about your neighbors?

RESPONSE: The cabin is owned by a couple and a brother and sister. I think they all live in Boulder. Every once in a while we are both here on the same weekends. We know the men are hunters, and come up more during the hunting season. We do not know them very well, but we wave or say "hi" when we see each other.

QUESTION: Were your neighbors here this week?

RESPONSE: We saw one of the men a few times.

QUESTION: What was he doing when you saw him?

RESPONSE: We saw him going in and out of the forest. He was carrying a backpack. One early morning he was coming out of the forest on his ATV. Once at dusk someone left the cabin and walked into the forest. It was probably him. For several nights we were awakened by what sounded like gunshots.

That would have been between October 17 and 19. There was a MailExpress truck at the house yesterday morning. We have not seen anyone since then.

QUESTION: What wildlife do you normally see around your cabin?

RESPONSE: Mule deer, elk, raccoons, coyotes, hawks, owls, ravens and other birds, and squirrels. We've heard there are mountain lions, bobcats, and black bears, but we have never seen them.

QUESTION: How often do you come to the cabin?

RESPONSE: About once a month, usually only on weekends. We decided to take a longer vacation during the kids' fall break this year. It's the first time we've been up here during the week. It's so quiet! No one is here, except our neighbors.

4. Interview of Meagan Dixon

Interviewed by: Wildlife Officer Mark Rucks

Location: The Lucero/Dixon cabin in Ward, Colorado

Date: October 23

Meagan Dixon is co-owner (with her husband Ryan Dixon and Corey and Eliza Lucero) of the cabin next to the Tweeds' cabin. Her cabin appeared to be the destination of tire tracks coming from the alleged bait station and carcasses. She volunteered to come to the cabin from her home in Boulder to be interviewed.

QUESTION: There have been some unusual wildlife deaths in the area. I am interviewing cabin owners to see if they have seen or heard anything unusual. Who owns this cabin?

RESPONSE: My husband Ryan and I co-own it with Cory and Eliza Lucero.

QUESTION: Was anyone at this cabin during the past month?

RESPONSE: Ryan and Cory were here hunting last week. They did not mention seeing or hearing anything unusual.

QUESTION: Do you let other people stay at your cabin if you are not here?

RESPONSE: No.

Handout f
Initial Crime Reports

Evidence collected with signed search warrant:

- MailExpress packing slip receipt
- Rifle
- Antler/horn
- Tire tread prints found in shed
- Tire tracks from driveway

Handout I
Big Game Hunting Season for Colorado: Rifle Seasons

- CRIME SCENE - DO NOT CROSS - CRIME SCENE - DO NOT CROSS - CRIME SCENE - DO NOT CROSS - CRIME SCENE - DO NOT CROSS - CRIME SCENE - DO NOT CROSS -

Combined Deer and Elk

First:	Oct. 12–16
Second:	Oct. 19–30
Third:	Nov. 2–10

Black Bear

First:	Oct. 12–16
Second:	Oct. 19–30
Third:	Nov. 2–10

Moose

First:	Oct. 12–16
Second:	Oct. 19–30
Third:	Nov. 2–10

American Pronghorn (antelope)

First:	Sept. 28–Oct. 4
Second:	Oct. 5–11

Mountain Lion

Jan. 1–March 31

Handout h
Hunting Laws and Regulations for Colorado

- CRIME SCENE - DO NOT CROSS - CRIME SCENE - DO NOT CROSS - CRIME SCENE - DO NOT CROSS - CRIME SCENE - DO NOT CROSS - CRIME SCENE - DO NOT CROSS -

License Requirements

1. You must have a license to hunt.

2. You must carry your license while hunting.

3. You can hunt only the animal and season specified on your license.

4. Licenses expire at the end of the season printed on them.

5. You can submit only one application in the license drawing per species per year.

6. You must complete a hunter education course before purchasing a hunting license.

Hunting Hours

One-half hour before sunrise to one half-hour after sunset.

Carcass Tag

You must attach your carcass tag (the lower part of the hunting license) to big game animals you kill until meat is processed.

It's Against the Law to:

1. Have a loaded rifle or shotgun in or on a motor vehicle.

2. Hunt carelessly or discharge a firearm or release an arrow disregarding human life or property.

3. Shoot from or use a motor vehicle, motorcycle, off-highway vehicle, snowmobile or aircraft to hunt, intercept, chase, harass, or drive wildlife.

4. Use aircraft to hunt, to direct hunters on the ground, or to hunt the same day or day after a flight was made to locate wildlife.

5. Hunt under the influence of alcohol or controlled substances.

6. Use electronic night-vision equipment, electronically enhanced light-gathering optics, or thermal imaging devices as an aid in hunting or taking wildlife.

7. Use dogs or bait to hunt bears, deer, elk, pronghorn, or moose. Bait means to put, expose, deposit, distribute, or scatter salt, minerals, grain, animal parts, or other food as a lure, attraction, or enticement for big game. Scent sticks that smell like food are illegal for bears.

8. Use poison, drugs, or explosives to hunt or harass wildlife.

9. Fail to make a reasonable attempt to track and kill animals you wound.

10. Fail to use edible wildlife meat for human consumption.

Handout h

Hunting Laws and Regulations for Colorado

11. Kill and abandon big game. Killing big game, removing only hide, antlers, or other trophy parts and leaving the carcass in field are illegal. (felony)

12. Sell, purchase, or offer to sell or purchase big game. (felony)

13. Sell, trade, barter, or offer to sell, trade, or barter bear gall bladders or edible portions of bears.

14. Kill cubs or black bears accompanied by one or more cubs. A cub is a bear less than a year old.

15. Have carcass, hide, skull, claws, or parts of bears or mountain lions without a valid hunting license or unless authorized by Division of Wildlife.

16. Hunt on private land without first obtaining permission from landowner or person in charge.

Penalties

Convictions of felony violations may result in lifetime suspension of hunting privileges, jail time, and fines.

Handout 1

MailExpress Receipt

CRIME SCENE - DO NOT CROSS - CRIME SCENE - DO NOT CROSS - CRIME SCENE - DO NOT CROSS - CRIME SCENE - DO NOT CROSS - CRIME SCENE - DO NOT CROSS -

MailEx *US Airbill*   Tracking Number **4615393285**

Sender's Copy

1 From (please print)

Date **Oct. 21**   Sender's Account Number

Sender's Name **E. Lucero**   Phone **(999) 999-9999**

Company _____ Dept/Floor/Suite/Room

Address **P.O. Box 22**

City **Ward**   State **CO**   Zip **80413**

2 Your Internal Billing Reference Information
(Optional) (First 24 characters will appear on invoice)

3 To (please print)

Recipient's Name **Mr. Ed Lee**   Phone **(999) 999-9999**

Company _____ Dept/Floor/Suite/Room

Address **782 Saddlebrook Circle**
(To "HOLD" at location, print address here)   (We Cannot Deliver to P.O. Boxes or P.O. Zip Codes)

City **San Francisco, CA**

For HOLD at
☐ Hold Weekday (Not available with First Overnight)
Location check here
☐ Hold Saturday (Not available with First Overnight or Standard Overnight) (Not available at all locations)

For Saturday Delivery check here
☐ (Extra Charge. Not available to all locations) (Not available with First Overnight or Standard Overnight)

4a Express Package Service *Packages under 150 lbs.*   Delivery commitment may be later in some areas

☒ Priority Overnight (Next business morning)   ☐ Standard Overnight (Next business afternoon)   ☐ 2Day* second business day

☐ NEW First Overnight (Earliest next business morning delivery to select locations) (Higher rates apply)   Letter Rate not available Minimum charge One pound 2Day rate

4b Express Freight Service *Packages over 150 lbs.*   Delivery commitment may be later in some areas

☐ Overnight Freight (Next business day service for any distance)   ☐ 2Day Freight (Second business day service for any distance)   ☐ Express Saver Freight (Up to 3 business day service based upon distance)
(Call for delivery schedule See back for detailed descriptions of freight products.)

5 Packaging
☐ Letter   ☐ Pak (Declared value limit $500)   ☐ Box   ☐ Tube   ☒ Other Pkg.

6 Special Handling
Does this shipment contain dangerous goods?
☒ Dry Ice   ☐ Yes (As per attached Shipper's Declaration)   ☐ Yes (Shipper's Declaration not required)
Dry Ice, 9, UN 1845 III
(Dangerous Goods Shipper's Declaration not required)   kg 904   CA   ☐ Cargo Aircraft Only

7 Payment
Bill to:
☐ Sender (Account no in section 1 will be billed)   ☐ Recipient   ☐ Third Party   ☐ Credit Card   ☒ Cash/Check
(Enter FedEx account no or Credit Card no below)

Account No.
Credit Card No.   Exp. Date

Total Packages	Total Weight	Total Declared Value	Total Charges
1	11	$ 99 00	$ 123.00

*When declaring a value higher than $100 per shipment, you pay an additional charge. See SERVICE CONDITIONS, DECLARED VALUE AND LIMIT OF LIABILITY section for further information.

8 Release Signature *Sign to authorize delivery without obtaining signature.*

Your signature authorizes us _____ to deliver this shipment without obtaining a signature and agrees to indemnify and hold harmless _____ from any resulting claims

272

Rev. Date 6/96
PART #147957
©1994 96 FedEx
PRINTED IN U.S.A.
GBFE 3/97

Service Conditions, Declared Value, and Limit of Liability – By using this Airbill you agree to the service conditions in our current Service Guide or U.S. Government Service Guide. Both are available on request. SEE BACK OF SENDER'S COPY OF THIS AIRBILL FOR INFORMATION AND ADDITIONAL TERMS. We will not be responsible for any claim in excess of $100 per package whether the result of loss, damage, or delay, non-delivery, misdelivery, or misinformation, unless you declare a higher value, pay an additional charge, and document your actual loss in a timely manner. Your right to recover from us for any loss includes intrinsic value of the package, loss of sales, interest, profit, attorney's fees, costs, and other forms of damage, whether direct, incidental, consequential, or special, and is limited to the greater of $100 or the declared value but cannot exceed actual documented loss. The maximum declared value for any Letter and Pak is $500. You may, upon your request, and with some limitations, refund all transportation charges paid. **See the Service Guide for further details.**

Questions? Call

Timeline of Wildlife Crime in Ward, Colorado

Name _____ Date _____

- CRIME SCENE - DO NOT CROSS - CRIME SCENE - DO NOT CROSS - CRIME SCENE - DO NOT CROSS - CRIME SCENE - DO NOT CROSS - CRIME SCENE - DO NOT CROSS -

Timeline of Wildlife Crime in Ward, Colorado
October/November

As you read voluntary statements and gather information from interviews, record what you were told happened on certain dates.

Sunday	Monday	Tuesday	Wednesday	Thursday	Friday	Saturday
9	10	11	12	13	14	15
16	17	18	19	20	21	22
23	24	25	26	27	28	29
30	31	1	2	3	4	5

Investigation Day 1: Has a Wildlife Crime Been Committed?

Teacher Guidelines

Overview

Student investigative teams are introduced to the wildlife crime. They will review the "Initial Crime Reports" (Handout f) and other handouts, record information they feel is important, and begin filling out a blank calendar to map out the crime timeline.

Teaching Plan

1. Review "Preparing for the Wildlife Crime Investigation—Teacher Guidelines" (pp. 188–189). Put students into assigned groups. Give each group a numbered Investigative Team Envelope as described on page 189. Students should have their Investigator Notebooks ready.

2. Introduce the crime by showing a transparency or web image of a map of Colorado. Locate Denver, Boulder, and Ward. Explain that officers from the Colorado Division of Wildlife suspect that a wildlife crime has occurred in the mountain town of Ward.

   Tell student teams that today they will begin investigating the possible crime by reading the "Initial Crime Reports," comparing legal hunting seasons (Handout g) with the dates of the crime, and reviewing Colorado hunting laws (Handout h). On Day 2 of the investigation, teams will interview witnesses and suspects. On Day 3 they will pool their interview information. On Days 4 and 5, they will analyze evidence using forensic lab techniques. On Day 6 teams will identify the prime suspect or suspects and determine what crimes were committed. Finally, the team with the strongest and most accurate case will make an arrest.

3. Let students know that they will be evaluating their own par-

ticipation and team members' participation when the investigation is complete (see Section 4).

4. Also tell students that they will have one or more assessments that test their lab skills and knowledge of the investigation (see Section 4).

5. Explain the daily routine for the investigation. Each team will use its Investigative Team Envelope to hold all investigation papers. All papers must be available each day of the investigation. No papers or Investigator Notebooks are to leave the classroom during the investigation. Each student will record personal case notes, questions, and summaries of interviews and evidence in his or her Investigator Notebook. These will be used to prepare an individual Final Case Report on the crime.

   Each student will write in his or her Investigator Notebook at the beginning and end of each day as instructed by the teacher. (See "Keeping an Investigator Notebook," p. xxv.)

6. Begin the investigative work: Students follow the steps in "Investigation Day 1: Has a Wildlife Crime Been Committed? Student Instructions," which they will find in their Investigative Team Envelopes.

7. When finished, students should return team papers to their envelope and put any loose individual notes into their folders.

Investigation Day 2: Interviewing the Cast of Characters (Suspects and Witnesses)

Teacher Guidelines

Overview

Each team member picks two of the eight cast members (who will be parents and teachers and are also known as "suspects and witnesses") to interview. Representatives from each team work together in groups to write interview questions for two cast members. Interview groups then go to designated locations around the school to find and interview the suspects and witnesses. Students then return to their original investigative teams to compile the information they have gathered.

Preparing for Interviews of Suspects and Witnesses

On the day of the interviews, investigative teams will get information from eight suspects and witnesses (the "cast members").

Note: The following procedures are written for student team interviews conducted around the school. If for some reason your class is not able to carry out that plan—perhaps parents or teachers are not available to act as cast members—consider these alternatives: (1) *read only*—investigative teams simply read statements (Handout b, "Cast of Characters [Suspects and Witnesses] and Character Statements." Be sure to black out the list of suspects and witnesses at the beginning because it reveals the "bad guys.") or (2) *classroom interviews*—students from another class act as cast members and come to your classroom to be interviewed by the entire class.

Materials for the Cast of Characters

Each cast member:
- See page 188, #1 for a list of the handouts that go to each suspect and witness (cast of characters).

Cast member playing Becky Lee:

- Four small labeled containers or film canisters for each interview group
  - Asthma Treatment (ground Tums or other antacid)
  - Liver Treatment (baking soda)
  - Eye Treatment (powdered milk)
  - Heart Treatment (ground aspirin)

Cast member playing Cory Lucero:

- Two hunting licenses for each interview group (Handout n).

Cast member playing Ryan Dixon:

- Two hunting licenses for each interview group (Handout o).

Cast member playing Jack(ie) Wilmore:

- Handwritten letter to Ed Lee from Ryan Dixon—one copy for each interview group (Handout p).

Materials for Investigative Teams and Interview Groups

- Each investigative team will need
  - "Interview Group Assignments" (Handout k, p. 215)
  - "Investigation Day 2: Interviewing Suspects and Witnesses: Student Instructions" (Handout l, p. 219)
- Each interview group will need
  - 2 "Permission for an Interview" forms (Handout m, p. 221)
  - Wildlife Officer badges (hall passes; one for each interview group member) (Handout q, p. 225)
- Groups interviewing cabin owners will need
  - 4 blank fingerprint cards (one card for each cabin owner) (Handout r, p. 226)
  - Ink pad
  - Wet wipes
  - Alternate plan: If you don't want to get actual fingerprints from suspects, you can use the prepared fingerprint evidence (p. 273).

Materials for the Teacher

- A transparency or paper copy of "Interview Group Assignments" (Handout k) to project onto a screen for students (see Step 1 under Teaching Plan)

Teaching Plan

1. Give each investigative team a copy of "Interview Group Assignments" (Handout k). Use a visual projector to review this handout and show students where to find each character.

2. Have teams assign each member to a pair of people to be interviewed.

3. Have students regroup themselves into interview teams.

4. Go over the student instructions for "Investigation Day 2: Interviewing Suspects and Witnesses: Student Instructions."

5. Have students write down questions for the people they will interview.

6. Review rules for student conduct outside of the classroom. Hand out Wildlife Officer badges (hall passes) and dismiss students to conduct interviews.

7. Check on students as they move throughout the school conducting interviews.

8. When students return, collect their notebooks with individual interview notes, any evidence, and other interview materials, including fingerprint cards and "medicines" (which will become part of class evidence for the forensic lab stations on Days 4 and 5).

Handout K
Interview Group Assignments

- CRIME SCENE - DO NOT CROSS - CRIME SCENE - DO NOT CROSS - CRIME SCENE - DO NOT CROSS - CRIME SCENE - DO NOT CROSS - CRIME SCENE - DO NOT CROSS -

Interview Group 1:

Eliza Lucero

(cabin co-owner, wife of Cory Lucero and sister of Ryan Dixon. Lives in Boulder, Colorado.)

Needs to be fingerprinted.

Where to find her: _____ .

Erika Crocker

(Boulder neighbor of the Luceros)

Where to find her: _____ .

What to take:

- Wildlife badge for each investigator
- Fingerprint materials (1 fingerprint card, ink pad, wet wipe) for Eliza Lucero
- Investigator Notebook with questions
- Two "Permission for an Interview" handouts

Handout k
Interview Group Assignments

- CRIME SCENE - DO NOT CROSS - CRIME SCENE - DO NOT CROSS - CRIME SCENE - DO NOT CROSS - CRIME SCENE - DO NOT CROSS - CRIME SCENE - DO NOT CROSS -

Interview Group 2:

Cory Lucero

(cabin co-owner, husband of Eliza Lucero. Lives in Boulder, Colorado.)

Needs to be fingerprinted.

Where to find him: _____ .

Linda Klemp

(MailExpress courier)

Where to find her: _____ .

What to take:

- Wildlife badge for each investigator
- Fingerprint materials (1 fingerprint card, ink pad, wet wipe) for Cory
- Investigator Notebook with questions
- Two "Permission for an Interview" handouts

National Science Teachers Association

Handout k
Interview Group Assignments

- CRIME SCENE - DO NOT CROSS - CRIME SCENE - DO NOT CROSS - CRIME SCENE - DO NOT CROSS - CRIME SCENE - DO NOT CROSS - CRIME SCENE - DO NOT CROSS -

Interview Group 3:

Meagan Dixon

(cabin co-owner, wife of Ryan Dixon. Lives in Boulder, Colorado.)

Needs to be fingerprinted.

Where to find her: _____ .

Ryan Dixon

(cabin co-owner, husband of Meagan Dixon and brother of Eliza Lucero. Lives in Boulder, Colorado.)

Needs to be fingerprinted.

Where to find him: _____ .

What to take:

- Wildlife badge for each investigator
- Fingerprint materials (two fingerprint cards, ink pad, wet wipes) for both Dixons
- Investigator Notebook with questions
- Two "Permission for an Interview" handouts

Handout k
Interview Group Assignments

Name _____ Date _____

CRIME SCENE - DO NOT CROSS - CRIME SCENE - DO NOT CROSS - CRIME SCENE - DO NOT CROSS - CRIME SCENE - DO NOT CROSS - CRIME SCENE - DO NOT CROSS -

Interview Group 4

(You will fly to San Francisco, California!)

Jack(ie) Wilmore

(San Francisco police officer)

Where to find him/her: _____ .

Becky Lee

(Becky Lee, wife of Ed Lee and co-owner of Traditional Asian Medicines store in San Francisco.)

Where to find her: _____ .

What to take:

- Wildlife badge for each investigator
- Investigator Notebook with questions
- Two "Permission for an Interview" handouts

National Science Teachers Association

Handout 1
Investigation Day 2:
Interviewing Suspects and Witnesses

- CRIME SCENE - DO NOT CROSS - CRIME SCENE - DO NOT CROSS - CRIME SCENE - DO NOT CROSS - CRIME SCENE - DO NOT CROSS - CRIME SCENE - DO NOT CROSS -

Student Instructions

Your Job

You are a wildlife investigator. Each member of your team will be assigned two different people to interview. You will prepare questions with members of other investigative teams. Then your interview group will find and question these suspects and witnesses.

Your Steps

1. Complete your "Interview Group Assignments" handout with new information from your teacher and assign each team member two suspects or witnesses (cast members) to interview. Your "Interview Group Assignments" handout will tell you exactly what you need for your interviews.

2. Sit with the members of the other teams who are interviewing the same people (e.g., everyone who will be interviewing Eliza Lucero and Erika Crocker should sit together). This new group is called your "interview group." As an interview group, decide what questions you should ask these people. Write them down in your Investigator Notebook.

3. Collect any materials listed on your "Interview Group Assignment" handout.

4. Find out how long you have for each interview. Select a timekeeper to let the group know when you need to be at the first interview, second interview, and back in the classroom.

5. Put on a Wildlife Officer badge (hall pass).

6. As a group, go to the location of the first interview. Ask for the person you need to talk with.

7. Be polite! Introduce yourselves—for example, "Hello. We are wildlife officers investigating a possible crime."

Handout 1
Investigation Day 2:
Interviewing Suspects and Witnesses

8. Explain why you need to talk with this person.

9. Fill out the "Permission for an Interview" handout with the names of all the wildlife officer interviewers. Leave the paper with the person being interviewed.

10. Ask the questions your interview group prepared, as well as any other questions that you think of during the interview.

11. Record all information in your Investigator Notebooks, even if it does not sound important right now.

12. If the person being interviewed answers "I don't know" or "I don't remember," this means he or she cannot tell you or does not have the information you are asking for. The person being interviewed will tell you all he or she knows if asked.

13. If you are interviewing Eliza Lucero, Cory Lucero, Meagan Dixon, and/or Ryan Dixon, you will fingerprint them. After obtaining the fingerprints, give them wet wipes to clean off ink. Collect hunting licenses from Cory Lucero and Ryan Dixon.

14. Thank the person for the interview.

15. Go to the location of the second person your group needs to interview.

16. Repeat the procedure.

17. Return to the classroom and turn in all papers, evidence, and materials.

National Science Teachers Association

Handout m
Permission for an Interview

(Wildlife Investigator: Leave this form with the person being interviewed.)

I, _____, voluntarily agree to talk with these wildlife investigators.

Wildlife investigators conducting the interview:

_____

_____

_____

_____

_____

_____

Comments:

Handout n

Hunting Licenses for Cory Lucero

License 1

COLORADO HUNTING LICENSE

D.C.T. 12345

Species
- ☒ Deer
- ○ Elk
- ○ Bear
- ○ Antelope
- ○ Mountain Lion
- ○ Turkey
- ○ Mountain Sheep
- ○ Mountain Goat

Lic. Type
- ☒ Antlered
- ○ Antlerless
- ○ Either Sex
- ○ Other

- ☒ Resident
- ○ Nonresident

Lic. Type
- ☒ Regular Rifle
- ○ Muzzle Loading
- ○ Archery

SEASON/DATES October 12-16
○ Limited license for Unit # _____ License # _____

NAME: Cory (FIRST) Boulder (MIDDLE) Lucero (LAST)
ADDRESS: Boulder (STREET) Boulder (CITY) (STATE) (ZIP)
DRIVER'S LICENSE: _____
LENGTH OF RESIDENCY IN STATE: (YRS) (MOS)
DATE AND HOUR OF ISSUE: 9 (MO) 15 (D) ☒ A.M. ○ P.M.
SEX: M WEIGHT HIGHT HAIR EYES DATE OF BIRTH
HUNTER SAFETY CARD NO.: _____
ISSUED BY: L. MOORE TITLE DWM STATION Boulder

CARCASS TAG D.C.T. 12345

License 2

COLORADO HUNTING LICENSE

D.C.T. 12345

Species
- ○ Deer
- ☒ Elk
- ○ Bear
- ○ Antelope
- ○ Mountain Lion
- ○ Turkey
- ○ Mountain Sheep
- ○ Mountain Goat

Lic. Type
- ○ Antlered
- ○ Antlerless
- ☒ Either Sex
- ○ Other

- ☒ Resident
- ○ Nonresident

Lic. Type
- ☒ Regular Rifle
- ○ Muzzle Loading
- ○ Archery

SEASON/DATES October 12-16
○ Limited license for Unit # _____ License # _____

NAME: Cory (FIRST) Boulder (MIDDLE) Lucero (LAST)
ADDRESS: Boulder (STREET) Boulder (CITY) (STATE) (ZIP)
DRIVER'S LICENSE: _____
LENGTH OF RESIDENCY IN STATE: (YRS) (MOS)
DATE AND HOUR OF ISSUE: 9 (MO) 15 (D) ☒ A.M. ○ P.M.
SEX: M WEIGHT HIGHT HAIR EYES DATE OF BIRTH
HUNTER SAFETY CARD NO.: _____
ISSUED BY: L. MOORE TITLE DWM STATION Boulder

CARCASS TAG

ORIGINAL LIC. # _____

D.C.T. 12345

IMPORTANT: DO NOT DETACH OR SIGN THIS TAG UNTIL KILL HAS BEEN MADE. SEE TAGGING INSTRUCTIONS ON BACK OF THIS TAG.

ISSUING OFFICER'S SIGNATURE _____

COLORADO

LIC. TYPE	PUNCH MONTH AND DAY OF KILL																																											
	JAN	FEB	MAR	APR	MAY	JUN	JUL	AUG	SEP	OCT	NOV	DEC	1	2	3	4	5	6	7	8	9	10	11	12	13	14	15	16	17	18	19	20	21	22	23	24	25	26	27	28	29	30	31

PUNCH SEX	MALE	FEMALE

National Science Teachers Association

Handout 0

Hunting Licenses for Ryan Dixon

License 1 (D.C.T. 12345)

COLORADO HUNTING LICENSE — D.C.T. 12345

Species
- o Deer
- ✗ Elk
- o Bear
- o Antelope
- o Mountain Lion
- o Turkey
- o Mountain Sheep ✗ Resident
- o Mountain Goat o Nonresident

Lic. Type
- ✗ Antlered
- o Antlerless
- o Either Sex
- o Other

Lic. Type
- ✗ Regular Rifle
- o Muzzle Loading
- o Archery

SEASON/DATES October 12-16
o Limited license for Unit # ____ License # ____

NAME: Ryan (FIRST) (MIDDLE) Dixon (LAST)
ADDRESS: Boulder (CITY) Boulder (COUNTY) (STATE) (ZIP)
NUMBER: LENGTH OF RESIDENCY IN STATE ___ YRS ___ MOS
DRIVER'S LICENSE:
SEX M WEIGHT HIGHT HAIR EYES DATE OF BIRTH
HUNTER SAFETY CARD NO.
DATE AND HOUR OF ISSUE: MO 9TH DAY 17 A.M. P.M.
ISSUED BY L. MOORE TITLE DWM STATION Boulder

CARCASS TAG D.C.T. 12345

License 2 (D.C.T. 12345)

COLORADO HUNTING LICENSE — D.C.T. 12345

Species
- o Deer
- o Elk
- ✗ Bear
- o Antelope
- o Mountain Lion
- o Turkey
- o Mountain Sheep ✗ Resident
- o Mountain Goat o Nonresident

Lic. Type
- o Antlered
- o Antlerless
- ✗ Either Sex
- o Other

Lic. Type
- ✗ Regular Rifle
- o Muzzle Loading
- o Archery

SEASON/DATES October 12-16
o Limited license for Unit # ____ License # ____

NAME: Ryan (FIRST) (MIDDLE) Dixon (LAST)
ADDRESS: Boulder (CITY) Boulder (COUNTY) (STATE) (ZIP)
NUMBER: LENGTH OF RESIDENCY IN STATE ___ YRS ___ MOS
DRIVER'S LICENSE:
SEX M WEIGHT HIGHT HAIR EYES DATE OF BIRTH
HUNTER SAFETY CARD NO.
DATE AND HOUR OF ISSUE: MO 9TH DAY 17 A.M. P.M.
ISSUED BY L. MOORE TITLE DWM STATION Boulder

CARCASS TAG D.C.T. 12345

- CRIME SCENE - DO NOT CROSS - CRIME SCENE - DO NOT CROSS - CRIME SCENE - DO NOT CROSS - CRIME SCENE - DO NOT CROSS - CRIME SCENE - DO NOT CROSS -

The person playing the role of Ryan Dixon needs to hand-write this note on a piece of paper. Then make a photocopy for each investigative team.

October 21

EL,

5 BBGBs are enclosed. Your payment of $2500 was received. Next order will arrive in the spring. I am increasing charges to $600 due to increased security risk.

20 paws also included. Send agreed-upon payment immediately.

RD

Handout 9
Wildlife Officer Badges

THIS CERTIFIES THAT

has been officially appointed as a *Colorado Division of Wildlife* Wildlife Officer and pledges to protect wildlife and the environment at all times

AUTHORIZED SIGNATURE

THIS CERTIFIES THAT

has been officially appointed as a *Colorado Division of Wildlife* Wildlife Officer and pledges to protect wildlife and the environment at all times

AUTHORIZED SIGNATURE

THIS CERTIFIES THAT

has been officially appointed as a *Colorado Division of Wildlife* Wildlife Officer and pledges to protect wildlife and the environment at all times

AUTHORIZED SIGNATURE

THIS CERTIFIES THAT

has been officially appointed as a *Colorado Division of Wildlife* Wildlife Officer and pledges to protect wildlife and the environment at all times

AUTHORIZED SIGNATURE

THIS CERTIFIES THAT

has been officially appointed as a *Colorado Division of Wildlife* Wildlife Officer and pledges to protect wildlife and the environment at all times

AUTHORIZED SIGNATURE

THIS CERTIFIES THAT

has been officially appointed as a *Colorado Division of Wildlife* Wildlife Officer and pledges to protect wildlife and the environment at all times

AUTHORIZED SIGNATURE

Using Forensics: Wildlife Crime Scene!

Handout r
Fingerprint Card

Fingerprint Card

Name _____

<u>Right Hand</u>

Thumb	1st Finger	2nd Finger	3rd Finger	4th Finger

Classification of Print Patterns _____ _____ _____

<u>Left Hand</u>

Thumb	1st Finger	2nd Finger	3rd Finger	4th Finger

Classification of Print Patterns: _____ _____ _____

Prints taken by: _____

226

Investigation Day 3: Sharing Interview Notes

Teacher Guidelines

Overview

Interview groups reconfigure back into the investigative teams. They share insights from their interviews, record interview summaries, and begin to piece together the crime.

Materials

- Each team will need
  - Its Investigative Team Envelope
  - Evidence from interviews—(a) handwritten letter from Ryan Dixon to Ed Lee, and (b) the four hunting licenses from Cory Lucero and Ryan Dixon
  - "Investigation Day 3: Sharing Interview Notes: Student Instructions" (Handout s, p. 229)
  - "Additional Interviews" (Handout v, p. 235) (Hand this out AFTER students have finished Steps 1–4 in the Student Instructions for Investigation Day 3)
- Each student will need his or her Investigator Notebook
- Give each student a copy of
  - "Witness List" (Handout t, p. 230)
  - "Evidence List" (Handout u, p. 232)

Teaching Plan

1. Have students put copies of the hunting licenses and the letter to Ed Lee in their Investigative Team Envelopes. All personal loose papers should be filed in students' individual folders.

2. Go over steps for "Investigation Day 3: Sharing Interview Notes: Student Instructions" and allow time for teams to complete note sharing.

3. Give groups the "Additional Interviews" handout. Explain that this information was collected by other investigators.

Have students add the new information from the "Additional Interviews" handout to the "Witness List," the calendars, and their Investigator Notebooks.

4. When student have completed the work in Steps 2 and 3 above, they should put all materials into the Investigative Team Envelope and individual folders.

Handout 8
Investigation Day 3: Sharing Interview Notes

Name _____ Date _____

CRIME SCENE · DO NOT CROSS · CRIME SCENE · DO NOT CROSS · CRIME SCENE · DO NOT CROSS · CRIME SCENE · DO NOT CROSS · CRIME SCENE · DO NOT CROSS ·

Student Instructions

You Need

- Your team's Investigative Team Envelope
- Your individual folder
- "Witness List" (from your teacher)
- "Evidence List" (from your teacher)
- Evidence collected during the interviews—(a) handwritten letter from Ryan Dixon to Ed Lee, and (b) the four hunting licenses from Cory Lucero and Ryan Dixon
- Your Investigator Notebook

Your Steps

1. Now that the interviewing is complete, you should be back in your investigative teams (no longer in interview groups). Add the new evidence of the four hunting licenses and the letter to your "Evidence List" along with evidence collected at the crime scene and Dixon/Lucero cabin.

2. Take turns having each team member report on the information gathered from the interviews. Each member will report on two of the eight interviews.

3. Record information about each interview on your "Witness List," and add information to the timeline as needed.

4. If you have additional questions for any of the eight people interviewed, write them down. Your teacher can ask those cast members to visit your classroom over the next few days so you can talk with them.

5. Ask your teacher for the "Additional Interviews" handout. Add any new information to your "Witness List."

6. Brainstorm and record ideas in your Investigator Notebook about what your team thinks might have happened based on the interviews and evidence. You will need to write the Final Case Report after you analyze the evidence on Days 4 and 5.

Handout t
Witness List

Investigators: _____

Team #: _____

Witness List

Fill in the "Information from interview" column after interviewing the individuals or reading voluntary statements. Fill in "How information relates to offense" column as you piece together the crime and analyze evidence.

Witness	Information from interview	How information relates to offense
Cory Lucero		
Eliza Lucero		
Ryan Dixon		
Meagan Dixon		
Erika Crocker		

Handout t
Witness List

Witness	Information from interview	How information relates to offense
Linda Klemp		
Jack(ie) Wilmore		
Becky Lee		
Adam and Patricia Tweed		
Additional Interviews		
Shane Potter		
Roger Moore		
Airlines servicing Denver International Airport		
Linda Jefferson		

Handout u
Evidence List

Investigators: _____ Team #: _____

Evidence List

The following is a list of evidence collected in the investigation of a wildlife crime in Ward, Colorado.

Complete "Where found" after the interviews. Complete the last two columns after the evidence has been analyzed by the Wildlife Forensic Lab.

Evidence	Where found	Results of analysis or examination	How evidence relates to offense
1. Antler/horn			
2. Animal tracks			
3. Bloody rag			
4. DNA from human hair			

National Science Teachers Association

Handout u

Evidence List

Evidence	Where found	Results of analysis or examination	How evidence relates to offense
5. Fingerprints on MailExpress receipt			
6. Fingerprints on rifle			
7. Hair			
8. Medicines			
9. Skull			
10. Tire tracks in forest (if available)			
11. Tire tracks from cabin driveway (if available)			

Handout u
Evidence List

Additional Evidence

Complete "Where found" and "Description" after examining the evidence. Add notes in the last column as you figure out how the evidence relates to the crime.

Evidence	Where found	Description	How evidence relates to offense
12. MailExpress package receipt			
13. Hunting licenses: Cory Lucero			
14. Hunting licenses: Ryan Dixon			
15. Handwritten letter to Ed Lee from Ryan Dixon			

National Science Teachers Association

Handout V
Additional Interviews

Name _____ Date _____

`- CRIME SCENE - DO NOT CROSS - CRIME SCENE - DO NOT CROSS - CRIME SCENE - DO NOT CROSS - CRIME SCENE - DO NOT CROSS - CRIME SCENE - DO NOT CROSS -`

Additional statements taken from:

- Shane Potter, cabin neighbor visited by Ryan Dixon, Ward, Colorado
- Roger Moore, owner of Town Market in Ward, Colorado
- Representatives of airlines that service Denver International Airport
- Cory Lucero, cabin owner, Ward, Colorado
- Linda Jefferson, Ryan Dixon's employer

Shane Potter, Cabin neighbor

Interviewed on October 25 in Boulder, Colorado.

"I know the Dixons and Luceros. They live several miles from my cabin in Ward. Sometimes we get together when we are both at our cabins. The last time I saw all of them was in August when we got together for a barbeque. I was at my cabin all day on October 16, but did not see Ryan that day."

Roger Moore, Owner of Town Market

Interviewed on October 26 in Ward, Colorado.

"Ryan Dixon came to the store several times between October 10 and 17. Besides small amounts of grocery items, he bought dozens of day-old donuts and several crates of over-ripe cantaloupe and apples that had been taken off display."

Representatives of all airlines with planes departing from Denver International Airport October 16–21.

Interviewed on October 26 in Denver, Colorado.

There is no record of Mr. Ryan Dixon purchasing or using a ticket from Denver to St. Louis between October 16 and October 21.

Cory Lucero

Interviewed on October 28 in Boulder, Colorado.

"My wife Eliza went to help out a sick friend for a few days. She left on October 20 and got in the evening of the 21st. I do not know the person she was with. She said it was someone from work."

Linda Jefferson, Ryan Dixon's employer

Interviewed on October 26 in Boulder, Colorado.

"Ryan was not at work from October 10 through October 21. He was hunting from the October 10 through October 14. He called in sick the next week. He said the week of hunting really wore him down. He was home in bed with a fever and a severe cold.

Preparing for Investigation Day 4: Forensic Lab Tests

Teacher Guidelines

Overview

Investigative teams are now ready to divide up the evidence and conduct 10 forensic labs simultaneously at stations around the room. The lab procedures and reference materials are the same as those in the training labs (Section 2). You need to set up materials and evidence on 10 lab trays before Day 4. (To look over Teacher Guidelines for Day 4, go to p. 279)

Steps for Setting Up Forensic Lab Stations

1. Clearly label 10 trays with the forensic lab test names. (Labels are on p. 241.)

2. Put materials for each lab, listed below, in the tray.

3. Keep the BBGB Indicator Test at a teacher-monitored table to control its use.

4. Put the forensic lab trays and other equipment on tables and counters throughout the room.

Each station should have room for two people to work.

Materials

- Forensic Lab Papers #1–9 (pp. 242–259) (one copy per team)

Tray 1: Animal Tracks and Tire Tracks

- Evidence (Make two copies of each piece of evidence so that two students can be conducting a lab at the same time.):
  - Bobcat track (or other native animal irrelevant to the case: deer, mountain lion, raccoon, porcupine) (p. 260)
  - Tire tracks (pp. 261–268)

- Ruler
- "Field Guide to Mammal Tracks" (in Lesson 8: Tracks and Trace Fossils, p. 175)

Optional evidence: Make tire tracks by first rubbing dirt on four car tires of different patterns and two or more ATV and tractor tires. Then roll the tires over several pieces of white paper to transfer the tire patterns. Cut a section of two car tire patterns and one ATV tire pattern to use as evidence. Use the full paper prints of all the patterns as the known tire track keys.

Tray 2: Blood Typing of Suspects

- Evidence:
  - 2 sets of simulated blood labeled with cabin owners' names (You can use the simulated blood you used in Lesson 2: Blood and Blood Typing.)

    KEY: * Ryan Dixon = Must be AB+   Meagan Dixon = B- (*)

                 Cory Lucero = A+ (*)   Eliza Lucero = O- (*)

        * Cory, Meagan, and Eliza can have any blood type except AB+
- "Forensic Lab Instructions: Blood Typing" (p. 269)
- 2 spot plates
- 2 magnifying lenses
- 2 sets of simulated antibody serum: anti-A, anti-B, anti-Rh
- Plastic stirrers

Tray 3: DNA From Human Hair

- Evidence:
  - "DNA Strand From Hair Evidence"* (Ryan Dixon) (p. 249)
- Scissors
- Clear tape
- Gel plate paper model (See Lesson 3: DNA Fingerprinting, p. 75.)
- Graph paper (small grid, 10 divisions/inch)

*If students are not trained to make a simulated DNA fingerprint, use the prepared DNA fingerprints as evidence (p. 272).

Tray 4: Fingerprints From MailExpress Receipt

- Evidence:
  - Card (MailExpress receipt) with inked prints of index finger and thumb from Eliza Lucero*
  - Fingerprint cards from the four cabin owners, obtained during interviews*
- Two magnifying lenses
- "Fingerprint Pattern Key" (See Lesson 4: Fingerprints, pp. 96–99)

* Prepare fingerprint evidence by having the Eliza Lucero cast member put ink fingerprints of her thumb and index fingers on an index card. If fingerprint cards were not made with Lucero and Dixon characters, use prepared prints by making copies of the fingerprint evidence and the comparison prints of suspects (p. 273).

Tray 5: Fingerprints From Rifle

- Evidence:
  - 1 (per team) glass, paper, or plastic item with Ryan Dixon's fingerprints. This represents the prints found on the rifle.*
  - Fingerprint cards from the four cabin owners obtained during interviews*
- 2–4 plastic surgical gloves
- Materials for powder dusting, iodine crystals, or superglue procedures (procedure chosen by teacher; see Lesson 4: Fingerprints)

* If fingerprint cards were not made with the Lucero and Dixon characters, or if students were not trained in lab techniques for latent fingerprints, prepare fingerprint evidence by having the Ryan Dixon cast member put fingerprints on one object per team. The object chosen (options: microscope slides, baby food jars, small beakers, filter paper, other paper, piece of plastic) depends on the lab procedure the students will use. An alternative is to use prepared prints by making copies of the rifle fingerprint evidence and the comparison prints of suspects (p. 273).

Tray 6: Hair

- Evidence:
  - Prepared slides of three hairs found at crime scene. Prepare as follows:
  a. Label slides: Hair Evidence 1, Hair Evidence 2, Hair Evidence 3.
  b. Paint a line of clear fingernail polish on the slide.
  c. Lay the hair on the wet polish and paint over the hair to seal it in.

- Hair Evidence 1 = deer hair (or other irrelevant animal)
- Hair Evidence 2 = black bear hair
- Hair Evidence 3 = human hair
- 2 rulers
- 2 microscopes
- "Anatomy of a Hair" (see pp. 112–114 in Lesson 5: Hair Identification)
- Labeled hair slides (see p. 107 in Lesson 5: Hair Identification)

Tray 7: pH Indicator Test of Medicines

- Evidence:
  - 4 labeled film containers of medicines from Ed and Becky Lee's Traditional Asian Medicines store (substances can be in solution or powder form)

    Key:
    Asthma Treatment = Ground Tums or other antacid (weak base)
    Liver Treatment = Baking soda (base)
    Eye Treatment = Powdered milk (neutral)
    Heart Treatment = Ground aspirin (acid)
- Forensic Lab Instructions: "pH Indicator Test of Medicines" (p. 275)
- Three pH indicators used in Lesson 6: pH and pH Indicators (bromthymol blue, phenolphthelein, Congo red, natural nontoxic solutions from red cabbage, beets, or tea)
- 2 small containers of water
- 2 droppers for water
- 2 spot plates
- Color codes for pH indicators from Lesson 6: pH and pH Indicators

Tray 7a: BBGB Indicator Test

- "The Gall Bladder" information sheet (p. 278)
- 1 small flask of vinegar labeled "BBGB Indicator"

Tray 8: Skull

- Evidence:
  - Bear skull
- Ruler
- Tape measure
- "Key to Skulls of North American Mammals" (see Lesson 7: Mammal Skulls)

Tray 9: Antler/ Horn
- Evidence:
  - Antler/horn of any North American species (irrelevant to crime)
- Ruler
- Tape measure
- Animal Headgear Identification Cards (see Lesson 1: Antlers and Horns, pp. 42–43)

Labels for the 10 Forensic Lab Trays

Animal Tracks and Tire Tracks

Blood Typing of Suspects

DNA From Human Hair

Fingerprints From MailExpress Receipt

Fingerprints From Rifle

Hair

pH Indicator Test of Medicines

BBGB Indicator Test

Skull

Antler/Horn

Investigator: _____ Team # _____

FORENSIC LAB PAPER #1

Evidence: Animal Tracks and Tire Tracks

A. ANIMAL TRACKS

Evidence Submitted

This animal track was found at a wildlife crime scene where four animal carcasses were left after being shot. The carcasses were about one-half mile behind the Lucero/Dixon cabin and Tweed cabin in Ward, Colorado.

Request to Wildlife Forensic Lab

Identify the species of animal that made the tracks. Use the "Field Guide to Mammal Tracks."

Lab Results

1. Draw the track, including measurements of length and width. (Do not include claws in measurement.)

2. Species identification: Common name: _____

   Scientific name: _____

   Track size given in field guide: _____

3. One or more unique characteristics that helped identify the track.

Lab Conclusions

Summary: This track was made by a(n) _____

Making Connections: Do these results relate to the crime? _____
Explain.

B. TIRE TRACKS

Evidence Submitted

1. Two sets of tire tracks were found in the driveway of the Lucero/Dixon cabin in Ward, Colorado. This location is under investigation in connection with a nearby wildlife crime.

2. Tire tracks were found between the Lucero/Dixon cabin and the site where four animal carcasses were found. .

Request to Wildlife Forensic Lab

Compare these tracks to tracks of known vehicles of suspects. Identify any track matches.

Lab Results

Track #	Drawing of unique feature	Vehicle ID	Owner ID

Lab Conclusions

Summary: The tire tracks in the driveway matched vehicles owned by _____ and _____.

The tire tracks in the forest matched a vehicle owned by _____.

Making Connections: Do the tire tracks in the driveway relate to the crime? _____ Explain.

Do the tire tracks from the crime scene relate to the crime? _____ Explain.

Investigator: _____ Team # _____

FORENSIC LAB PAPER #2

Evidence: Blood Typing of Suspects

Evidence Submitted

A bloody rag was collected from the site of four animal carcasses in the forest about one-half mile behind the Lucero/Dixon cabin and the Tweed cabin in Ward, Colorado.

Request to Wildlife Forensic Lab

While testing the rag's blood, the lab found it contained blood from two different species. One was human AB+ blood. The other was nonhuman. Here are blood samples from four suspects in the wildlife crime. Please identify the blood type and Rh factor on each and compare them to the human blood type found on the rag evidence. Follow the procedure in the "Forensic Lab Instructions: Blood Typing."

Lab Results

Name of suspect	Anti-A	Anti-B	Anti-Rh	Blood type
_____	◯	◯	◯	_____
_____	◯	◯	◯	_____
_____	◯	◯	◯	_____
_____	◯	◯	◯	_____

Lab Conclusions

Summary: Blood type found near crime scene _____

Suspect with matching blood type _____

Making Connections: Do the results relate to the crime? _____
Explain.

National Science Teachers Association

Investigator:_____   Team # _____

FORENSIC LAB PAPER #3

Evidence: DNA From Human Hair

Evidence Submitted

Human hair was collected from a wildlife crime scene in Ward, Colorado, where four unidentified animals had been killed. This hair was on a tarp covering a motion detector camera at a bait station in the National Forest. It has been identified as a human hair.

Request to Wildlife Forensic Lab

Because the hair structure cannot be matched to one individual, please create a DNA fingerprint from the hair to compare to possible suspects. Follow the procedure in the "Forensic Lab Instructions: Creating a DNA Fingerprint."

These materials are included:

- DNA fingerprints of four suspects
- DNA strand from hair

Lab Results

Gel Box Summary

# nucleotide base pairs	# DNA pieces
19+	
16–18	
13–15	
10–12	
7–9	
4–6	
1–3	

Attach the DNA fingerprint from the hair evidence.

Lab Conclusions

Summary: Write the names of suspects and mark if his or her DNA fingerprint matches the evidence.

Suspect	Matches Evidence?
1.	
2.	
3.	
4.	

Making Connections: Do these results relate to the crime? _____ Explain.

Handout W
DNA Strand From Hair Evidence

Name _____ Date _____

- CRIME SCENE - DO NOT CROSS - CRIME SCENE - DO NOT CROSS - CRIME SCENE - DO NOT CROSS - CRIME SCENE - DO NOT CROSS - CRIME SCENE - DO NOT CROSS -

AT (1)	CG (2)	TA (3)	CG (4)	TA (5)	GC (6)
CG	TA	CG	CG	CG	CG
TA	TA	CG	CG	GC	CG
AT	CG	GC	AT	AT	AT
AT	GC	AT	TA	CG	CG
CG	AT	AT	AT	GC	CG
TA	CG	CG	TA	TA	CG
AT	GC	CG	CG	CG	TA
AT	AT	AT	CG	CG	TA
CG	AT	AT	GC	CG	TA
CG	AT	AT	AT	CG	AT
CG	AT	TA	TA	TA	CG
TA	CG	AT	AT	CG	AT
CG	CG	GC	AT	AT	TA
CG	TA	AT	AT	AT	GC
GC	CG	TA	TA	GC	AT
AT	CG	CG	AT	AT	CG
AT	AT	AT	CG	AT	AT
AT	TA	GC	CG	GC	TA
TA	CG	AT	CG	CG	CG
GC	CG	CG	AT	CG	CG
AT	CG	TA	AT	AT	TA
TA	TA	CG	TA	AT	TA
GC	TA	CG	CG	CG	AT
AT	AT	CG	GC	AT	TA
AT	CG	GC	CG	CG	CG
TA	GC	TA	TA	CG	CG
GC	AT	AT	AT	TA	TA
CG	AT	AT	CG	CG	AT
AT	CG	CG	TA	CG	AT
TA	CG	GC	AT	AT	CG
CG	AT	AT	CG	AT	GC
AT	AT	AT	CG	GC	AT
AT	AT	CG	GC	GC	AT
AT	AT	CG	TA	CG	CG
AT	CG	GC	TA	AT	AT
CG	CG	CG	CG	AT	TA
TA	AT	TA	AT	CG	GC

Using Forensics: Wildlife Crime Scene!

Investigator:_____ Team # _____

FORENSIC LAB PAPER #4

Evidence:
Fingerprints on MailExpress Receipt

Evidence Submitted

This MailExpress receipt with fingerprints was found on the floor under a table in a cabin owned by the Luceros and Dixons in Ward, Colorado. The receipt is for a package sent to San Francisco.

Request to Wildlife Forensic Lab

1. Number the prints.
2. Identify the pattern of each.
3. Compare the patterns to the fingerprint cards of the four cabin owners: Cory Lucero, Eliza Lucero, Ryan Dixon, Meagan Dixon.
4. Identify the finger and hand for each print.
5. Determine the owner of the prints.

Lab Results

Print #	Pattern	Hand/finger

Owner of fingerprints: _____

Lab Conclusions

Summary: These prints belong to _____ .

Making Connections: Do these results relate to the crime? _____ Explain.

Investigator:_____ Team # _____

FORENSIC LAB PAPER #5

Evidence: Fingerprints on Rifle

Evidence Submitted

These fingerprints were found on a rifle. It has been determined that the rifle was used to kill animals in a crime. It was found in a large shed next to the cabin owned by suspects in a wildlife crime. The cabin is owned by the Luceros and Dixons and is located in Ward, Colorado.

Request to Wildlife Forensic Lab

Make latent fingerprints on the rifle (copy of fingerprints on glass, plastic, or paper) into visible prints. Identify the patterns and owner of the prints. The fingerprint cards of the four cabin owners (Cory Lucero, Eliza Lucero, Ryan Dixon, and Meagan Dixon) are enclosed. The head of the lab (teacher) will decide whether you will dust for prints, use the iodine crystal fuming test, or use the superglue fuming test.

Lab Results

Print #	Pattern	Hand/finger

Owner of fingerprints: _____

Lab Conclusions

Summary: These prints belong to _____ .

Making Connections: Do these results relate to the crime? _____ Explain.

Investigator:_____ Team # _____

FORENSIC LAB PAPER #6

Evidence: Hair

Evidence Submitted

Hairs were taken from the Ward, Colorado, wildlife crime scene. The first hair was taken from one of the four carcasses. All appear to be the same species. The second was from the ground near the carcasses. The third was on the tarp covering the motion detector camera at the bait station.

Request to Wildlife Forensic Lab

Identify the species of animal for each hair by comparing it with known hair samples. Record findings in the lab results table, Hair Characteristics, page 253.

National Science Teachers Association

Lab Results: Hair Characteristics

Hair #	Visual hair color	Human medulla: Absent, trace, broken, or continuous. DRAW	Nonhuman medulla: (amorphous, uni/multi-sertal, vacuolated, lattice). DRAW	Medullary Index: (estimate 0, 1/4, 1/2, 3/4, 1)	Species identification

Lab Conclusions

Summary:

Hair 1 belongs to a _____. Characteristics that helped identify it:

Hair 2 belongs to a _____. Characteristics that helped identify it:

Hair 3 belongs to a _____. Characteristics that helped identify it:

Making Connections:

1. Explain possible reasons for each hair being at the crime scene.

   a. Hair 1:

   b. Hair 2:

   c. Hair 3:

2. Do any of these hairs relate to this crime? _____ Explain:

National Science Teachers Association

Investigator:_____ Team # _____

FORENSIC LAB PAPER #7

Evidence: pH Indicator Test of Medicines

Evidence Submitted

Undercover investigators purchased four different medicines (Asthma Treatment, Liver Treatment, Eye Treatment, and Heart Treatment) from the Traditional Asian Medicines store in San Francisco, California, in October. The store is owned by Ed and Becky Lee. It is suspected that one or more of the medicines contain parts of the poached animals from Ward, Colorado.

Request to Wildlife Forensic Lab

Important information to know before testing:

- BBGB stands for _____.
- BBGBs are suspected of being in one or more of these medicines. They contain fluids that are (circle one) acidic / neutral / basic and would make the medicine have the same pH range.
- Therefore, you are looking for medicine with a pH between _____ and _____ .

Lab testing:

1. Use a combination of three pH indicators to determine the pH range of each medicine. Follow the Forensic Lab Instructions: pH Indicator Test of Medicine (p. 275).

2. Determine which, if any, medicines match the targeted pH range for BBGBs.

3. Perform the final BBGB indicator test on the medicine(s) that have the targeted pH to find out if BBGB is present.

Lab Results

Test 1: pH Ranges of Medicines

Medicine	Indicator	Color change from indicator	pH range (1–14)	pH range of medicine Acid, Base, Neutral
				_____
				_____
				_____

Test 2: Final Test for BBGB

1. Medicine(s) chosen to test for BBGB:

   _____ with pH range = _____

2. Medicine(s) with positive test (bubbling/fizzing) for BBGB:

   _____

Lab Conclusions

Summary: BBGB (_____) has been

identified in the medicine(s) _____.

Making Connections: Do these test results relate to the crime? ____
Explain.

Investigator:_____ Team # _____

FORENSIC LAB PAPER #8

Evidence: Skull

Evidence Submitted

This skull was collected on October 22 about a half mile behind the Tweed cabin and the Lucero/Dixon cabin in Ward, Colorado. It was found on the ground in a forested area. The entire body of this animal and three other similar animals were at this location.

Request to Wildlife Forensic Lab

Use the "Key to Skulls of North American Mammals" to identify the species of the skull. Record the number and description for each characteristic you choose in the key.

Lab Results

Step # in Key	Characteristic

Lab Conclusions

Summary: Species identification _____

Making Connections: Do these results relate to the crime? _____ Explain.

Investigator:_____   Team # _____

FORENSIC LAB PAPER #9

Evidence: Antler/Horn_____

Evidence Submitted

This antler/horn was found in a shed at the Lucero/Dixon cabin in Ward, Colorado, near other pieces of evidence taken for a wildlife crime investigation. It is from a recently killed animal.

Request to Wildlife Forensic Lab

Determine the animal species of the antler/horn. We will then determine if any of the cabin owners had licenses to hunt this animal.

Lab Results

1. Drawing of antler/horn.

2. Length of antler/horn. (Measure from the base to the most distant tip. Follow the main beam.)

    _____ ____   (to nearest cm)

3. Species: _____

4. Description that confirms its match to the species:

5. Answer the following questions to determine if this is a legal kill.

   • Did any cabin owner have a license to hunt this animal recently?
   _____

   • If yes, provide hunter's name: _____

   • Dates of hunting season on license: _____

   • Is this a possible legal kill? Yes / No

Lab Conclusions:

Summary: This antler is from a(n) _____.

Making Connections: Do these results relate to the crime? _____
Explain.

EVIDENCE: Animal Track

Animal track found at wildlife crime scene.

EVIDENCE: Tire Tracks

Evidence 1:
Tire track found in the
Lucero/Dixon driveway

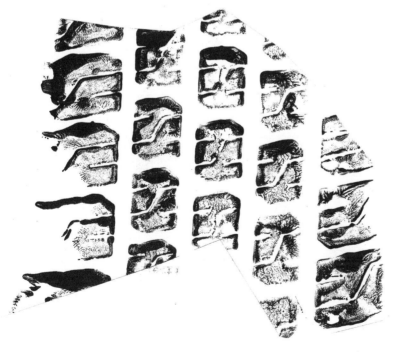

Evidence 2:
Tire track found in the
Lucero/Dixon driveway

EVIDENCE: ATV Tire Track

Evidence 3:
Partial tire track found at the crime scene (Ryan Dixon).

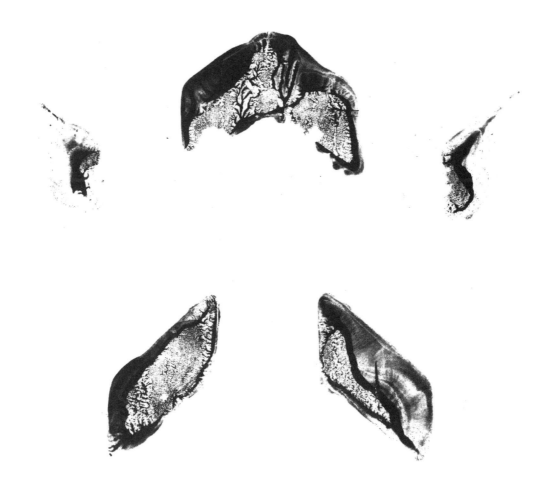

EVIDENCE: Tractor Tire Track

Tire track from Lucero tractor.

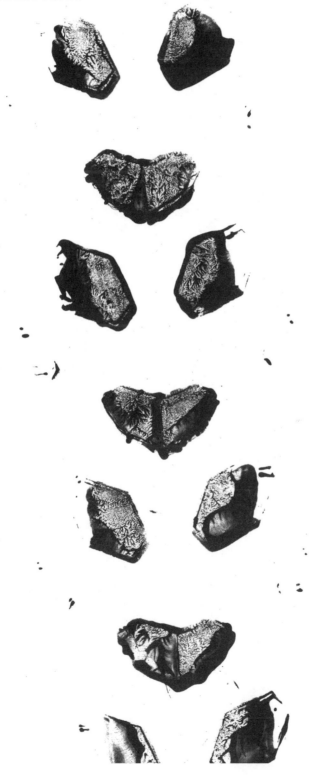

EVIDENCE: ATV Tire Track

Tire track from Dixon ATV.

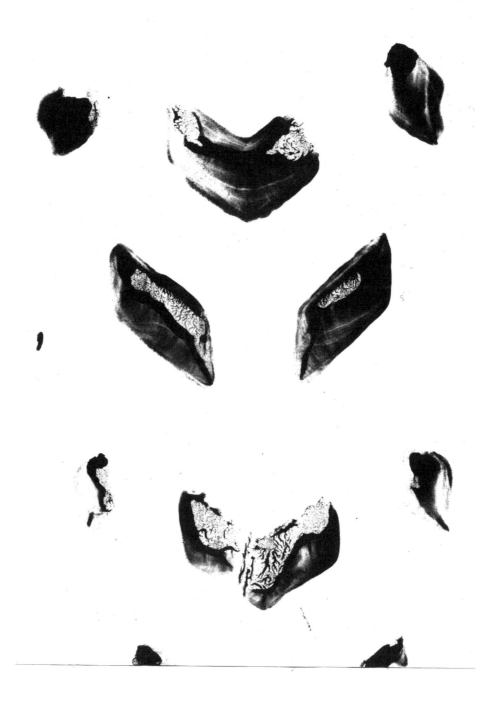

EVIDENCE: Tire Track

Tire track from Cory Lucero's vehicle.

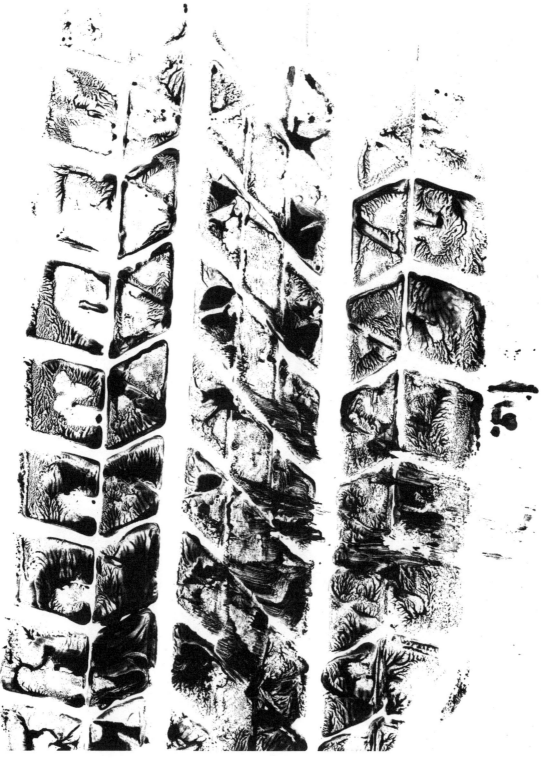

EVIDENCE: Tire Track

Tire track from Eliza Lucero's vehicle.

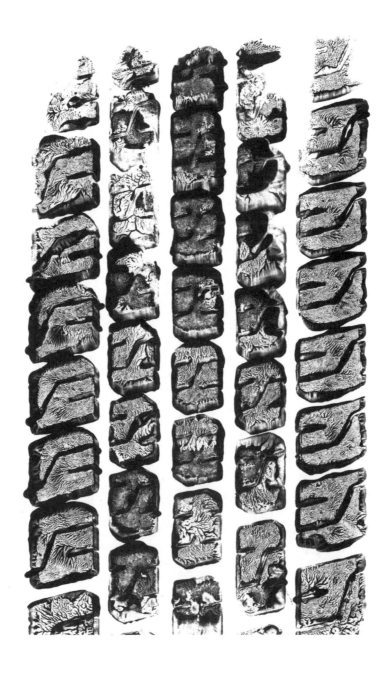

EVIDENCE: Tire Track

Tire track from Meagan Dixon's vehicle.

EVIDENCE: Tire Track

Tire track from Ryan Dixon's vehicle.

National Science Teachers Association

Forensic Lab Instructions

Blood Typing

Task

Test for blood types and Rh factors of four suspects in the wildlife crime. You are attempting to find someone who matches blood type AB+, found on the rag at the scene of the crime.

Materials

- 1 spot plate
- 4 blood samples
- Anti-A serum, anti-B serum, and anti-Rh serum
- Magnifying lens

Procedure

1. Set the spot plate in the center of the paper towel. Label the suspect names and anti-sera as shown in Forensic Lab Paper #2, "Evidence: Blood Typing the Suspects." Copy the set-up and results into your Investigator Notebook.

2. Put 2–3 drops from one person's blood into three cups of the spot plate.

3. Test the blood's reaction to each antibody serum by putting 1–2 drops of anti-A into the first well, 1–2 drops of anti-B in the second well, and 1–2 drops of anti-Rh into the third well.

4. Complete steps 2 and 3 for each person's blood.

5. Use the magnifying lens to confirm the presence of a precipitate.

6. Complete the lab results and conclusions.

Forensics Lab Instructions

Creating a DNA Fingerprint

Task

Create a DNA fingerprint "photograph" from a paper copy of DNA base pairs from a human hair.

Materials

- "DNA Strand From Hair Evidence" (Handout w, p. 249)
- Clear tape
- Scissors
- Gel box paper model
- Graph paper (10 divisions/inch or smaller)

Procedure

1. Create your DNA strand by cutting apart the columns of nucleotide pairs on "DNA Strand From Hair Evidence." Carefully tape them together end to end *in the order given* to form one long continuous strand. There should be no gap between bases when taped together.

2. Cut the DNA strand after every GC pair. Start at the top of your DNA strand. When you come to a GC, cut the paper *under* this pair. Do this for the entire strand.

3. Set all DNA pieces at the starting well of the gel box.

4. Count the nucleotide pairs for each DNA piece and move it into the correct section of the gel box. For instance, pieces with 1–3 pairs are light and move to the end of the gel box. Pieces with 19+ pairs are too heavy to move out of the starting well.

5. After all DNA pieces have been moved to their correct location in the gel box, count the number of pieces in each section. Record these numbers in your lab results.

6. Use graph paper to "photograph" the DNA fingerprint shown on your gel box. Space the sections evenly up the page.

7. Compare the photograph of the DNA fingerprint from the evidence to DNA fingerprints of suspects. Determine if there is a match.

8. Complete "Lab Conclusions."

DNA Fingerprints From Suspects

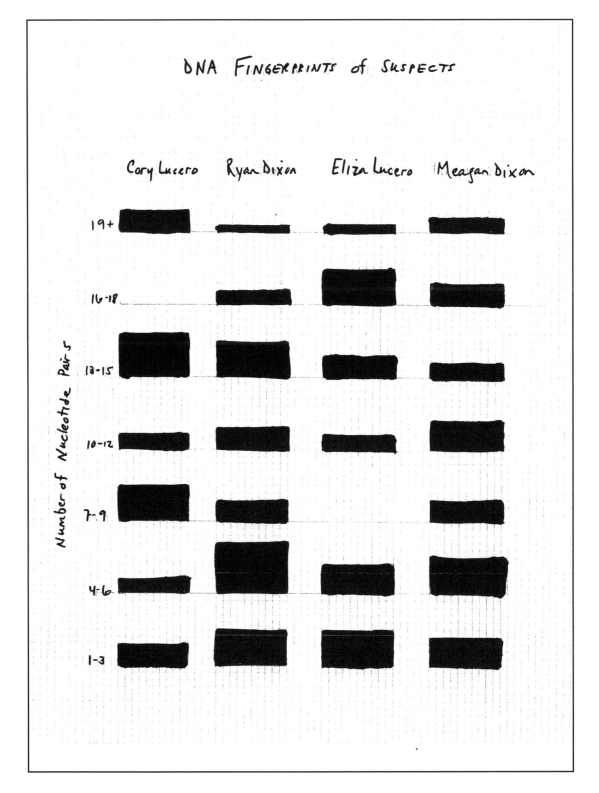

Fingerprints on MailExpress Receipt

(Alternative to using fingerprints from character)

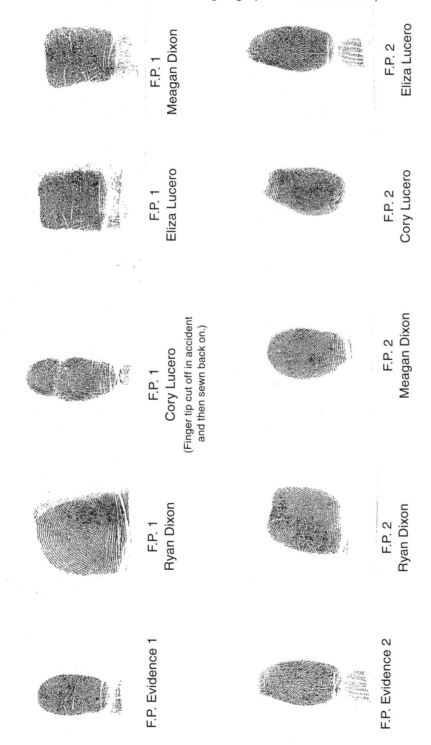

F.P. 1
Meagan Dixon

F.P. 2
Eliza Lucero

F.P. 1
Eliza Lucero

F.P. 2
Cory Lucero

F.P. 1
Cory Lucero
(Finger tip cut off in accident and then sewn back on.)

F.P. 2
Meagan Dixon

F.P. 1
Ryan Dixon

F.P. 2
Ryan Dixon

F.P. Evidence 1

F.P. Evidence 2

Fingerprints on Rifle

(Alternative to using fingerprints from character and using dusting, super-glue, or iodine crystals to make them visible.)

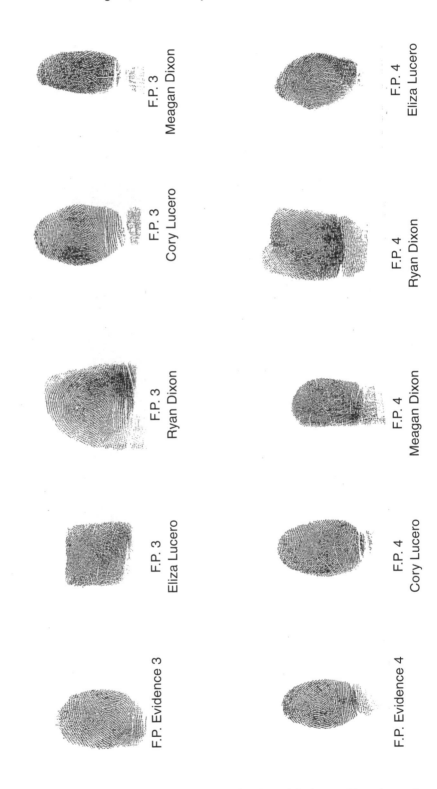

F.P. 3
Meagan Dixon

F.P. 4
Eliza Lucero

F.P. 3
Cory Lucero

F.P. 4
Ryan Dixon

F.P. 3
Ryan Dixon

F.P. 4
Meagan Dixon

F.P. 3
Eliza Lucero

F.P. 4
Cory Lucero

F.P. Evidence 3

F.P. Evidence 4

Forensic Lab Instructions

pH Indicator Test of Medicines

Task

Use pH indicators to determine if any of the four medicines matches the pH range for BBGBs. Test the matched medicine(s) with a final BBGB indicator test.

Materials

- 4 medicines
- Beaker of water
- Droppers
- Spot plate
- 3 pH indicators

Procedure

1. Determine what animal part (BBGB) you are looking for BEFORE running these tests. Clues are found in the "Initial Crime Reports," the handwritten letter found in the Lees' house, and introductory activities on crimes against wildlife in Section 1.

2. Ask for and read "The GB" information sheet (p. 278). Write the pH range of this body part on your lab sheet. This is the pH you are looking for in Test 1.

Test 1: pH Ranges of Medicines

3. Set the spot plate in the center of a paper towel. Label the medicine rows and pH indicator columns as shown in the spot plate drawing below. Complete columns 1 and 2 of the data table in Forensic Lab Paper #7.

Spot Plate for pH Indicator Testing

pH Indicator

Medicine   _____ _____ _____

_____   ◯   ◯   ◯

_____   ◯   ◯   ◯

_____   ◯   ◯   ◯

_____   ◯   ◯   ◯

4. Put a pinch of the first powdered medicine into three labeled cups of the spot plate.

5. Add one drop of pH indicator to the cups as shown by your labels.

6. Record the color changes of the solutions in your data table.

7. Use class notes from your pH training lab (Lesson 3) to estimate the pH of the substance based on the combined color results. *Important:* If the indicators show pH ranges that do not overlap (e.g., one says acid and the other says base), clean the spot plate and rerun tests.

8. Repeat 4–7 for the other three medicines.

9. Determine which medicine(s) has/have the targeted pH for GB and run the BBGB Indicator Test on it/them.

Test 2: BBGB Indicator Test

A test has been developed specifically for BBGBs. Because the test materials are very expensive and produced in small amounts, the test is used only with medicines having the targeted pH. The test solution contains a chemical that only reacts with BBGB proteins.

a. Place a pinch of the powdered medicine(s) in a clean spot plate cup.

b. Take it to the BBGB indicator test station.

c. Add 2–4 drops of the BBGB indicator. If BBGB is present, the mixture will bubble or fizz.

d. Record your results and conclusions on your lab sheet.

The Gall Bladder

You now know that "BBGBs" are black bear gall bladders.

Bile is produced in the liver and stored in the gall bladder, a small greenish organ that sits under the liver (see drawing below). Bile helps with food digestion in the small intestine. It contains sodium bicarbonate, a base that neutralizes stomach acid, and a mix of salts that breaks down fat. (The pancreas also helps with digestion in the small intestine. It sends fluid that neutralizes stomach acids and contains digestive enzymes.)

Acids in the stomach help breakdown food. When the partially digested food moves to the small intestine, it is highly acidic. The basic fluids from the gall bladder and pancreas flow into the section of the small intestine that connects to the stomach. The acidic food is quickly changed to a neutral level between pH 7 and 8 so that the intestine's digestive enzymes can work most effectively.

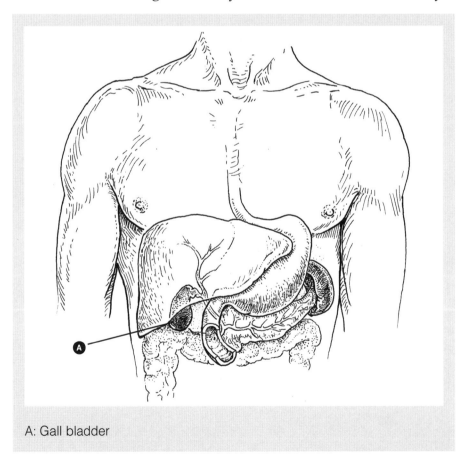

A: Gall bladder

Investigation Day 4: Forensic Lab Tests of Evidence

Teacher Guidelines

Overview

Investigative teams will divide evidence among members to test and identify.

Teaching Plan

1. Give each investigative team a Forensic Lab Plan (Handout x, p. 281). They can staple the plan to the front of their Investigative Team Envelopes.

2. Each member must choose a lab to complete from both Evidence Group 1 and Evidence Group 2 in the Forensic Lab Plan.

3. Give each team a set of the nine forensic lab papers (pp. 242–259). Students write their names on their assigned lab papers and put them in their personal folders.

4. Explain guidelines for working at the lab stations:

   • All labs were practiced in the eight forensic training lessons in Section 2. Refer students to the notes they took during those lessons.

   • No more than two students work at a station at a time.

   • When done, clean all equipment and return it to the tray.

5. Special instructions for pH lab:

    •   As a team, students must determine what BBGB means before the pH lab can be completed. Once they do, give them a "The Gall Bladder" information sheet (p. 278). They must figure out the pH of gall bladders and match it with the pH of one or more medicines.

    •   The student assigned to the pH lab will put a pinch of the matching medicine(s) in a spot plate and take it to the BBGB Indicator Test station. A positive test is obtained when the medicine and indicator mixture (baking soda + vinegar*) bubble.

    *   If other chemicals are available, you may choose a different reaction to substitute for the baking soda/vinegar reaction.

6. Completion of all labs should take a team 1½–2 days to complete. *Remind students to not share findings with other teams.* The team with the most accurate lab results and crime scenario will get to arrest the suspect(s)!

Handout X
Forensic Lab Plan

Name_____ Date_____

- CRIME SCENE - DO NOT CROSS - CRIME SCENE - DO NOT CROSS - CRIME SCENE - DO NOT CROSS - CRIME SCENE - DO NOT CROSS - CRIME SCENE - DO NOT CROSS -

Team # _____

Team Members: _____

<u>Instructions</u>: Write your name beside one piece of evidence in Group 1 and one in Group 2. You will be responsible for completing these labs. Attach this paper to the front of your Investigative Team Envelope.

Evidence Group 1 (shorter labs)

_____ 1. Fingerprints from MailExpress receipt (Identify the owner of the prints.)

_____ 2. Fingerprints from rifle (Make latent prints visible and identify the owner.)

_____ 3. Skull (Identify the species using a dichotomous key.) AND

_____ 4. Antler/Horn (Identify species.)

_____ 5. Animal Tracks and Tire Tracks

> **IMPORTANT:**
> One student does both skull and antler/horn.

- • Animal tracks (Identify species.)
- • Tire tracks from cabin driveway (Identify the owner.)
- • Tire tracks from crime scene (Identify the owner.)

Evidence Group 2 (longer labs)

_____ 6. Ph Indicator Test of Medicines (and final BBGB Indicator Test)

_____ 7. Three hairs (Use microscope to identify the species.)

_____ 8. DNA from human hair (Create a DNA "fingerprint" and match to the owner.)

_____ 9. Blood typing of suspects

Investigation Day 5: Forensic Lab Tests Continue

Teacher Guidelines

Overview

Investigative teams share any forensic lab test findings on evidence they have completed so far, and discuss new ideas about the crime. Then they continue completing their assigned labs.

Materials

Investigation Day 5: "What Do We Know So Far?" (p. 283)

Teaching Plan

1. Give each investigative team "What Do We Know So Far?" Team members should answer the questions by sharing the results of labs they've completed so far. This can be done at the beginning or end of class, depending upon how much they got done on Day 4. Ideally, each person should have completed one lab before working on this sheet.

2. Have students continue working on their assigned labs.

3. As students finish their labs, they can record their findings on the "Evidence List" and look over the wildlife laws and regulations to determine how the evidence shows the violation of certain laws. If the results from a piece of evidence seem incorrect, students can redo the lab as time and materials allow.

Investigation Day 5: What Do We Know So Far?

1. What animals were the victims of this crime?

2. What evidence supports this?

3. San Francisco connection:

   a. Who was involved in San Francisco?

   b. What role did this person (these persons) play in the crime?

   c. What is BBGB?

   d. Why do you think this person or these people wanted BB-GBs?

4. Separating legal and illegal hunting:

   a. What animals did Cory and Ryan have hunting licenses to kill?

   b. What were the hunting season dates for their hunting licenses?

   c. When was the crime committed?

   d. Could the dead animals be legal kills? Explain.

5. What offenses do you think were committed (see "Hunting Laws and Regulations in Colorado").

6. Suspects:

   a. Who is your main suspect?

b. What evidence do you have to prove the person committed a crime?

c. If you have another suspect, who is it?

d. What evidence do you have to prove the person committed a crime?

Investigation Day 6 and 7: Summarizing Findings and Charging Suspects

Teacher Guidelines

Overview

Teams complete the "Witness List" and "Evidence List" by determining how each piece of information relates to the offenses. Teams will determine criminal offenses, suspects, and victims.

Materials

- "Final Case Report on Wildlife Crime Investigation" (Handout y, p. 286)

Teaching Plan

1. After students complete all forensic labs, have teams work together to fill in the last columns of the "Witness List" and "Evidence List."

2. Give each student a "Final Case Report on Wildlife Crime Investigation." This report is made up of three parts: Summary of Offenses, Proof of Offenses, and Summary of Crime. Students can fill out these three parts individually or as a team.

Handout Y
Final Case Report on Wildlife Crime Investigation

Name _____ Date _____

- CRIME SCENE - DO NOT CROSS - CRIME SCENE - DO NOT CROSS - CRIME SCENE - DO NOT CROSS - CRIME SCENE - DO NOT CROSS - CRIME SCENE - DO NOT CROSS -

Summary of Offenses

Investigators: _____ Team #: _____

Date(s) of Offense: _____

Location of Offense: _____

Victim(s): _____

Suspect 1: _____

Offense(s): _____

_____

_____

Suspect 2: _____

Offense(s): _____

_____

_____

Proof of Offenses

For each charged offense, explain the evidence and witness information that supports the charge.

Write on your own paper.

Offense: _____

Suspect: _____

Evidence supporting charge: _____

National Science Teachers Association

Handout Y
Final Case Report on Wildlife Crime Investigation

Witness information supporting charge: _____

_____

_____

_____

_____

Summary of Crime

1. Who: _____

2. What: _____

3. When: _____

4. Where: _____

5. Why: _____

6. *Final Case Report.* Write the story of the crime or chronologically list what happened, based on your investigation.

287

Investigation Day 8: Presentation of Case to the Prosecuting Attorney

Teacher Guidelines

Overview

Teams present their case to the prosecuting attorney to explain evidence that supports the charges being made. The teams with the most accurate case will make the arrest.

Materials

- "Summary of Evidence: Wildlife Crime in Ward, Colorado" (p. 289). **Make a transparency or paper copy of this form for each team.**
- "Case Solved" (pp. 290–291) **Copy or make a transparency of these two pages, which the teacher will use at the end of the lesson.**
- Transparency marker for each team.

Teaching Plan

1. Have each team record their conclusions on the "Summary of Evidence: Wildlife Crime in Ward, Colorado" transparencies or papers.

2. Using a visual projector, each team will present to the class, with you as the prosecuting attorney. Determine which team has the most accurate evidence results and clearest explanation of victims, suspects, and offenses.

3. After all presentations are given, show the class the facts in "Case Solved."

4. The team that was most accurate in solving the crime will lead the class to the suspects and make the arrest. Give that "winning" team the handout "Making the Arrest" (Handout z, p. 292) so they know what to do. "Making the Arrest" calls for student to put handcuffs on the suspects; you can skip this part, buy two sets of handcuffs at a toy store, or ask an actual police officer to come in to advise and assist in the arrests.

(Teacher makes a transparency or paper copy of this form for each team.)

Summary of Evidence:
Wildlife Crime in Ward, Colorado

Evidence	Results of analysis or examination
1. Antler/horn	
2. Animal Tracks	
3. Bloody rag	
4. DNA from human hair	
5. Fingerprints on MailExpress receipt	
6. Fingerprints on rifle	
7. Hair	
8. Medicines	
9. Skull	
10. Tire tracks: crime scene	
11. Tire tracks: driveway	
12. MailExpress package receipt	
13. Hunting licenses: Cory Lucero	
14. Hunting licenses: Ryan Dixon	
15. Handwritten letter to Ed Lee	

Case Solved!

Do Not Share This Handout With Students Until Investigation Is Complete. An asterisk next to an offense means that that offense is most significant.

Suspect: Ryan Dixon

(All laws cited below are found in "Hunting Laws and Regulations for Colorado," Handout h, p. 206)

Offenses:
1. Using bait to hunt bears. (Law 7)

2. Failure to use edible wildlife meat for human consumption. (Law 10)

*3. Killing and abandoning big game. Killing big game to remove body parts and leaving the carcass in the field ("willful destruction"). (felony) (Law 11)

*4. Selling big game. (felony) (Law 12)

*5. Selling gall bladder and other edible portions of bears. (Law 13)

6. Having parts of bear without a valid hunting license. (Law 15)

Suspect: Eliza Lucero

Offenses: *1. Selling big game. (felony) (Law 12)

*2. Selling gall bladder and other edible portions of bears. (Law 13)

Evidence Results:

1. Antler/horn: Mule deer (or elk—not relevant to case)

2. Animal Tracks: Bobcat (or other native animal not relevant to case)

3. Bloody rag from crime scene: Ryan Dixon with AB+

4. DNA from human hair: Ryan Dixon

5. Fingerprints on MailExpress receipt: Eliza Lucero

6. Fingerprints on rifle: Ryan Dixon

7. Hair from carcass disposal site: Human, elk or other irrelevant native animal, black bear

8. Medicines: Liver Medicine tested positive for black bear gall bladder

9. Skull: Black bear

10. Tire tracks—Crime scene: Ryan Dixon's ATV

11. Tire tracks—Driveway: Ryan Dixon's and Eliza Lucero's vehicles

12. MailExpress package receipt: From Eliza Lucero to Ed Lee

13. Hunting licenses: Cory Lucero—1 elk, 1 deer (killed). Ryan Dixon—1 elk (killed), 1 bear (killed)

14. Handwritten letter to Ed Lee: From Ryan Dixon to Ed Lee explaining payment for black bear gall bladders

Handout 4
Making the Arrest

Name _____ Date _____

- CRIME SCENE - DO NOT CROSS - CRIME SCENE - DO NOT CROSS - CRIME SCENE - DO NOT CROSS - CRIME SCENE - DO NOT CROSS - CRIME SCENE - DO NOT CROSS -

1. Ask the suspect to confirm his/her name. "Are you _____?"

2. Read the offense(s) you are charging him/her with. "You are under arrest for _____."

3. Handcuff the suspect.

4. Read the Advisement of Rights:

   - You have the right to remain silent.
   - Anything you say can be used against you in court.
   - You have the right to talk to an attorney before you are questioned and to have your attorney present with you during any questioning.
   - If you want an attorney, but cannot afford to hire one, an attorney will be appointed by a court to represent you before you are questioned and to be with you during any questioning.
   - If you decide to start answering questions, you will still have the right to stop answering questions and the right to talk to an attorney at any time.
   - Do you understand your rights?

5. Lead him or her to the principal's office or other predetermined location.

6. Remove handcuffs and turn him or her over to the higher authority.

Section 4

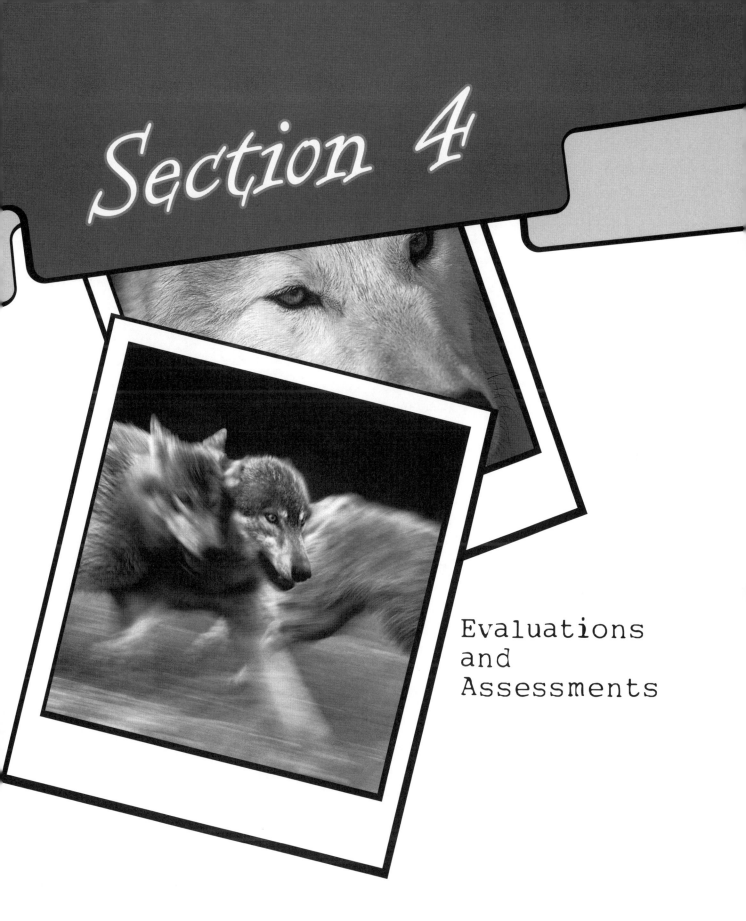

Evaluations
and
Assessments

Overview

Handout 4-A
Investigator's
Summary Packet Checklist

- CRIME SCENE - DO NOT CROSS - CRIME SCENE - DO NOT CROSS - CRIME SCENE - DO NOT CROSS - CRIME SCENE - DO NOT CROSS - CRIME SCENE - DO NOT CROSS -

Investigator _____

Complete and check off all papers listed below. Organize and bind them to show your role in solving the wildlife crime. When they are bound, these papers become your "Investigator's Summary Packet."

__ Cover Page (title, investigator's name, team members' names in parentheses, date, illustration [optiona])

__ 1. "Investigator's Summary Packet Checklist" (this page)

__ 2. "Investigator's Self-Evaluation" (Handout 4-B, pp. 297–298)

__ 3. "Final Case Report on Wildlife Investigation"

__ 4. "Evidence List" (Circle the names of the evidence you analyzed.)

__ 5. Completed forensic lab sheet for one piece of evidence you analyzed
      (Name of evidence: _____)

__ 6. Completed forensic lab sheet for another piece of evidence you analyzed (Name of evidence: _____)

__ 7. Summary of Evidence You Analyzed. Summarize three pieces of evidence—the two listed above and one of the following: MailExpress receipt, letter to Ed Lee, hunting licenses. For each, explain:

   • What is the evidence?
   • What were the results of your analyses?
   • How did it help (or not help) you solve the case?

__ 8. "Witness List" (Circle the names of the two people you interviewed.)

Handout 4-A
Investigator's Summary Packet Checklist

___ 9. Summary of your witness interviews. For each explain:

- Who is the person?
- What information did the person give that related to the case?

___ 10. Explanation of reasons for any differences between the actual results—presented in "Case Solved!"—and your team's lab findings.

Handout 4-B
Investigator's Self-Evaluation

- CRIME SCENE - DO NOT CROSS - CRIME SCENE - DO NOT CROSS - CRIME SCENE - DO NOT CROSS - CRIME SCENE - DO NOT CROSS - CRIME SCENE - DO NOT CROSS -

Investigator _____

Evaluate the completeness of your Investigator's Summary Packet and your participation in solving the wildlife crime.

Investigator's Summary Packet

__ 1. All entries are present.

__ 2. Each entry is complete and thorough.

__ 3. Each entry is neat and organized.

The grade I deserve on this packet is _____.

The reason that I deserve this grade is

_____

_____

_____

_____

_____

_____

_____

Handout 4-B
Investigator's
Self-Evaluation

Participation in Solving Crime

__ 1. I participated in two interviews, took notes, and shared information with my team.

__ 2. I thoroughly completed analysis of two pieces of evidence, recorded the findings, and shared them with my team.

__ 3. I participated in daily assignments and discussions of the case with my team.

__ 4. I was a positive contributor to my investigation team.

__ 5. I was present every day. If I was absent, I made up my work on time and shared it with my team.

The grade I deserve for my participation in solving the crime is _____

The reason that I deserve this grade is

_____

_____

_____

_____

_____

_____

Handout 4-C
Group Evaluation

Name_____ Date_____

All team members must complete this evaluation together and agree with the points assigned each member. If you can not reach agreement, explain the reason for your disagreement on a separate paper.

1. Each member of your team can be given from 0 to 16 points for participation in the team's efforts to solve the wildlife crime. Discuss each statement below for each team member. Circle the number from 1 to 4 that best describes each member's participation and effort (1 = lowest participation and effort, 4 = highest participation and effort).

    A. Participated in two interviews, took notes, and shared the information with the team.

    B. Thoroughly completed labs for two pieces of evidence, recorded the findings, and shared them with the team.

    C. Participated in daily assignments and discussions of the case with the team.

    D. Was a positive contributor to the investigation team.

    E. Was present every day. If absent, made up the work on time and shared it with the team.

Team Member Name	A	B	C	D	E	Total (0–16)
_____	1 2 3 4	1 2 3 4	1 2 3 4	1 2 3 4	1 2 3 4	_____
_____	1 2 3 4	1 2 3 4	1 2 3 4	1 2 3 4	1 2 3 4	_____
_____	1 2 3 4	1 2 3 4	1 2 3 4	1 2 3 4	1 2 3 4	_____
_____	1 2 3 4	1 2 3 4	1 2 3 4	1 2 3 4	1 2 3 4	_____
_____	1 2 3 4	1 2 3 4	1 2 3 4	1 2 3 4	1 2 3 4	_____

Handout 4-C
Group Evaluation

2. Make the circle into a pie chart. The chart represents each member's contribution to completing all team requirements for solving the crime. Total participation of all members equals 100%. Divide the pie into sections that represent the portion of work done by each team member. If all participated equally, the divisions should be the same size. The pie sections could be larger or smaller if a member did more or less work than required.

(Write member's name by pie section.)

Member signatures: _____

_____

_____

_____

_____

Discuss your responses to 3–6 as a team. Record comments.

Handout 4-C
Group Evaluation

3. Describe a part of the crime investigation that worked well for your team.

4. Describe a part of the crime investigation that did not work well for your team.

Handout 4-C
Group Evaluation

5. What did you like most about the forensic training lessons and wildlife crime investigation?

6. What did you like least about the forensic training lessons and wildlife crime investigation?

Setting Up a Lab Practical Assessment

Teacher Guidelines

In a lab practical assessment, students move from station to station to demonstrate their lab skills and content knowledge by answering questions or interpreting lab evidence.

Materials

- Card for each station with one question or lab directions, taken from the "Lab Practical Assessment" (pp. 306–311).
- Items for some of the lab stations (see "Lab Practical Assessment")
- Clock with second hand, or stopwatch

Getting Ready

1. Choose all or some of the lab stations on pages 306–311 for your assessment. There needs to be at least as many stations as students. Tape a card with each station's question or directions on the station. Place any required materials at appropriate lab stations.

2. Make a map of your room showing where each station will be found and how the students will move from one station to another. The map can look something like the one at right. Draw the map on the board for students to refer to.

3. Remove all irrelevant items from counters, desks, and tables being used for lab stations.

4. Decide how long students will have at

Map of Stations at Lab Tables
Arrows show flow of students from station to station.

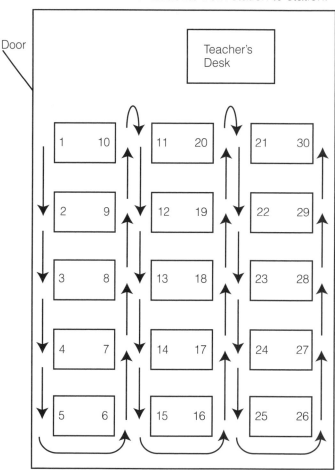

each station before being required to move to the next (usually one to two minutes). You might need to modify this as you watch the students at the first few stations. Select a time interval that allows students to get to all stations during the class period, with a little time at the end for collecting papers and allowing students to return to questions that they did not finish.

5. In the class period before the practical, tell students they will be locked out of the room until the assessment begins. All they need is lined paper and pencil.

Steps

1. Meet students outside the door of the assessment room. Have them get out lined paper (referred to below as their "test paper") and a pencil, and number their papers on every other line from 1 to the total number of lab stations.

2. Explain the testing procedure they will follow when they enter the room:

   • No talking.
   • When you enter the room, walk to a station. Only one person can be at a station.
   • Circle your beginning station number on your test paper. Each student will begin the assessment at a different question. (Remind students frequently to make sure their station/question number matches the number on the test paper where they are writing their answers.)
   • Stay at your station until the teacher announces, "Move to the next question." Some questions can be answered quickly; others will take a minute or two. If you do not finish answering a question, mark it and move on. You will have time at the end of the assessment to return to stations that you did not finish.

3. Open the door and let students silently move to stations.

4. Show them the map of stations and how they will move through the room. They will always be moving to the next higher number. When they leave the station with the highest test number, they will go to station #1.

5. When all student clarification questions are answered, remind them to write their first response next to the circled number on their test paper. Also remind them not to move from that station until you say to. They can use extra time to check answers. Then say, "Begin."

6. Watch how quickly students at the longer questions finish. Pick a time interval that works for your students. Every one to two minutes say, "Move to the next question. Check the number on your test paper."

7. After students have moved through all stations, collect papers of students who are done and have them go back outside the classroom door. Any students who need to finish a question will keep their papers and silently move around the room to those stations. Only one student is allowed at a station. Collect papers.

Lab Practical Assessment

Station 1.   Materials: Spot plate of blood typing

Question: What is the blood type on this spot plate?

Station 2.   Materials: None

Question: Why does blood clot when some blood types are mixed?

Station 3.   Materials: None

Question: Which antigens and antibodies are found in type A blood?

a.    b.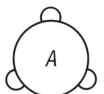

c. 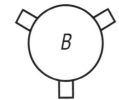   d.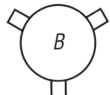

Station 4.   Materials: Microscope and a copy of "Anatomy of a Hair" (pp. 112–114)

Directions: Draw the hair and identify the animal it came from.

Station 5.   Materials: Microscope and a copy of "Anatomy of a Hair" (pp. 112–114)

Directions: Draw and identify the type of medulla in this human hair.

Station 6.   Materials: None

Questions:

    a. T/F Hair structure can be matched to one individual.

    b. Why is a DNA fingerprint of hair stronger evidence than hair structure?

Station 7.   Materials: Skull

Questions:

    a. Is this skull from a carnivore or herbivore?

    b. How do the teeth prove this?

Station 8.   Materials: Skull

Directions: Count the number of

    a. incisors

    b. canines

    c. molars and premolars

Station 9.   Materials: Track Patterns

Directions:

    a. Measure the length and width of this track.

    b. Name two types of information you can learn from a track or track pattern.

Station 10. Materials: Antler or horn and a copy of the Animal Headgear Information Cards (pp. 42–43)

Question: This antler/horn came from what animal?

Station 11. Materials: Antler or horn

Question: What is the length of this antler/horn?

Station 12. Materials: None

Question: What is pH a measure of?

Station 13. Materials: None

Question: How many times more acidic is pH2 than pH4?

Station 14. Materials: Spot plate and a copy of "How Do pH Indicators Work?" pages 126–127

Questions: The pH of this solution was tested with bromthymol blue.

a. What is the numerical pH range of this solution?

b. Is it acidic, neutral, or basic?

Station 15. Materials: Spot plate and and a copy of "How Do pH Indicators Work?" pages 126–127

Question: An unknown solution was tested for pH using several different pH indicators. Complete the chart. (This question will be continued at the next station.)

Indicator	Color	pH Range	Acid/Base/Neutral
Congo Red	_____	1-3	_____
BTB	Yellow	_____	_____
_____	Hot pink	10 +	_____

Station 16. Materials: Spot plate and and a copy of "How Do pH Indicators Work?" pages 126–127

Questions (continuation of station 15):

a. Which pH indicator gave test results different from the other two?

b. If you got these results in a lab, what would you need to do?

Station 17. Materials: None

Question: DNA can be separated from _____ and used as evidence in a crime.

a. Skin

b. Saliva

c. Hair

d. a and c

e. all of the above

Station 18. Materials: None

Questions: Which step happens first when making a DNA fingerprint?

a. DNA pieces form bands in the gel plate.

b. DNA is put into the starting well of an electronic gel plate.

c. A photograph is taken that shows unique banding of the DNA fingerprint.

d. An enzyme cuts the DNA into different sized pieces.

Station 19. Materials: Ink fingerprint and a copy of the "Fingerprint Pattern Key" (pp. 96–99).

Directions: Draw the basic fingerprint pattern and identify the pattern name.

Station 20. Materials: None

Questions:

    a. T/F   One person's fingers can have different print patterns.

    b. T/F   A fingerprint can be matched to one individual.

Station 21. Materials: None

Question: Which statements describe fingerprints?

    a. Dry fingers make clearer prints on objects.

    b. Ridges of skin on the fingertips create the fingerprint pattern.

    c. Body oil pools between the ridges and makes a print when the finger touches an object.

    d. The skin of fingertips is smooth across the fingerprint pattern.

Station 22. Materials: None

Questions:

    a. What animal is heavily poached for gall bladders?

    b. What are the gall bladders used for?

Station 23. Materials: None

Directions: Name two pieces of evidence used to investigate the Ward wildlife crime.

Station 24. Materials: None

Directions: Name one piece of evidence that directly linked Ryan Dixon to the crime.

Station 25. Materials: None

Directions: Name one piece of evidence that directly linked Eliza Lucero to the crime.

Station 26. Materials: None

Question: What felony was confirmed in the hand-written message from Ryan Dixon to Ed Lee?

Station 27. Materials: None

Directions: Name one offense that was committed when Ryan Dixon killed five bears, took only the gall bladders, and left the bodies in the forest?

Station 28. Materials: None

Directions: Name one animal species, other than black bear, that is killed for body parts.

Animal: _____

Why poached: _____

Station 29. Materials: None

Question: What are common crimes committed against these animals?

a. Alligators and crocodiles _____

b. Monkeys and apes _____

Station 30. Materials: None

Directions: Describe something you could do to help reduce the black market (illegal) trade of wildlife and animal parts.

Lab Practical Assessment

Answer Key

1. Lab set-up—Answer varies by teacher's choice.

2. The antibodies attach to the antigens.

3. b

4. Lab set-up—Answer varies by teacher's choice.

5. Lab set-up—Answer varies by teacher's choice.

6. a. False

   b. It can be matched to one individual.

7. a. Lab set-up—Answer varies by teacher's choice.

   b. Varies depending on teacher's choice of skulls.

8. Lab set-up—Answer varies by teacher's choice.

9. a. Lab set-up—Teacher's choice.

   b. Species, weight and size of animal, direction of travel, behavior, activity, health, number of animals found together, and more.

10. Lab set-up—Answer varies by teacher's choice.

11. Lab set-up—Answer varies by teacher's choice.

12. Potential hydrogens

13. 100

14. Lab set-up—Answer varies by teacher's choice. Have spot plate with solution of your choice with BTB.

15.

Indicator	Color	pH Range	Acid/Base/Neutral
Congo Red	Blue	1–3	acidic
BTB	Yellow	1–6	acidic
PHT	Hot pink	10+	basic

16. a. PHT

   b. Do the tests again.

17. e

18. d

19. Lab set-up—Answer varies by teacher's choice.

20. a. True

   b. True

21. b and c

22. a. Bears (black bears)

   b. Medicines

23. (any of the 13 pieces of evidence)

24. DNA fingerprint from hair, fingerprint on rifle.

25. Fingerprint on MailExpress receipt.

26. Sell, purchase, or offer to sell or purchase big game.

27. Three possibilities:

    • Hunting without a license.

    • Killing and abandoning any big game wildlife.

    • Taking any big game wildlife for the purpose of removing only the hide, antlers, or other trophy parts and leaving the carcass in the field.

28. A few of many options: cats for fur, elephants for tusks, alligators and crocodiles for skins, rhinos for horns.

29. a. Use of skin products, trophy parts.

    b. Meat or pets

30. Any of the following:

    • Do not buy products made from wildlife parts.

    • Do not support pet stores that offer questionably obtained wildlife for sale.

    • Do not buy food of wildlife that might have been hunted illegally.

    • Hunt only in season with proper license.

    • Tell authorities of suspected illegal hunting activities.

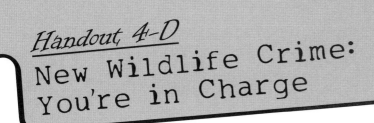

Handout 4-D
New Wildlife Crime: You're in Charge

Name _____ Date _____

- CRIME SCENE - DO NOT CROSS - CRIME SCENE - DO NOT CROSS - CRIME SCENE - DO NOT CROSS - CRIME SCENE - DO NOT CROSS - CRIME SCENE - DO NOT CROSS -

Apply What You Know to a New Crime

Your Job

You are a wildlife investigator. Your state has a wildlife crime reporting program called Operation Game Thief (OGT). This lets the public anonymously report suspected crimes against wildlife. Since wildlife officers have such huge territories to patrol, they rely on and greatly appreciate these tips.

You have been assigned as lead investigator on a new crime. Use all your experiences (questioning suspects and witnesses, gathering and analyzing evidence, piecing together all the pieces to the crime puzzle, and presenting your case) to design an investigation strategy for your new case.

Your Crime Assignment

For a State Crime:

Go to your state's OGT website (Search "Operation Game Thief (state)") or talk with your local wildlife agency to find information about current crimes under investigation in your state. Forty-nine out of 50 states have OGT. Many websites have brief descriptions of current cases or cold cases.

Note: If your state does not have crimes listed on the website, look at Operation Game Thief websites of neighboring states or check one of the OGT websites of these states: Colorado, New Mexico, Maine, Nevada, Kansas, or Wyoming.

For an International Crime:

- Go to TRAFFIC (The Wildlife Trade Monitoring Network) at *www.traffic.org.* Find an article about a crime in the "News Room."
- Go to National Geographic News at *http://news.nationalgeographic.com.* Find an article about a crime or threats to wildlife in the "Animals and Nature News."

Handout 4-D
New Wildlife Crime: You're in Charge

Investigator's Report on the Crime

1. What do the authorities know about the crime? (who, what, when, where, why, how?)

2. What types of evidence do they have to help solve this crime? (Including but not limited to antlers, human blood, DNA, fingerprints, animal and human hair, unidentified liquid and powders, animal skull, animal tracks)

3. What wildlife laws might have been broken?

4. What questions do investigators need to answer in order to solve the crime?

5. What are the next steps the investigators should take?

Appendixes

DO NOT give this appendix to students until AFTER they complete the investigation.

CRIME SCENE - DO NOT CROSS - CRIME SCENE - DO NOT CROSS - CR

Bears: Loved Alive or Dead!

People love bears! They are the favorite animal of nature programs, stuffed toys, and zoos. Unfortunately, bears are also loved for the unique body parts they provide when dead. It is this huge international demand for bear parts that has pushed many species to the edge of extinction (Wildlife trade: Bear trade, n.d.; Third International Symposium on Trade in Bear Parts 2000).

Why are bear numbers dropping?

Many bear species are threatened or endangered because of loss of habitat, fragmentation of populations, illegal or unmanaged hunting, and the capture of cubs to sell to zoos, circuses, and bear farms.

Bear body parts are popular in illegal animal trade markets. Bear fat, spinal cords, brains, bones, blood, and gall bladders are all bought and sold for medical treatments. Bear meat and bear paw soup are eaten as gourmet foods at restaurants around the world. Claws, teeth, and fur are sold for decorations, trophy showcases, and jewelry. But of all these, the gall bladder is in highest demand, bringing in the most money. In the United States, one can sell for $300–$500, while in some Asian markets one gall bladder can go for $4,000–$10,000!

Are bears protected by laws?

All bears and their body parts are protected under a treaty by CITES (Convention on International Trade in Endangered Species of Wild Fauna and Flora), signed by 162 countries. It prohibits international trade of bear species, except with a special permit. Unfortunately, the restrictions have not stopped bear trade but have simply moved it to illegal markets. Another problem is that countries who have not become members of CITES (such as South Korea and Taiwan) can continue to sell bear parts legally (Mills 1992).

The United States has not been able to pass a federal law protecting all bears in our country, so most of the 40 states who have native bear populations have passed laws to protect them. Unfortunately, since some states do not have such laws, the illegal market is difficult to control (Roberts 1999).

Why do people want bear gall bladders?

Gall bladders produce bile, a fluid that flows into the small intestine to help neutralize stomach acid and break down fat. Bear bile is unique because it also contains the chemical *ursodeoxycholic acid* (UDCA) that no other animal is known to produce.

Clinical research has confirmed that UDCA is an effective treatment for liver problems, cancers, burns, asthma, eye and sinus problems, coughs, and gall stones (*TRAFFIC Network Report* 1995; World Wildlife Fund n.d.; Raloff 2005). Contrary to popular belief, it is not an aphrodisiac.

Who is buying bear gall bladders?

Bear bile has been used in traditional Asian medicines for over 2,000 years. Though it is now illegal to buy and sell bear parts, people in 18 Asian countries still actively do so, with China, Vietnam, Korea, Japan, Indonesia, Malaysia, Singapore, and Taiwan leading the market. Illegal sales also occur in the United States, Canada, and Australia (World Wildlife Fund n.d.).

How is bile taken from bear gall bladders?

There are two ways to get the bile from bears: Kill wild bears and remove the gall bladders or keep bears alive on farms while continually draining their bile.

- Wild bears: Wild bears are killed legally (with a hunting license) and illegally in the United States and across the world. In the United States, licensed hunters must take the entire body and prepare the meat for eating, even though most just want trophy parts. People involved in the sale of bear gall bladders often remove the gall bladder and leave the rest of the body in the field. This is a felony in the United States.

- Farmed bears: Bear farms began in Asian countries in 1984 to try to lessen the illegal killing of wild bears. A loophole in the CITES law allows bile from farmed bears to be collected and sold legally (Raloff 2005; Mills 1992). One farmed bear can make the same amount of bile as 220 killed wild bears. Unfortunately, as the farmed bears have produced more bile, the demand for bear bile has also increased. Now, in Asian countries, bear bile is advertised to be in everything from luxury shampoos to wines.

  "Milking the bear" is the phrase describing the procedure for draining bile from a live bear. The bear is kept isolated in a small

cage to keep it from walking around. A tube is inserted into its gall bladder through a cut in its abdomen, which is kept open or reopened regularly. The bile drains into a container outside of the cage. These bears can be kept alive for years, until bile production or the animals' health deteriorates (Raloff 2005).

Is there any other chemical that can replace bear bile?

In 1955, scientists synthesized (chemically made) bile that had the same medical benefits as bear bile. It is made from cow bile and is much less expensive that bear bile. Substitutes for bear bile have also been made from plants. Unfortunately, many people still prefer to pay higher prices for real bear bile.

What is being done to stop the illegal trade of bears and bear parts?

Reduce demands: Synthesized "bear bile" from cow bile and plants is marketed. It has the same medicinal benefits as actual bear bile.

Catch smugglers and sellers: Efforts continue to strengthen laws, increase law enforcement, and prosecute more criminals.

Identify products with bear bile: A bear bile identification kit is being developed that allows law enforcement officers to quickly test suspicious materials for the presence of bear bile. Results are available in five minutes. The test uses antibodies that match proteins found only in bears. When the antibodies are mixed with a substance that contains bear proteins, they lock onto the proteins and create a visible change in the solution. (This is similar to the tests for blood types.)

Student Questions: What Does It All Mean?

1. What are reasons that bears are loved, alive and dead?

2. Why is there a demand for bear bile?

3. Two sides of the issue:

    a. Why were bear farms started?
    b. Why have bear farms not solved the problem of harming or killing bears to get bile?

4. Which effort described above in "What is being done to stop the illegal trade of bears and bear parts?" do you think has the most promise? Why?

5. Optional research: Read one of the articles on bear trade listed below, or find another article by doing an online search.

BEAR TRADE REFERENCES

Castle, T. 2005. State Battles Lucrative Bear Bile Trade. *San Francisco Chronicle.* April 25. *www.sfgate.com/cgi-n/article.cgi?file=/c/a/2005/04/25/MNG9ACEIJF1.DTL*

International illegal trade in bears. 2005. World Society for the Protection of Animals. *www.wspa.org.uk*

Mills, J. 1992. Milking the bear trade. *International Wildlife* (May/June). National Wildlife Federation. *www.nwf.org/wildlife/grizzlybear/milking-bears.cfm*

Nette, T. 2000. Bear gallbladders to sell or not to sell. Department of Natural Resources, Nova Scotia (July 19). *www.gov.ns.ca/natr/wildlife/lgmams/beargalls.htm*

Raloff, J. 2005. A galling business: The inhumane exploitation of bears for traditional Asian medicine. *Science News* 168 (Oct. 15): 25–52.

Roberts, A. 1999. Bear poachers busted as Congress considers federal bear bill. *AWI Quarterly* 48:2. *www.awionline.org/wildlife/aw-sp99b.htm*

The terrible fate of the world's bears: International bear-part trade. n.d. National Wildlife Federation. *www.nwf.org/wildlife/grizzlybear/bearparttrade.cfm*

The Third International Symposium on Trade in Bear Parts (April 2000). *TRAFFIC Bulletin* 18:2. *www.traffic.org/bulletin/archive/april2000/news-bearparts.html*

Wildlife trade: Bear trade. n.d. World Wildlife Fund. *www.worldwildlife.org/trade/faqs_bear.cfm*

Meet the Experts

What's it like to devote your career to protecting and caring for wildlife? Here are profiles of five people who do just that, presented in a question-and-answer format.

Ken Goddard

Director, National Fish and Wildlife Forensics Laboratory, Ashland, Oregon

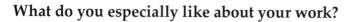

What is your job?

I direct the activities of the National Fish and Wildlife Forensics Laboratory [part of the U.S. Fish and Wildlife Service] and maintain the laboratory facility—all in an ethical manner, within our budget, and according to federal government rules and regulations. I'm ultimately responsible for all activities, operations, and/or problems at the lab. So I have to be thoughtful, patient, and persistent—and, of course, fair and impartial in my decisions.

What do you especially like about your work?

I enjoy the fact that the National Fish and Wildlife Forensics Lab is the only such lab in the world and that we're supposed to provide forensic support for wildlife law enforcement agencies in all 50 states and the 162 CITES [Convention on International Trade in Endangered Species of Wild Fauna and Flora] countries. I enjoy our being pioneers in the field by coming up with new protocols and procedures that meet national and international forensic and law enforcement standards. The work is challenging and fascinating (if occasionally frustrating and irritating), but I'd be bored silly with a normal nine-to-five job.

What is the hardest part of your job?

The hardest part of the job is determining priorities: what research gets done, which cases get worked, who goes to what training classes, and (most importantly) what doesn't get done. These de-

cisions can be impacted by unpredictable courtroom subpoenas and priorities set by my boss (the chief of law enforcement for the U.S. Fish and Wildlife Service).

What education, skills, or experience did you need to get your job?

I have a BS degree in biochemistry and MS degree in criminalistics. My experiences include CSI (crime scene investigation) and forensic work with California sheriff and police departments and the U.S. Fish and Wildlife Service.

What is one of the most memorable experiences you have had on the job?

It was an investigation into illegal walrus hunting in Alaska. I flew along the coast of the Steward Peninsula, landing on the beaches and conducting necropsies (autopsies) on the dozens of decomposed and headless walruses that had washed ashore. In doing so, we crashed an airplane (no one was hurt), got our jeep stuck in an arctic stream, and had to wade across another nearly frozen arctic stream to get to our survival and CSI gear.

I have also been part of an international team of marine biologists trying to develop CSI techniques to investigate damaged coral reefs. This has been an interesting experience because most CSI techniques that work on land don't work well (if at all) in the water. The work is complicated by the continual flow of corrosive saltwater through the scene, the need to keep track of your depth and the amount of air remaining in your scuba tank, and the occasional appearance at the scene of things that bite!

What thoughts would you like to share with students about wildlife and crimes against wildlife?

My view of wildlife law enforcement is that we'll never resolve the underlying conflicts and issues of wildlife preservation through our investigative and forensic efforts alone. The best we can do is try to keep things from getting worse until smarter and more thoughtful people show up on the planet and take charge of things. I'm still enough of an idealist to believe that will happen some day, especially if all of us refuse to give up.

Bernadette Atencio

Supervisor, National Eagle and Wildlife Property Repository, Denver, Colorado.

What is your job?

I supervise all activities at this one-of-a-kind U.S. Fish and Wildlife Service facility in Denver, Colorado. When wildlife parts and products are confiscated by law enforcement officers or found abandoned anywhere in the United States, they end up here to be stored or disposed of. I spend much of my time educating the public about wildlife laws, biodiversity, wildlife conservation, threatened and endangered species, and eagles.

I also supervise the National Native American Eagle Feather program that distributes legally protected eagle feathers to Native Americans for ceremonies.

As a wildlife inspector I monitor the multibillion-dollar world market of legal and illegal trade of wildlife and wildlife products by clearing legal shipments of wildlife and stopping shipments that violate our wildlife laws. I inspect live animals imported and exported for pet trade, manufactured products (such as boots, handbags, clothing, jewelry, and caviar), and other wildlife items such as hunting trophies, feathers, furs, raw coral and shells.

What education, skills or experience did you need to get your job?

All of my skills have come from on-the-job training and experience. I don't have a college degree, though today it would be very helpful. Wildlife inspectors need knowledge of wildlife taxonomy, zoology, ornithology, criminal justice, smuggling techniques, interviewing and profiling techniques, courtroom testimony, and wildlife laws and regulations. Communication and computer skills are also essential.

My career began as a federal government clerk typist transcribing wildlife case reports and working with migratory bird permits. Later, I became supervisor of the wildlife inspection program for the Denver International Airport, where I inspected wildlife shipments and confiscated any illegal wildlife parts or products. Over

the years, I have developed a great appreciation for our wildlife and am totally committed to continuing my contribution by educating the public and being a "voice for the voiceless."

What is the most challenging part of your job?

It is most challenging to identify the species for the many different kinds of international wildlife products (whole skins, mounts, and products containing a small piece or part of an animal), and determine if the animal parts are authentic or manmade.

What is one of the most memorable experiences you have had on the job?

As a wildlife inspector, I have confiscated a number of illegal wildlife shipments, including products made from a threatened zebra, African elephant ivory, crocodile, lizard, alligator, python, parrot feather, coral, iguana, and sea turtle. I have confiscated numerous illegal trophy skins, skulls, and mounts. I have also assisted in setting up in federal and state roadblocks to look for illegal hunting trophies within the United States.

What advice or wisdom could you give students?

Stay in school and learn all you can about our natural resources so that you, too, can help protect and preserve what is so necessary to our survival. Acquire an appreciation for wildlife and pass it on to your children and your children's children.

Mark Lamb

District Wildlife Manager (DWM), Colorado Division of Wildlife

What is your job?

The job duties of a DWM can be divided into four areas:

1. law enforcement—Wildlife officers in Colorado are considered peace officers. This means we can enforce all of the laws of the state (writing speeding tickets, investigating burglaries or other crimes), but we concentrate our time and efforts on enforcing wildlife laws and regulations.

2. biology—This is the part of the job most people associate with what we do. This includes conducting research studies (collaring elk and bighorn sheep) on animal movements and behavior and learning more about different animals. We also spend time in planes or helicopters counting herds or identifying areas for law enforcement or habitat projects.

3. education—We spend a lot of time educating the public in classrooms, campground talks, or community presentations on bears or lions or some other wildlife topic. We also teach hunter education and assist with 4-H shooting sports or other outdoor classes.

4. land use—Land use is a crucial part of the job and maybe the toughest. This is where you try to identify how activities will impact wildlife, both negatively and positively. There could be a new subdivision being planned, a controlled burn, or a timber cut. What we try to do is figure out how to minimize the impacts to wildlife and sometimes how to improve the plan.

What education, skills, or experience does a person need for your job?

A college degree in one of the biological fields (e.g., wildlife, fisheries, microbiology, or forestry) is required to even be considered for this job. It is helpful to have experience in hunting, fishing, orienteering, and other outdoor skills. A lot of wildlife officers

got field experience in college or summer jobs by working with different government agencies.

What do you especially like about your job?

Everything! The best thing is that no two days are alike. That keeps the job fun and exciting. I like the flexible hours. Some days start at 4:00 a.m., some start at 10:00 a.m., and others may even start in the afternoon. This job requires that you spend time outdoors. Whether counting elk or checking fishing licenses, I am outdoors and love it!

What is the most challenging part of your job?

Sometimes the flexible hours can be a pain, like when I get the call at 2:00 a.m. about a deer that was hit by a car and is still alive or when I spend the night in my DOW (Division of Wildlife) truck waiting for a bear so I can try to prevent it from breaking into a house.

What are the most memorable experiences you have had on the job?

I could write a book about the memorable experiences I've had on my job. Here's a short list:

- Watching a peregrine falcon circle a raft of ducks on a lake and then swoop down and take one.
- Assisting with bighorn sheep trapping and collaring.
- Reintroducing river otters into the wild.
- Learning how smart and adaptive black bears really are.
- Getting a poacher to confess to the illegal taking of numerous big game animals.
- Getting the public to understand the importance of wildlife in their communities.
- Being the advocate and voice for wildlife.

What advice or wisdom could you give students?

Appreciate what we have! Wildlife is one of our most awesome

resources and at times we don't appreciate it. I don't know any-one who doesn't get excited to see a herd of elk or a bald eagle spread its wings and slowly land on a tree branch. Something that everyone can do is to be vigilant and call if someone is doing something wildlife-related that doesn't seem right. Being protective can be as simple as a phone call.

Shirley McGreal

Founder and head of the International Primate Protection League, Summerville, South Carolina

What is your job?

I work to help nonhuman primates. I say "nonhuman primates" because you and I are primates too! Primates includes apes, monkeys, and lemurs, plus some smaller ones like tiny tarsiers and lorises. Protecting primates means working to keep their forest homes safe for them and taking care of animals that have been treated cruelly by humans. It also means finding out the names of primate smugglers and turning them in to the wildlife police.

What do you especially like about your job?

Rescuing animals from abuse and seeing wildlife smugglers going to prison so that they learn what it is like to lose their freedom and live behind bars like the apes and monkeys they catch and ship round the world.

What is the hardest part of your job?

Seeing primates suffering in bad zoos and in labs and seeing wild primates kept as pets. They deserve better.

What education, skills, or experience did you need to get your job?

I started my own organization, International Primate Protection League (*www.ippl.org*), because I was concerned about the condi-

tions of the capture, transport, and captive lives of primates. It really helps to speak French and some other languages and to learn to investigate wildlife crime.

What is one of the most memorable experiences you have had on the job?

Bringing our first laboratory gibbon to our sanctuary so we could provide a healthy, safe place for him to live the rest of his life. He was a baby who banged his head all the time and had been kept in isolation for his first two years of life. Working to make him happy was a wonderful experience that lasted for many years. We saw him enjoying life with his companion, another lab gibbon.

Another memorable experience was catching a smuggling gang that had shipped six baby orangutans from Asia to Europe. Three of the international smuggling gang, one in the United States, one in the Netherlands, and one in Germany, landed up in prison.

If you could give students one piece of advice or wisdom about wildlife, crimes against wildlife, or their role in wildlife protection, what would it be?

Always carry a camera so you have proof of any animal cruelty you see. Learn one or two foreign languages. Never buy wildlife as pets or wildlife products such as fur coats, tortoiseshell ornaments, or ivory decorations.

Jeff Rucks

Wildlife Education Manager, Colorado Division of Wildlife

What do you do as a wildlife education manager?

My staff coordinates all the education and outreach efforts for the Colorado Division of Wildlife. The programs I supervise are Hunter Education, Angler Education, Wildlife Viewing, Hunter Outreach, and Project WILD. Our goal in these programs is to help people learn about wildlife and wildlife-related recreation, including hunting, fishing, and wildlife viewing.

What do you especially like about your work?

My work is very rewarding because we help people get excited about wildlife.

What is the hardest part of your job?

As the supervisor of many programs and staff I am responsible for managing the budget and making sure we have enough money to run these programs. Each year I have to develop a detailed budget for each program. Many time there is not enough money to do everything we would like to do and I have to decide what programs will not be funded.

What education, skills, or experience did you need to get your job?

This job requires knowledge about wildlife and about education. It also requires skills in supervision and leadership. I have a bachelor's degree in wildlife management and a master's degree in education administration and supervision.

What is one of the most memorable experiences you have had on the job?

Whenever I take a group out to experience wildlife, I love watching people get excited about what they discover. Whether it is the

first time they see a bald eagle or they catch their first fish, the amazement and joy in their eyes is fun to watch.

If you could give students one piece of advice or wisdom about wildlife, what would it be?

I miss Steve Irwin, the Crocodile Hunter. I wish everyone could experience the child-like enthusiasm and sheer joy he had about all things wild.

Many resources are listed throughout this book under the relevant topic. Here are additional resources for teaching wildlife forensics.

All about blood, blood types: What are they. n.d. Australian Red Cross. *www.arcbs.redcross.org.au/Donor/aboutblood/bloodtypes.asp*

Brickson, B. 1994. A drop of blood, a tuft of hair, and a little DNA. *Pacific Discovery* (Fall): 25–30.

Buyer beware! n.d.. World Wildlife Fund. *www.worldwildlife.org/buyerbeware*

Digest of federal resource laws of interest to the U.S. Fish and Wildlife Service. n.d. U.S. Fish and Wildlife Service. *www.fws.gov/laws/lawsdigest/indx.html*

Dendy, L. 1994. Animal crimes animal clues. *Ranger Rick* (Jan.): 36–44.

Dunn, T. 2003. Caught, after the act: How crime solvers use scientific sleuthing to stay hot on the trail of wildlife criminals. *Smithsonian National Zoological Park ZooGoer* 32(6).

Endangered species handbook. n.d. *www.endangeredspecieshandbook.org/legislation*

Federal laws and related laws handbook. n.d. New Mexico Center for Wildlife Law. *http://ipl.unm.edu/cwl/fedbook/airhunt.html*

Facts about federal wildlife laws. n.d. U.S. Fish and Wildlife Service. *www.turnerlearning.com/efts/species.970730/wildlaw.html*

Helmenstine, A. M. n.d. Acid/base indicators. About.com. *www.chemistry.about.com/library/weekly/aa112201a.htm*

Helmenstine, A. M. n.d. How to make red cabbage indicator. About.com. *www.chemistry.about.com/library/weekly/aa012803a.htm*

I would like to donate blood—do they need all blood types or just certain ones? n.d. How Stuff Works. *www.howstuffworks.com/question593.htm*

International illegal trade in bears. 2005. World Society for the Protection of Animals. *www.wspa.org.uk*

Jackson, D. M. 2000. *The wildlife detectives: How forensic scientists fight crimes against nature.* New York: Houghton Mifflin.

Kelly, B., ed. 2005. *Big game 2005.* Denver, CO: Colorado Division of Wildlife.

Meadows, D. H. Feb.14, 2000. Dead in the water. Daily Grist. *www.grist.org/comments/citizen/2000/02/14/in/index.html*

Ridges and furrows. n.d. *www.ridgesandfurrows.homestead.com/index.html*

Schefter, J. 1994. DNA fingerprints on trial. *Popular Science* (Nov.): 60–64.

Spinning skulls. n.d. University of Michigan Museum of Zoology. *www.animaldiversity.ummz.umich.edu/site/topics/skullpromo.html*

Tracking, tracks and signs: Mammal tracks and signs. n.d. Wildwood Survival: Wilderness Survival, Tracking, Nature, Wilderness Mind. *www.wildwoodsurvival.com/tracking/mammals/index.html*

Wertheim, P. A. n.d. Atmospheric superglue method. Crime and clues: The art and science of criminal investigation. *www.crimeandclues.com/superglue.htm*

Wild about elk: An educator's guide. 1994. Missoula, MT: Project Wild, Western Regional Environmental Education Council, Rocky Mountain Elk Foundation.

Index

Index

Index

Index

Index

National Science Teachers Association